STRAYER-UPTON
PRACTICAL ARITHMETICS
SECOND BOOK
PART 1

BY

GEORGE DRAYTON STRAYER

Profesor of Education, Teachers College

Columbia University

AND

CLIFFORD BREWSTER UPTON

Profesor of Mathematics, Teachers College

Columbia University

YESTERDAY'S CLASSICS

ITHACA, NEW YORK

This edition, first published in 2022 by Yesterday's Classics, an imprint of Yesterday's Classics, LLC, is an unabridged republication of the text originally published by American Book Company in 1934. For the complete listing of the books that are published by Yesterday's Classics, please visit www.yesterdaysclassics.com. Yesterday's Classics is the publishing arm of the Gateway to the Classics which presents the complete text of hundreds of classic books for children at www.gatewaytotheclassics.com.

ISBN: 978-1-63334-083-1

Yesterday's Classics, LLC
PO Box 339
Ithaca, NY 14851

PREFACE

This series of books aims to give the child the ability to compute easily and accurately, and to enable him to interpret and solve the quantitative situations which he will meet in everyday life. In the achievement of this aim, these books incorporate the most valuable findings of modern experimentation in the teaching of arithmetic, including the results of important researches conducted by the authors themselves. These books present only those methods and materials which have been thoroughly tested in the classroom by many experienced teachers.

It is an established principle of teaching that nothing stimulates a pupil's interest so much as the satisfaction he gets from his ability to do things successfully. If he finds himself steadily perfecting new skills in arithmetic, he will look forward to his arithmetic period and will approach each new problem with intelligent interest. In accordance with this principle, these texts require the pupil to take only one new step at a time and supply him with enough exercises to assure mastery of that step before proceeding to the next one. Thus the constant stimulus of success is made possible for the pupil.

In this book the following features are worthy of note:

1. This book is written for children, in language with which they are familiar. The greatest care has been taken in the selection of vocabulary.

2. The problems relate to the life and interests of the pupils. They are *real problems* in every sense of the word.

3. Motivation is the keynote of successful work in arithmetic. When a new topic is being presented, the pupils should know why the topic is important and how it is used in life. This fundamental principle of teaching is

applied throughout this series of books by presenting every new operation or detail of a process in connection with an interesting motivating problem that treats of some situation with which the child is familiar.

4. The explanations of new principles and processes have been made as simple and clear as possible.

5. All the abstract exercises have been scientifically constructed so as to provide drill on all the fundamental number combinations, with ample repetition of those recognized as most difficult. The pupil thereby acquires that automatic mastery of the basic computations which is so essential to rapid and accurate computation.

6. The total number of abstract exercises in this book is far greater than that usually found in elementary school texts. All these exercises have been graded with extreme care with reference to the difficulty of the steps involved.

7. The checking of computations is one of the most important habits that a child can form. Throughout this book checking is taught early in the presentation of each new operation and is constantly required in connection with all exercises.

8. A series of 84 Improvement Tests covering whole numbers, fractions, and decimals is included. These tests provide the most efficient and interesting means yet devised for keeping alive skills already learned while the pupil is studying new topics. For example, when the pupil is studying the addition and subtraction of fractions, the Improvement Tests provide the drill on whole numbers that is necessary to keep these skills active. These tests have the further advantage that the total time required to give and score them is less than 30 minutes a week thus leaving ample time to be devoted to the new work of the grade. For further information concerning these tests, see pages 16-20 of this book.

9. This book provides an exceptionally full and generous program of diagnostic and remedial work. Frequent diagnostic tests are given throughout the book, with keyed references to remedial exercises.

10. The carefully planned instruction in problem solving, which was given in the First Book of this series, is continued in this book. In addition to a large number of one-step problems in which the technical language expressions of arithmetic are frequently reviewed, special attention is now given to the solution of problems of two or more steps, with emphasis upon those types of two-step and three-step problems that occur most frequently in everyday life.

There are very few pages in the book on which all the problems may be worked by using the same operation, such as addition only. There are, on the other hand, many pages containing problems of different kinds, each of which the pupil has to study carefully before selecting the operation to be performed. By developing the pupil's initiative in this way and also by centering attention on the more common types of problems, as stated above, the pupil's ability in problem solving is developed as systematically as his skill in computation.

11. A series of tests on problem solving is also provided throughout the book. These tests cover types of problem situations with which every pupil should be familiar. An important feature of these tests is that they not only measure the pupil's mastery of types of thinking frequently employed in problem solving, but they also check his ability to interpret important language expressions and technical phrases peculiar to arithmetic. These tests are arranged in groups known as Groups A, B, and C. Each group consists of three tests; thus Group A consists of Tests A1, A2, and A3. The problems on Test A1 cover the same variety and types of problem situations and the same range of difficulty as those found on Tests A2 and A3. A pupil, therefore, should do better on the second and third tests of any group than on the first test. Thus the pupil has the satisfaction of seeing himself grow in problem-solving ability. The problems on the tests of Groups B and C cover, in similar manner, other sets of type problems.

12. This book contains many interesting projects and units of work involving quantitative relationships.

13. Full provision has been made for pupils of varying levels of ability. For those of average and below-average ability a large number of well-graded exercises is provided. For pupils of superior ability more difficult exercises marked with a star (✶), are furnished. The diagnostic tests indicate the needs of each pupil and give references to suitable remedial work.

GEORGE DRAYTON STRAYER

CLIFFORD BREWSTER UPTON

CONTENTS

Chapter I

CHAPTER I

OUR NATURE STUDY CLUB

1. Our Nature Study Club has 35 members who pay weekly dues of $.05 each. How much does Ted, the treasurer, collect in dues in 1 week? in 4 weeks?

2. During the first four weeks Ted pays out the following amounts. How much does he pay in all?

(*a*) $1.15 for glass and cement to make an aquarium.

(*b*) $1.50 for bird records for the phonograph.

(*c*) $.75 for a blue print outfit.

(*d*) $.49 for a box of blue print paper.

(*e*) $2.75 to rent a motion picture film of wild animals.

3. If the total amount Ted receives during the four weeks is $7.00, how much has he left after paying out the amounts mentioned in ex. 2?

The next page shows how Ted keeps his accounts.

1

TED'S ACCOUNT BOOK

As treasurer of the Nature Study Club, Ted keeps this account of all the money he receives and spends.

Received					Paid Out			
Sept.	12	Dues	1	75	Sept.	15	Glass and cement	1	15
"	19	Dues	1	75	"	20	Phonograph records	1	50
"	26	Dues	1	75	"	28	Blue print outfit		75
Oct.	3	Dues	1	75	Oct.	2	Blue print paper		49
					"	6	Film rent	2	75
						6	Cash on hand		36
			7	00				7	00
Oct	6	Cash on hand		36					

How much in all does Ted receive during the four weeks? How much in all does he spend?

Ted subtracts the $6.64 he spends from the $7.00 he receives, which gives $.36 as the amount of cash he *should have* on hand. This is his **balance.** He counts his cash and finds that he really has $.36 left. Then he writes " Cash on hand, $.36 " on the right side of his book, as shown above, and adds that side. The sum is $7.00 and his book *balances* because the left side also totals $7.00. He draws double lines under $7.00 on both sides to show that the account above these lines is correct.

He now starts a new section of his account by writing " Cash on hand, $.36 " on the left side under $7.00.

In balancing his book, if Ted finds that he has not $.36 left, he tries to discover his mistake. If he has *less* than $.36, he may have forgotten to record some amount that he has spent; if he has *more* than $.36, he may have failed to record some amount that he has received.

TED CHECKS HIS ADDITION

Ted finds that the best way to add is to begin at the bottom of each column and add up. After obtaining the sum, he checks the work by beginning at the top of each column and adding down. If he gets the same sum each time, he considers that his work is correct.

Exercises

1. Here is the next section of Ted's account. Copy it, balance the account, and check the addition.

Received					Paid Out				
Oct.	6	Cash on hand		36	Oct.	14	Book of birds	1	45
"	10	Dues	1	75	"	18	Rock specimens	2	40
"	17	Dues	1	75	"	25	Postage		12
"	24	Dues	1	75	"	31	Trip to park	2	50
"	31	Dues	1	75	Nov.	1	Cash on hand		

2. For the next four weeks Ted starts with a balance of $.89 and receives $1.75 in dues each week. He pays $.65 for express on lantern slides, $.95 for a class excursion, $1.35 for "Book of Trees," $.85 for lumber for bird houses, $.75 for fish for the aquarium. Insert dates and make out and balance Ted's account. Check the work.

3. On Dec. 1 Ted has a balance of $3.34. On Dec. 5 he collects dues of $1.75 and each of the next two weeks he collects the same amount. He spends $.75 for food for squirrels, $1.65 for paper for costumes for a bird play, $.95 for pictures of trees, $.65 for express, $1.00 for a prize for the best photograph of animals. Balance the account to find the amount he should have left. Check the work.

ANNA'S CASH BOOK

1. Here are two pages from Anna's cash book. On the left-hand page she writes the amounts she receives. On the right-hand page she writes what she spends.

Received					Paid Out				
Sept.	1	Cash on hand	2	06	Sept.	7	Story book	1	07
"	5	Allowance	1	00	"	12	Ice cream		10
"	9	For old reader		35	"	18	Picnic		35
"	11	Errands		30	"	23	Red Cross Fund		40
"	19	Allowance	1	00	"	24	Set of paints	1	04
"	26	From Aunt Jess		50	"	30	Cash on hand		

Balance Anna's account to show that she should have $2.25 on hand on Sept. 30.

2. On Sept. 30 Anna counts her money and finds that she has only $2.15 (see ex. 1). Grace says that this might mean that she lost $.10. Is Grace right?

3. Anna is sure that she did not lose any money. Then she remembers that she spent $.10 for candy on Sept. 29. How does this change her account?

4. Show how Anna should keep her cash account for January. She has $1.19 on hand on Jan. 1. She receives $5.00 as a New Year's present, $1.75 on Jan. 7 for running errands, and $1.91 on Jan. 16 for helping her aunt. She spends $2.25 on Jan. 5 for a pair of skates, $.75 on Jan. 16 for a present for her sister, $.84 on Jan. 19 for a game, and $.65 on Jan. 24 for ribbon. How much cash should she have on hand on Jan. 31?

5. Keep a cash account as Anna did. As soon as you receive or spend any money, make a record of it.

COLUMN ADDITION

Add the following and check the work:

	1.		2.		3.		4.		5.		6.		7.		8.
	4		3		6		9		5		9		9		7
	9		6		7		0		1		3		2		9
	8		7		0		8		8		1		0		1
	2		4		7		2		4		7		8		5
	3		0		2		2		8		7		7		3

	9.		10.		11.		12.		13.		14.		15.		16.
	9		8		5		7		5		4		3		3
	0		2		0		2		2		4		0		1
	8		3		2		1		1		0		6		4
	3		8		6		8		6		6		3		9
	3		8		8		9		9		7		9		6

	17.		18.		19.		20.		21.		22.		23.		24.
	6		5		4		8		9		4		7		9
	5		5		2		6		4		5		6		3
	5		1		3		1		0		7		3		7
	4		8		5		7		9		1		7		2
	6		3		9		6		5		6		5		1

	25.		26.		27.		28.		29.		30.
	49		29		22		93		68		72
	33		59		78		16		95		80
	84		12		44		62		38		61
	81		80		96		80		90		79
	42		70		42		57		31		29

	31.		32.		33.		34.		35.		36.
	31		97		54		62		16		37
	63		27		62		21		57		71
	40		50		76		10		44		16
	48		33		31		69		65		57
	58		18		81		74		87		23

DRILL IN ADDITION

Add orally, starting at the bottom.   Check by adding down:

1.	2.	3.	4.	5.	6.	7.	8.
8	7	9	3	4	3	8	8
4	5	6	4	6	8	2	0
2	0	6	5	5	4	4	4
5	9	8	8	0	6	9	8
0	6	2	6	9	7	8	6
9	7	7	2	7	9	4	5
5	3	8	5	2	0	4	7

Copy and add, starting at the bottom.   Check the work:

9.	10.	11.	12.	13.	14.
89	19	83	31	70	66
43	93	29	16	33	72
20	77	28	55	62	81
69	45	32	28	84	46
98	78	64	57	11	42
53	32	68	34	19	57

15.	16.	17.	18.	19.	20.
99	97	27	92	24	43
70	41	96	59	61	17
75	47	61	94	36	88
31	98	42	25	80	50
60	60	80	75	58	78
47	21	92	10	59	98

21.	22.	23.	24.	25.	26.
388	680	360	569	390	968
330	575	457	792	915	287
661	394	778	725	645	626
125	203	303	502	473	250
674	882	544	396	779	183

COLUMN ADDITION

Add the following and check the work:

	1.		2.		3.		4.		5.		6.
	294		470		522		226		822		829
	841		133		937		590		584		606
	598		658		731		616		364		145
	430		472		630		360		731		878
	122		319		819		658		875		910
	373		470		259		789		569		710

	7.		8.		9.		10.		11.		12.
	505		524		873		198		953		694
	424		772		283		606		521		348
	454		588		135		962		723		311
	920		349		779		380		836		740
	809		990		940		536		114		753
	677		944		261		709		616		257

	13.		14.		15.		16.		17.		18.
	841		924		719		610		322		259
	350		842		516		332		477		916
	186		903		971		916		793		112
	626		460		482		887		541		616
	112		734		960		480		220		550
	975		507		609		203		473		405
	685		798		598		855		658		154

	19.		20.		21.		22.		23.		24.
	603		722		716		473		820		881
	314		598		527		300		607		213
	134		174		306		438		813		919
	518		415		460		544		233		660
	890		870		851		413		297		722
	203		101		452		810		120		637
	651		729		845		345		534		207
	986		686		214		809		696		727

THE EXPENSES OF A TOY STORE

1. Mr. Grant runs a small toy and stationery store in Johnstown. During August he spends $276.20 for supplies, $10.14 for lighting, $60.00 for rent, $9.00 for advertising, and $37.60 for help. How much are the expenses of his store during August?

Here are the August expenses of some other small stores. Copy them and find the total expenses of each store. Check the answers:

2.	3.	4.	5.
$167.05	$178.37	$146.26	$221.93
39.54	13.03	20.59	77.80
16.82	75.69	86.69	54.79
85.78	68.47	51.90	65.58

6.	7.	8.	9.
$189.49	$101.95	$200.94	$330.40
33.23	24.30	69.23	26.96
20.41	51.74	53.80	42.57
14.68	68.92	12.77	99.08
47.89	42.39	30.95	74.80

10.	11.	12.	13.
$330.77	$162.51	$257.80	$ 79.67
158.83	350.09	43.52	110.67
80.40	46.39	40.44	188.06
64.18	71.53	18.07	45.23
25.68	26.00	189.16	89.59

ANSWERING QUESTIONS BY SUBTRACTING

1. Emma had $3. She gave $.14 to her little brother. How much had Emma left?

First write $3 as $3.00. Then subtract $.14 from $3.00, making sure that the decimal points are under each other.

$3.00	Minuend
.14	Subtrahend
$2.86	Remainder

You find that Emma had $2.86 left.

To *check* the answer, add $2.86 and $.14, beginning at the bottom and adding up, thus: $6 + 4 = 10$; 1 (carried)$+ 8 + 1 = 10$; 1 (carried) $+ 2 = 3$. The sum is $3.00, which is the same as the minuend; hence the work is right.

In the above problem, $2.86 is called the **remainder.**

2. Tony has saved $4.20. Jim has saved $2.57. How much less has Jim saved than Tony?

Here you subtract to find the *difference* between Tony's and Jim's savings.

$4.20	
2.57	
$1.63	Difference

3. Alfred has $6.42. He needs $8.50 to buy a coaster. How much more does he need?

4. Mollie has $7.45. She spends $2 and puts the rest in a savings bank. How much does she put in the bank?

5. Abraham Lincoln was born in 1809. He was killed in 1865. How old was he at the time of his death?

6. In 1927 Lindbergh flew about 3647 mi., without stopping, in going from New York to Paris. A few weeks later Chamberlin flew about 4400 mi. from New York to Germany. How much longer was Chamberlin's trip than Lindbergh's?

7. Subtraction answers several kinds of questions, like "How much is left?" "How much farther?" and "What is the difference?" Make up six subtraction problems, each having a different kind of question.

A SUBTRACTION RACE

Do not copy these problems. Place the edge of your paper under the top row of problems. Write the answers along that edge of the paper, checking your work as you do it. Then fold the answers under and write the next row of answers along the folded edge.

As soon as one pupil finishes, the entire class stops. The one who then has the most problems correct wins.

Subtract the following and check the work:

1. 2967
      585
	2. 6384
	      747
		3. 7475
		      3994
			4. 6354
			      5549

5. 7253
      324
	6. 8252
	      482
		7. 9629
		      7656
			8. 9215
			      2631

9. 4850
      170
	10. 4126
	       881
		11. 5001
		      3331
			12. 7009
			      5247

13. 5647
       388
	14. 8446
	      3666
		15. 7275
		      2299
			16. 8910
			      1429

17. 8913
       972
	18. 3263
	      1871
		19. 8526
		      7894
			20. 5419
			      2888

21. 4301
       750
	22. 5800
	      2611
		23. 8000
		      2546
			24. 7912
			      4886

25. 9094
       765
	26. 9319
	      3650
		27. 4314
		      3491
			28. 3209
			      1669

PRACTICE IN SUBTRACTION

Subtract the following and check the work:

1. $77.64
   47.87
	2. $80.00
	   19.05
		3. $50.00
		   23.83
			4. $76.32
			   57.75

5. $70.04
   35.66
	6. $82.43
	   44.87
		7. $66.34
		   19.48
			8. $51.33
			   14.36

9. $73.41
   15.40
	10. $93.64
	   29.69
		11. $82.32
		   22.86
			12. $40.70
			   11.02

13. $41.78
   9.99
	14. $32.81
	   7.89
		15. $50.03
		   7.63
			16. $87.44
			   8.95

Subtract the following and check the work:

17. $361.03
   237.44
	18. $921.27
	   668.89
		19. $860.00
		   141.25
			20. $796.21
			   658.35

21. $700.00
   289.72
	22. $924.34
	   438.66
		23. $534.25
		   399.59
			24. $770.10
			   363.06

25. $627.48
   78.77
	26. $392.78
	   6.79
		27. $300.08
		   46.48
			28. $821.65
			   8.67

29. $554.35
   96.75
	30. $660.00
	   3.51
		31. $132.87
		   89.89
			32. $473.43
			   95.45

ON A FRUIT FARM

1. Bob and Mary spent the summer with Uncle Ned on his fruit farm. There are 25 acres of fruit trees, 14 acres of berry vines and bushes, and 17 acres of grain fields. How many acres are there in Uncle Ned's farm?

2. One of the biggest crops he has is his peach crop. Last year he shipped 1895 bu. of peaches to market and this year he shipped 1977 bu. How many more bushels did he ship this year than last year?

3. Mary picked 53 qt. of strawberries and 87 qt. of blackberries while she was on the farm. How many quarts of berries did she pick in all?

4. Bob picked 217 qt. of berries in all. How many more quarts did he pick than Mary?

5. They helped Uncle Ned pack berries for the market. Uncle Ned packed 43 crates, Bob packed 27 crates, and Mary packed 32 crates. How many crates in all did they pack to send to market?

6. Bob weighed 81 lb. when he came to the farm and 88 lb. when he left. How many pounds did he gain?

HOW WE MAKE CHANGE

Fred is a clerk in a grocery store. Anna buys a dozen eggs for 38¢ and gives him a 1-dollar bill.

To make change for Anna, Fred first thinks 38¢; then he takes 2 cents and thinks 40¢; then he takes a dime and thinks 50¢; then he takes a half dollar and thinks $1. As he gives Anna the coins, he counts them again, saying, "38, 40, 50, $1." Anna counts with him to make sure that the change is right.

To check your change, start with the cost of your purchase and add to it the coins that the clerk gives you. The sum should equal the amount that you gave the clerk.

Making Change

1. Tess buys a basket of apples for 69¢. She gives the clerk $1. He gives her a cent, a nickel, and a quarter. Count the change as the clerk did. Is it right?

2. Martha buys a 7-cent notebook and gives the clerk a quarter. The clerk gives her 3 cents, a nickel, and a dime. Count out the change with the clerk.

3. Edward buys 15¢ worth of rolls and hands the clerk $1. The clerk gives him 2 nickels, 2 dimes, and a half dollar as change. Count the change. Is it right? What change should the clerk give Edward?

Tell what coins you would give as change for $1 on each of these purchases:

4. 83¢ **6.** 59¢ **8.** 91¢ **10.** 72¢ **12.** 68¢ **14.** 60¢

5. 22¢ **7.** 41¢ **9.** 29¢ **11.** 33¢ **13.** 9¢ **15.** 16¢

Make change from $5 for these purchases:

16. $1.23 **17.** $2.07 **18.** $3.12 **19.** $2.28 **20.** $3.64

MAKING CHANGE

Mary spent 22¢ for colored paper and 15¢ for paste. If she gave the clerk 50¢, how much change did she get?

This problem has two steps. The first step is to find how much Mary spent in all and the second step is to find how much change she got.

First Step. To find how much Mary spent in all, you add 22¢ and 15¢. This gives 37¢ as the answer to the first step. You use this answer to work the second step of the problem.

$$\begin{array}{r} 22 \\ \underline{15} \\ 37 \end{array}$$

Second Step. To find the amount of Mary's change, you subtract 37¢ from 50¢. This gives 13¢ for the answer to the second step. This is also the answer to the problem. You see that Mary got 13¢ change.

$$\begin{array}{r} 50 \\ \underline{37} \\ 13 \end{array}$$

Work these two-step problems:

1. Robert paid $.45 for a book and $.12 for a ruler. How much change did he get from $1.00?

2. For his lunch to-day Frank bought soup for 7¢, milk for 5¢, a sandwich for 9¢, and ice cream for 10¢. If he paid for his lunch with a half dollar, how much change did he get?

3. To-day Mrs. Case went to the grocery store. She bought 2 doz. oranges at $.29 a dozen. How much did she have left from $1.00?

4. Mrs. Wilson sent Ann to the store for ½ lb. of tea. If the tea was $.70 a pound, how much change did Ann get from a half dollar?

5. Mary's mother bought her a sweater for $2.50, a dress for $3.98, and a hat for $1.19. How much money did she have left from a 10-dollar bill?

TWO-STEP PROBLEMS

1. Jim and Tom went fishing. Jim caught 8 fish and Tom caught 9 fish. They kept 10 fish and gave the rest away. How many fish did they give away?

2. Alice bought 3 yd. of blue ribbon and 5 yd. of pink ribbon. She paid 8¢ a yard for each kind. How much did she pay for all the ribbon?

3. Joe keeps hens. He got 17 eggs yesterday and 26 eggs to-day. If he sold 30 eggs to Mrs. King, how many eggs did he have left?

4. Mary bought $\frac{1}{4}$ lb. of salted nuts at $.80 a pound and a box of candy for $.50. How much in all did she pay for these things?

5. Jack had 150 stamps. He gave Bob 25 stamps. Now he has a new stamp book that holds 400 stamps. How many more stamps does he need to fill the book?

6. Mrs. West paid $.05 for a spool of thread, $.35 for a dress pattern, and $1.74 for cloth for a dress. How much change did she get from a 5-dollar bill?

7. John sold 6 qt. of berries at 15¢ a quart. He put $\frac{1}{2}$ of the money he got in his bank. How much money did he put in his bank?

8. Betty earned a quarter running errands. She spent 5¢ for an ice-cream cone and 8¢ for popcorn. How much money did she have left?

9. There were 5 boys and 7 girls who went to Squirrel Pond for a picnic. It cost 12¢ each to go there and back on the bus. How much did all the fares cost?

HOW TO IMPROVE YOUR SKILL IN COMPUTING

You are all anxious to improve your skill in computing. You can do this if you practice faithfully; but you may find that you do not improve very much *unless you practice in the right way.* Suppose that you wish to improve your ability in the standing broad jump. You will improve somewhat if you practice jumping each day; but you will make the fastest progress if you *carefully measure* the longest distance you jump to-day, and write it down, and *then try hard to jump a little farther to-morrow.* Every athlete watches his record carefully in this way and *always tries to improve it.*

If you wish to add as well as or better than any other pupil in your class, you must watch your record and *always try to improve it.*

A good way to do this is by means of Improvement Tests, such as Test 1 A in Addition, given on page 17. When you try this test, the teacher will time you, telling you when to start and when to stop. At the end of the 4 minutes allowed for the test, the teacher will read the correct answers and you should see how many examples you have right. Then find your score on the test.

Try the same test again *the next day, doing your best to improve your score.* Repeat the test as often as the teacher directs, trying to get all the problems right, if possible, in 4 minutes.

The teacher will tell you when to try Test 1 B. Write down your score each time that you take a test, keeping your record as shown on page 20. See pages 18 and 19.

Always try to improve upon your best previous record.

NOTE. See Suggestions to Teachers on the page before the Index.

17

IMPROVEMENT TEST No. 1

Test 1 A — Addition   (Time 4 min.)

1. 287	2. 791	3. 578	4. 148	5. 284
395	706	845	263	495
906	268	659	587	509
331	519	763	264	787

6. 217	7. 267	8. 149	9. 666	10. 838
143	654	804	397	343
294	495	755	360	529
949	801	803	373	418

Test 1 B — Subtraction   (Time 4 min.)

1. 1141	2. 4065	3. 8223	4. 9169	5. 6824
372	530	3284	974	885

6. 1342	7. 2000	8. 7011	9. 9817	10. 3570
786	1262	1043	5919	2856

11. 1688	12. 7863	13. 2009	14. 8493	15. 5492
391	355	460	2909	662

Test 1 C — Addition   (Time 4 min.)

1. 128	2. 959	3. 897	4. 698	5. 169
407	257	332	725	370
826	349	806	590	138
532	160	758	844	901
790	741	391	104	749
336	254	217	476	776
901	162	743	835	819
290	908	489	948	346

HOW TO TAKE AN IMPROVEMENT TEST

When you are taking an Improvement Test in addition, subtraction, or short division, like Test 1 A, 1 B, or 3 A, do not copy the examples. Instead, place the edge of a sheet of paper directly under the first row of examples in the test, and write only the answers along that edge of the paper. Then fold these answers under and write the next row of answers along the folded edge.

For an Improvement Test in multiplication or long division, like Test 2 C or 3 C, the examples should be copied on paper before the test begins. In copying, spread the examples out so as to give sufficient space for working them. The time allowed for the tests in multiplication and long division does not include the time required for copying.

Work on each test only the number of minutes permitted for that test, and stop work *immediately at the end of that time*, even if you are just finishing an example. Otherwise it will not be possible to compare your scores from day to day on the same test.

If you finish a test before the signal to stop, check as many of the examples as you can in the remaining time. Occasionally the teacher will have you check the entire test, allowing you twice as long for doing and checking all the examples as for only doing them once.

FINDING YOUR SCORE IN AN IMPROVEMENT TEST

This table shows how to find your score on a test.

NUMBER OF EXAMPLES IN TEST	NUMBER OF EXAMPLES RIGHT																
	0	1	2	3	4	5	6	7	8	9	10	11	12	13	14	15	16
3	0	3	7	10													
4	0	3	5	8	10												
5	0	2	4	6	8	10											
6	0	2	3	5	7	8	10										
8	0	1	3	4	5	6	8	9	10								
9	0	1	2	3	4	6	7	8	9	10							
10	0	1	2	3	4	5	6	7	8	9	10						
12	0	1	2	3	3	4	5	6	7	8	8	9	10				
15	0	1	1	2	3	3	4	5	5	6	7	7	8	9	9	10	
16	0	1	1	2	3	3	4	4	5	6	6	7	8	8	9	9	10

1. Suppose that you take Test 1 B, which contains 15 examples, and get 12 examples right. Look down the first column to the *row* beginning with 15 (shown by Arrow A). Look *along that row* until you reach the *column* with 12 at the top (shown by Arrow B), and you will find the number 8 (shown by Arrow C). This means that your score is 8 on that test.

2. In Test 1 A (containing 10 examples), if you get 8 examples right, your score is 8; if you get 10 examples right, your score is 10, or perfect.

3. In finding your score, count only the examples that are entirely right. A partly finished example does not count.

Use the above table to find Frank's scores in these tests:

Number in test	5	8	8	9	10	10	12	12	12	15
Number right	4	5	7	5	7	9	8	10	12	14

GRAPHS OF RECORDS IN IMPROVEMENT TESTS

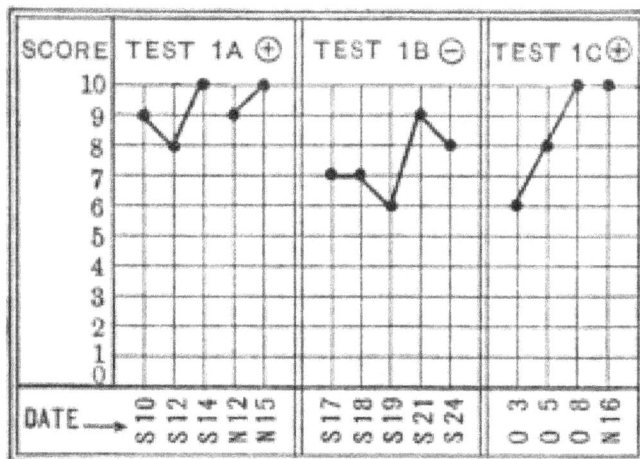

Here is a picture, or **graph**, of Carl's daily scores. Such a picture is the best way to keep your record.

The dates on which Carl tried each test are given below the bottom line of the graph. S 10 means Sept. 10, which is the first day on which Carl tried Test 1 A. The heavy black dot above S 10, on the horizontal line marked 9, shows that Carl got a score of 9 on Sept. 10. The months are abbreviated as shown at the right.

S = Sept.	F = Feb.
O = Oct.	M = Mar.
N = Nov.	A = Apr.
D = Dec.	My = May
J = Jan.	Ju = June

Reading the Graph of Carl's Record

1. What was Carl's score on Sept. 12? Did he do as well then as on Sept. 10? Did he improve on Sept. 14?

2. How many times did he try Test 1 A before he got a score of 10, or a perfect score?

3. How long after he first got a score of 10 did he try Test 1 A again? What was his score on Nov. 12?

4. Did Carl do as well on Test 1 B as on 1 A? What was his first score on Test 1 B? his lowest score? his last score? Does he need more practice on Test 1 B?

5. Tell his lowest and his highest score on Test 1 C.

6. On which test did Carl improve the most rapidly?

THE 100 MULTIPLICATION COMBINATIONS

Try to multiply all these orally in 2 min. Give the answers only. The last 4 rows are the hardest. Practice on those combinations that you get wrong or do slowly:

1.	1 2	2 0	6 2	9 0	3 6	2 1	2 9	1 0	6 0	2 6
2.	2 2	6 1	1 1	9 1	0 2	5 1	0 1	2 3	1 3	5 2
3.	5 0	4 1	0 4	3 5	9 2	4 5	8 2	3 4	8 0	4 2
4.	5 3	0 3	1 5	3 3	0 9	5 4	1 4	2 8	0 6	8 1
5.	1 6	2 4	1 7	0 5	1 9	4 3	5 5	0 8	7 2	0 7
6.	3 2	7 0	3 1	1 8	4 4	2 7	4 0	7 1	3 0	2 5
7.	4 8	5 7	4 6	5 8	0 0	8 4	6 6	3 8	6 3	7 5
8.	7 3	6 5	7 7	3 9	3 7	9 3	9 9	8 3	6 4	9 7
9.	8 8	4 9	5 6	8 5	9 4	6 9	4 7	8 9	7 8	7 4
10.	7 6	9 6	6 8	5 9	6 7	7 9	8 7	9 8	8 6	9 5

BUYING THINGS FOR THE SCHOOL STORE

1. At the beginning of the school year, our school store buys 25 fountain pens at $1.46 each. How much do the pens cost in all?

You do the work as shown here. Check the work by going over it.

$$\begin{array}{r} \$1.46 \quad \text{Multiplicand} \\ 25 \quad \text{Multiplier} \\ \hline 7\,30 \\ 29\,2 \\ \hline \$36.50 \quad \text{Product} \end{array}$$

In this example, $1.46 and 25 are called the **factors** and the answer is the **product**.

Find the cost of these things for the school store:

2. 35 geographies at $1.27 each.
3. 78 arithmetics at $.72 each.
4. 95 readers at $.84 each.
5. 62 spelling books at $.43 each.
6. 50 writing pads at $.18 each.
7. 12 dozen red pencils at $.58 a dozen.
8. 18 water-color paint sets at $.45 each.
9. 24 dozen notebooks at $1.08 a dozen.

PRACTICE IN MULTIPLICATION

Copy these examples. Then multiply as rapidly as you can. Check each example by going over your work carefully:

1. 576 43	**6.** 725 29	**11.** 918 82	**16.** 862 75	**21.** 829 45
2. 275 86	**7.** 517 57	**12.** 942 63	**17.** 316 59	**22.** 609 38
3. 346 27	**8.** 316 38	**13.** 603 76	**18.** 248 83	**23.** 347 56
4. 436 59	**9.** 809 65	**14.** 754 28	**19.** 509 69	**24.** 945 17
5. 489 91	**10.** 829 47	**15.** 134 94	**20.** 476 34	**25.** 827 29

Multiply and check. Be sure to put the decimal point and the dollar sign where they belong in the product:

26. $62.51 39	**30.** $16.87 96	**34.** $12.68 36	**38.** $38.53 73
27. $46.93 82	**31.** $49.05 65	**35.** $92.05 19	**39.** $57.12 67
28. $49.17 37	**32.** $35.28 48	**36.** $26.70 48	**40.** $30.26 47
29. $59.24 69	**33.** $68.05 47	**37.** $70.52 83	**41.** $81.07 76

ANOTHER WAY TO CHECK MULTIPLICATION

Multiplication can always be checked by going over
the work again. Another way to
check multiplication is to change
the position of the factors and
multiply again. This is called *re-*
versing the factors. If you have
found 75 × 83, you can check the

Example	Check
83	75
75	83
415	225
581	600
6225	6225

result by finding 83 × 75. The product will be the same
both ways if the work is correct.

Use the method of checking explained above when both
factors have the same number of figures. Otherwise
check by going over the work again.

Exercises

Multiply. Check the work by reversing the factors:

1. 54	**2.** 76	**3.** 48	**4.** 52	**5.** 87	**6.** 85
98	43	52	26	19	37

Multiply. Check by going over the work again:

7. 9421	**8.** 2843	**9.** 3176	**10.** 3756	**11.** 6382
65	74	92	15	68

*Multiply the following. Tell which check you will use
for each problem, and then check it:*

12. 197	**13.** 496	**14.** 209	**15.** 623	**16.** 5926
86	7	89	83	9

17. 731	**18.** 459	**19.** 492	**20.** 376	**21.** 806
217	342	571	356	684

TAKING CARE OF 0's IN MULTIPLICATION

Unless you watch the 0's in a multiplication example they may cause you trouble. Study these examples carefully so that you will know what to do with the 0's.

```
  456                                    456
  730 ← This 0 stands out                703
       at the right.
─────                                   ─────
13680                                   1368
 3192 ← This 2 comes under              3192 ← This 2 comes under
        the 7 of 730.                          the 7 of 703.
──────                                  ──────
332880                                  320568
```

Exercises

Check these problems the new way shown on page 24.

1. Herman has a news stand at Red Oaks Station. He sells, on an average, 126 papers a day. If he works 350 days in a year, how many papers does he sell in a year?

2. The Westfield School has 409 pupils. The cost of the school is estimated at $105 a year for each pupil. How much does the school cost in a year?

3. May Jones makes about 108 paper flowers a day. When she works 230 days in a year, how many flowers does she make in a year?

Multiply. Check by reversing the factors:

4.	683 740	**7.**	649 690	**10.**	803 609	**13.**	579 408	**16.**	357 407
5.	459 380	**8.**	503 260	**11.**	298 203	**14.**	207 702	**17.**	245 208
6.	409 570	**9.**	836 850	**12.**	457 503	**15.**	506 708	**18.**	653 309

SAVING TIME IN MULTIPLICATION

The owner of a radio shop is finding how much 132 storage batteries will cost him at $9 each.

He must multiply $9 by 132. This could be done as shown in A, but it is much easier to multiply as shown in B. Notice that 9×132 gives the same product as 132×9, just as 5×7 equals 7×5.

When you do the work as shown in B, remember that the result, 1188, stands for *dollars* because you are finding the cost.

A	B
9	132
132	9
18	1188
27	
9	
1188	

If one factor has fewer figures than the other, it is always quicker to multiply by the factor with the fewer figures.

Exercises

Multiply the quicker way. Then decide if the answer stands for dollars, yards, or some other unit.

1. Find the cost of 48 hats at $5 each.

2. There are 304 girls in the Fitch School. Each girl needs 2 yd. of light blue paper for a parade costume. How many yards of light blue paper are needed?

3. Richard sells magazines at 15¢ each. How much will he collect for 185 magazines?

4. David has 14 chickens. A poultry farm has 258 times as many. How many chickens has the poultry farm?

Have a race with a boy or a girl in your class to see who can do these examples more quickly:

5. 186×4 hr.	**8.** $182 \times \$2$	**11.** 432×3¢
6. 901×7 ft.	**9.** $156 \times \$5$	**12.** 287×4¢
7. 165×9 yd.	**10.** $307 \times \$8$	**13.** 129×11¢

MRS. FISKE'S CANDY SHOP

1. Mrs. Fiske has a candy store near our school. One day she made 48 boxes of nut fudge, which she sold at 19¢ a box. How much did she get for the fudge?

2. The same day she made 104 bars of molasses taffy for which she charged 5¢ a bar. If she sold all the taffy, how much did she receive for it?

3. Mrs. Fiske used 65 lb. of sugar for candy last week and 52 lb. this week. How many pounds of sugar did she use in the two weeks?

4. To-day Mrs. Fiske took in $14.56 and last Saturday she took in $38.69. How much more did she take in on Saturday than she did to-day?

★5. At Easter she bought from a candy factory 36 one-pound boxes of chocolates at $.78 a box and 27 two-pound boxes at $1.39 a box. What was her total bill?

6. Bert bought a box of small mints from Mrs. Fiske. He counted 210 mints in the box. How many mints would there be in 35 of these boxes? in 50 boxes? in 100 boxes? in 125 boxes?

7. Mary bought a box of candy for $.25 and some salted peanuts for $.19. She gave Mrs. Fiske a half dollar. How much change did Mary get?

THE 90 DIVISION COMBINATIONS

Try to divide all the following orally in 2 min. Give the answers only. Practice on those combinations that you get wrong or do slowly:

1.	2)4	4)28	7)49	8)64	9)0	1)5
2.	1)6	3)27	7)28	5)15	2)6	5)0
3.	4)4	3)12	6)18	2)12	8)48	3)6
4.	4)0	9)36	4)16	5)30	7)14	1)9
5.	3)3	4)20	8)16	2)18	5)45	2)2
6.	9)9	6)24	6)42	5)20	3)18	4)8
7.	1)3	4)24	4)36	3)21	5)35	8)0
8.	3)9	6)30	2)16	7)63	5)25	1)2
9.	1)7	7)35	7)56	6)12	8)24	5)5
10.	7)0	9)27	3)24	7)42	9)18	3)0
11.	1)4	7)21	3)15	9)54	2)14	1)8
12.	8)8	5)10	8)40	9)72	9)63	2)0
13.	6)0	6)48	8)32	9)81	4)12	1)1
14.	7)7	8)56	2)10	8)72	6)54	2)8
15.	1)0	9)45	5)40	6)36	4)32	6)6

GETTING READY FOR SHORT DIVISION

The uneven division combinations below are used over and over again in short division. If you can give the answers to 3 rows of these combinations in 1 minute, you should have no trouble with short division.

Give the quotients and remainders orally:

For example, in 5)37, say "7 and 2 over."

1. 6)7	5)37	6)29	5)19	6)57	5)17
2. 5)4	3)23	3)17	4)14	6)38	4)37
3. 3)8	5)48	5)23	3)20	3)29	6)19
4. 4)1	6)47	4)17	6)11	5)31	6)40
5. 4)7	4)35	6)27	6)22	4)30	5)13
6. 6)3	4)39	6)13	2)19	3)14	2)13
7. 3)5	5)36	4)11	6)58	5)34	6)53
8. 4)2	6)43	4)27	4)25	4)19	3)25
9. 5)9	6)34	6)59	3)22	5)42	6)55
10. 4)9	6)25	5)24	6)51	5)26	5)38
11. 2)7	6)17	6)41	4)33	4)22	6)15
12. 7)9	5)12	5)29	3)10	5)44	6)45

UNEVEN DIVISION COMBINATIONS

Here are some harder uneven division combinations. Give the quotients and remainders orally:

1. 7)53   9)77   8)58   8)74   8)51   8)27

2. 9)14   7)34   9)17   9)57   9)46   9)59

3. 8)79   9)33   9)28   8)60   8)23   7)17

4. 7)41   8)30   8)65   9)31   9)84   7)26

5. 9)67   7)57   7)29   7)38   9)69   9)40

6. 7)20   9)80   8)11   9)61   8)54   8)39

Short Division

Find the quotients. Check the work by multiplying the quotient by the divisor:

1. 2)48   6)60   3)963   2)806   4)840

2. 2)86   2)62   5)550   3)663   3)906

3. 3)84   6)72   2)136   7)735   9)954

4. 4)60   8)96   5)315   7)504   6)288

5. 7)84   4)96   8)960   9)927   6)636

6. 5)75   7)91   5)475   8)656   7)665

7. 4)72   5)80   9)792   7)756   9)918

BUYING REMNANTS

1. Janet bought a remnant containing 4 yards of green silk for $3.93. How much did she pay per yard?

Divide $3.93 by 4. The answer is $.98, with a remainder of $.01.

Hence Janet paid a little over $.98 a yard.

To check, multiply

Divisor 4)$3.93 Dividend
$ .98 Quotient
$ .01 Remainder

Check
$ .98
4
$3.92
.01
$3.93

the quotient, $.98, by the divisor, 4, and add the remainder, $.01. Since the result, $3.93, equals the dividend, the work is right.

To check division, multiply the quotient by the divisor and add the remainder. The result should equal the dividend.

2. Albert buys felt to make school banners. How much does he pay per yard if he gets a 7-yard piece for $18.55? if he gets a 3-yard piece for $7.50?

3. If a 9-yard remnant costs $18.27, what is the cost per yard?

4. If a 3-yard remnant costs $5.70, what is the cost per yard?

Other Problems

1. Six boys bought a football for $2.94. How much did each pay if they shared the expense equally?

★2. Rose made a train trip of 290 mi. in 9 hr. The train traveled a little over how many miles an hour?

3. Mrs. Allen's 8 grandchildren are saving money to buy her a rocking chair costing $32.40. How much will each need to save if they divide the cost equally?

4. The 226 girls of the Park School plan to march in rows of 7's in a parade. How many rows will they make? Will any girls be left over?

PRACTICE IN SHORT DIVISION

Divide the following. Check the work by multiplying:

1. $2\overline{)108}$ $6\overline{)854}$ $2\overline{)1342}$ $9\overline{)9540}$ $5\overline{)5350}$

2. $4\overline{)252}$ $8\overline{)316}$ $8\overline{)2165}$ $4\overline{)1360}$ $4\overline{)3043}$

3. $3\overline{)216}$ $9\overline{)367}$ $7\overline{)1449}$ $5\overline{)1047}$ $2\overline{)1186}$

4. $8\overline{)544}$ $4\overline{)239}$ $3\overline{)2550}$ $5\overline{)2532}$ $6\overline{)3606}$

5. $5\overline{)525}$ $2\overline{)578}$ $7\overline{)4335}$ $8\overline{)2528}$ $5\overline{)3745}$

6. $6\overline{)504}$ $3\overline{)494}$ $8\overline{)8064}$ $6\overline{)6036}$ $9\overline{)3672}$

7. $9\overline{)540}$ $5\overline{)348}$ $6\overline{)2430}$ $7\overline{)3049}$ $6\overline{)6001}$

8. $7\overline{)525}$ $8\overline{)438}$ $9\overline{)2133}$ $3\overline{)1251}$ $2\overline{)1750}$

9. $4\overline{)115}$ $9\overline{)981}$ $5\overline{)5150}$ $5\overline{)4045}$ $3\overline{)1874}$

In these division examples the answers are given. Tell which answers are wrong and correct them:

10. $7\overline{)483}$ $9\overline{)4716}$ $6\overline{)4938}$ $9\overline{)1845}$ $2\overline{)1116}$
       69   524   823   25   558

11. $3\overline{)927}$ $6\overline{)1242}$ $8\overline{)4344}$ $2\overline{)1810}$ $6\overline{)2502}$
      308   207   543   905   418

12. $4\overline{)188}$ $5\overline{)2185}$ $9\overline{)1413}$ $5\overline{)2140}$ $3\overline{)2811}$
       47   439   147   428   937

13. $8\overline{)856}$ $4\overline{)3608}$ $7\overline{)7490}$ $7\overline{)1456}$ $9\overline{)1089}$
       17   902   107   208   121

IMPROVEMENT TEST No. 2

Test 2 A — Addition   (Time 4 min.)

1.	2.	3.	4.	5.
5267	3746	1479	1796	6692
2090	9604	5610	7360	8787
4128	5534	3562	3918	9943
6896	8175	8884	9583	5019
7137	4955	4469	5377	2671
8502	2002	7335	2768	5936

Test 2 B — Subtraction   (Time 4 min.)

1.	2.	3.	4.	5.
4910	9571	7412	6075	6635
1340	5681	2543	4172	4539

6.	7.	8.	9.	10.
6375	9300	8243	5517	9822
1777	4587	4696	2980	6942

11.	12.	13.	14.	15.
7501	4000	8423	3168	9349
6340	1527	3182	2898	3187

Test 2 C — Multiplication   (Time 5 min. after copying)

1.	2.	3.	4.
765	915	508	790
35	46	72	83

5.	6.	7.	8.
948	826	467	975
65	94	27	49

Test 2 D — Multiplication   (Time 4 min. after copying)

1.	2.	3.	4.	5.
975	769	716	543	674
805	314	195	792	806

NOTE.   For directions for taking the above tests, see page 18.

DIAGNOSTIC TEST

*If you miss exercises in any row, you need more practice.
The Help Pages tell you where to find it.*

Add the following and check the work:

1.	970	639	340	640	858	
	183	846	577	616	549	
	778	693	940	537	394	**6, 7**
	462	150	796	290	511	
	821	507	335	872	364	
	682	188	462	547	329	

Subtract the following and check the work:

2.	8653	7000	9694	5825	**10, 11**
	1769	4984	6995	2885	

Multiply the following and check the work:

3.	327	865	1467	2368	**23, 24**
	24	38	45	72	

4.	632	526	742	506	**24, 25**
	418	846	503	290	

Find the quotients and remainders, if any.   Check:

5. 3)78   5)750   4)408   6)9180   **30**

6. 5)87   4)807   7)936   9)2896   **32**

MIXED PRACTICE

Copy these numbers in columns and add them:

1. 318 + 246 + 514 + 700 + 109 + 927 + 185
2. 621 + 378 + 223 + 805 + 573 + 445 + 528
3. 631 + 154 + 346 + 401 + 855 + 984 + 356
4. $12.65 + $945.03 + $263.42 + $68.18 + $55.60
5. $11.64 + $100.27 + $48.53 + $2.65 + $111.83
6. Find the quotient when the dividend is 1704 and the divisor is 8.
7. What is the difference between 1836 and 1249?
8. How much less is 4826 than 6000?
9. What is the product of 378 and 426?
★10. What is the remainder when 6824 is divided by 9?
11. How many inches are there in 2 ft. 7 in.?
12. Add 109 and 368. From the sum subtract 467.
13. Divide 1827 by 3. Add 391 to the quotient.
14. Beginning with 7, write the numbers by 5's to 57.
15. Beginning with 9, write the numbers by 4's to 53.
16. Find the sum of 137 and 27. Then divide the result by 2.
17. If you take 49 from 164, what is the remainder?

Find the answers to the following:

18. $\frac{1}{3}$ of 108 = ?	22. 134 − 89 = ?	26. 286 × 470 = ?
19. 35 × 89 = ?	23. 733 ÷ 8 = ?	27. 837 − 145 = ?
20. 97 + 68 = ?	24. $\frac{1}{5}$ of 205 = ?	28. 1485 ÷ 9 = ?
21. 612 ÷ 6 = ?	25. 7 + 9 + 6 = ?	29. 19 + 78 + 4 = ?

CAN YOU DO THESE PROBLEMS?

1. Four girls paid $1.40 for their mother's birthday present. If they shared the cost of the present equally, how much did each girl pay?

2. How many 3-cent stamps can you buy for 50¢? How many cents will you have left over?

3. Mrs. Lee bought 2 lb. of raisins at $.10 a pound and 4 lb. of sugar at $.05 a pound. How much did she pay for these things?

4. Fred saved $1.38 in September, $1.75 in October, and $1.54 in November. How much money in all did Fred save in these three months?

5. Jane made 128 pieces of fudge. She put 24 pieces in a box and had 5 boxes in all. How many pieces did she have left over?

6. Ned and Jack bought a bicycle for $19.50. If they shared the expense equally, how much did each boy pay?

7. Ann got $5.00 for a present. She bought a pair of roller skates for $2.75 and a book for $1.19. How much money did she have left?

8. The fourth grade sold 237 tickets for the school play and the fifth grade sold 315 tickets. How many more tickets did the fifth grade sell than the fourth grade?

9. This year Ted is putting $.25 in the school bank each week. How much money will he have at the end of 19 wk.? at the end of 38 wk.?

★10. Mrs. Adams bought 3 yd. of muslin at $.17 a yard, 5 yd. of ribbon at $.35 a yard, and a spool of thread for $.05. How much change did she get from $5.00?

PROBLEM TEST A1

1. The Red River is 1275 mi. long and the Rio Grande is 1650 mi. long. How many miles longer is the Rio Grande than the Red River?

2. Mary had $1.00 when she went to the store. She bought a book for $.48 and some paper for $.15. How much money did she have left?

3. Eight boys paid $12.00 for materials to build a hut in the woods. If the 8 boys shared the expense equally, how much did each one pay?

4. In June we made a three-day trip by automobile. The first day we went 308 mi.; the second, 295 mi., and the third, 327 mi. How many miles did we travel in all?

5. Alice spent most of her birthday money for books. She bought 2 books at $.59 each and 3 books at $.75 each. How much did she spend in all for her books?

6. George earns 25¢ a week working for a neighbor and 60¢ a week delivering papers. How much will he earn all together in 8 wk.?

7. Tom was measured in school to-day. He is 4 ft. 7 in. tall. How many inches tall is he?

8. John had 55¢. If he bought as many oranges as he could at 4¢ each, how many oranges did he get? How many cents did he have left over?

Standards	Excellent 8 right	Good 6 or 7	Fair 5	Poor 0 to 4

Write down the number of problems you got right on this test. Try to do better on your next problem test.

LONG DIVISION

Mr. Dane is driving from Savannah to California and back, a total distance of 7939 mi. If he drives about 23 mi. an hour, how many hours will he have to drive?

In dividing 7939 by 23, use the following rule:

When a two-figure divisor ends in 1, 2, 3, 4, or 5, divide by the first figure of the divisor to estimate each figure of the quotient.

1. Since the first figure of 23 is 2, divide by 2 to estimate quotient figures. The first partial dividend is 79. *Dividing* 7 by 2, you get 3 as the first quotient figure. Write 3 over 9 of 79. *Multiply* 23 by 3, which gives 69. *Subtract* 69 from 79, which gives a remainder of 10. *Compare* 10 with the divisor, 23. Since 10 is less than the divisor, this shows that 3 is the right quotient figure.

```
            345          Check
      23)7939            345
         69               23
        ----            ----
        103             1035
         92              690
        ----            ----
        119             7935
        115                4
        ----            ----
      R   4             7939
```

When you have the right quotient figure, the remainder will always be less than the divisor.

2. *Bring down* 3, which gives 103 as the next partial dividend. Dividing 10 by 2 would give 5 as the second quotient figure. But when you multiply 23 by 5, you get 115, which is too large to be subtracted from 103. Hence try 4. Why is 4 right?

When the rule gives a quotient figure that is too large, try the next smaller figure.

3. *Bring down* 9, which gives 119 as the next partial dividend. Divide 11 by 2, which gives 5 as quotient. Why is 5 right?

The quotient is 345, with a remainder of 4. Hence Mr. Dane will have to drive a little over 345 hr. in all.

Check the work by multiplying 345 by 23 and adding 4.

TRAVELING AT DIFFERENT SPEEDS

1. A fast airplane made a trip from Los Angeles to New York in 11 hr. The air-line distance between these two cities is about 2464 mi. How many miles an hour did the airplane travel on this trip?

2. The distance by train from Los Angeles to New York is about 3256 mi. If a fast train made this trip in 74 hr., how many miles an hour did it travel?

3. If you could walk the 3256 mi. from Los Angeles to New York at the rate of 22 mi. a day, how many days of walking would the trip require?

Exercises

Divide and check, using the rule on page 38 to find the quotient figures. Write R before the remainder, if any:

1. 5124 ÷ 21	**12.** 1911 ÷ 21	**23.** 18,396 ÷ 42
2. 7136 ÷ 32	**13.** 1935 ÷ 55	**24.** 18,414 ÷ 62
3. 1584 ÷ 22	**14.** 9961 ÷ 43	**25.** 28,861 ÷ 73
4. 2688 ÷ 64	**15.** 3330 ÷ 74	**26.** 15,264 ÷ 53
5. 5775 ÷ 25	**16.** 5719 ÷ 42	**27.** 55,876 ÷ 61
6. 6466 ÷ 53	**17.** 4768 ÷ 91	**28.** 29,736 ÷ 63
7. 7949 ÷ 81	**18.** 9072 ÷ 24	**29.** 18,975 ÷ 75
8. 1798 ÷ 35	**19.** 9980 ÷ 34	**30.** 62,560 ÷ 85
9. 8835 ÷ 95	**20.** 2436 ÷ 42	**31.** 19,932 ÷ 44
10. 5325 ÷ 75	**21.** 1045 ÷ 55	**32.** 26,424 ÷ 72
11. 8879 ÷ 72	**22.** 9021 ÷ 31	**33.** 26,979 ÷ 51

LONG DIVISION

Mrs. Blake is buying a small house costing $6815.   She is paying for the house at the rate of $29 per month.   How many months will it take her to pay for it?

In dividing 6815 by 29, use this rule:

When a two-figure divisor ends in 6, 7, 8, or 9, divide by **1** *more than the first figure of the divisor to estimate each quotient figure.*

Since the first figure of 29 is 2, use 3 as the trial divisor.   You may do this since 29 about equals 30.
1. To find the first quotient figure, think "6 ÷ 3 = 2." Trying 2 as the quotient, you get the remainder 10, which is less than the divisor.   Hence 2 is the right quotient.
2. How is 3 obtained as the second quotient figure? Is the remainder less than the divisor?
3. For the third quotient figure, think "14 ÷ 3 gives 4."   Trying 4 as quotient, you get a remainder of 29, which *is equal* to the divisor.   Hence 4 is too small.   Try 5.

```
      235
29)6815
    58
    101
     87
    145
    145
```

It will take Mrs. Blake 235 mo. to pay for the house.

When the remainder is equal to or larger than the divisor. try the next larger figure as quotient.

Exercises

Divide, using the above rule.   Check by multiplying:

1. 1669 ÷ 79
2. 1654 ÷ 37
3. 9792 ÷ 28
4. 4632 ÷ 59
5. 4422 ÷ 56
6. 1779 ÷ 97
7. 1320 ÷ 28
8. 2686 ÷ 79
9. 5592 ÷ 69
10. 7310 ÷ 86
11. 16,504 ÷ 38
12. 35,154 ÷ 69
13. 26,136 ÷ 36
14. 18,984 ÷ 28
15. 17,591 ÷ 49

DRILL IN LONG DIVISION

Divide and check. Write R before the remainder:

1. 5145 ÷ 21	**23.** 6094 ÷ 27	**45.** 29,736 ÷ 63
2. 7471 ÷ 31	**24.** 3659 ÷ 57	**46.** 10,028 ÷ 23
3. 2035 ÷ 55	**25.** 3072 ÷ 48	**47.** 24,667 ÷ 43
4. 2052 ÷ 33	**26.** 8035 ÷ 45	**48.** 16,504 ÷ 38
5. 1230 ÷ 39	**27.** 9858 ÷ 53	**49.** 53,756 ÷ 89
6. 2412 ÷ 67	**28.** 6293 ÷ 73	**50.** 28,497 ÷ 69
7. 1751 ÷ 56	**29.** 1897 ÷ 59	**51.** 16,836 ÷ 92
8. 5876 ÷ 52	**30.** 3128 ÷ 46	**52.** 17,990 ÷ 35
9. 7810 ÷ 55	**31.** 9747 ÷ 68	**53.** 12,244 ÷ 44
10. 1216 ÷ 64	**32.** 5960 ÷ 41	**54.** 28,178 ÷ 73
11. 5644 ÷ 83	**33.** 4510 ÷ 92	**55.** 63,427 ÷ 91
12. 2736 ÷ 28	**34.** 5798 ÷ 78	**56.** 44,030 ÷ 85
13. 2795 ÷ 38	**35.** 6263 ÷ 88	**57.** 73,079 ÷ 89
14. 8227 ÷ 46	**36.** 9664 ÷ 64	**58.** 47,817 ÷ 77
15. 2790 ÷ 45	**37.** 8989 ÷ 24	**59.** 48,926 ÷ 77
16. 6408 ÷ 24	**38.** 3029 ÷ 39	**60.** 15,561 ÷ 21
17. 2410 ÷ 52	**39.** 2711 ÷ 37	**61.** 19,723 ÷ 62
18. 3589 ÷ 49	**40.** 4864 ÷ 76	**62.** 14,011 ÷ 19
19. 5592 ÷ 69	**41.** 5273 ÷ 19	**63.** 35,789 ÷ 89
20. 9108 ÷ 99	**42.** 5131 ÷ 74	**64.** 14,048 ÷ 42
21. 1701 ÷ 81	**43.** 5896 ÷ 47	**65.** 10,990 ÷ 52
22. 9834 ÷ 33	**44.** 4256 ÷ 56	**66.** 37,890 ÷ 59

NOTE. For all two-figure divisors above 18, the trial quotient figure, obtained by using the rules near the top of pages 38 and 40, is the correct quotient figure three times out of every four. When the divisor is 14, 15, 16, 17, or 18, the quotient figures must be found by trial, since no rule is satisfactory for these five divisors.

QUOTIENTS THAT CONTAIN ZEROS

1. The children in our class picked 880 daisies. If these were put in 22 bunches, how many daisies did each bunch contain?

The first figure of the quotient is 4. $4 \times 22 = 88$, and $88 - 88$ leaves no remainder.

Bring down the 0 of the dividend. Since $0 \div 22 = 0$, the second quotient figure is 0.

The quotient is 40.

Hence each bunch contained 40 daisies.

```
        40
   22)880
       88
        0
        0
```

2. In a large school assembly hall there are 25 seats in a row. How many rows do 2728 children fill?

The first quotient figure, 1, leaves a remainder of 2. Bring down the next figure from the dividend, making 22. There are no 25's in 22, hence $22 \div 25$ gives 0. Write 0 in the quotient. Bring down the 8.

To get the last quotient figure, divide 22 by 2, which gives 11. 11 must be wrong because the next quotient figure must be a single figure; hence try 9, which is the largest single figure below 11. When the rule gives 10 or 11 as a quotient figure, always try 9.

The quotient is 109, with a remainder of 3.

Hence 109 rows are filled, and 3 children are left over.

```
         109
   25)2728
       25
       ───
       228
       225
       ───
         3
```

Exercises

Divide and check. Watch out for the zeros:

1. $6798 \div 22$	**7.** $6018 \div 29$	**13.** $16{,}340 \div 43$
2. $7290 \div 81$	**8.** $7675 \div 25$	**14.** $16{,}096 \div 32$
3. $7313 \div 71$	**9.** $5014 \div 46$	**15.** $29{,}640 \div 76$
4. $7696 \div 37$	**10.** $7107 \div 69$	**16.** $44{,}856 \div 89$
5. $9328 \div 88$	**11.** $7800 \div 52$	**17.** $69{,}720 \div 83$
6. $8235 \div 27$	**12.** $1011 \div 98$	**18.** $15{,}990 \div 39$

BUYING IN LARGE QUANTITIES

1. Our class bought 36 flags for $4.32 for a celebration. How much did each flag cost?

Divide dollars and cents just as you divide any other numbers. Always write the *first* figure of the quotient over the *last* figure of the partial dividend; thus, write 1 in the quotient over the 3 of 43. Then place the decimal point in the quotient directly above the decimal point in the dividend.

```
      $ .12
36)$4.32
     3 6
     ──
      72
      72
      ──
```

Each flag cost $.12. To check, multiply $.12 by 36.

2. Vera's mother bought a 25-trip railroad ticket to Cobb for $26.50. How much was the fare for each trip?

★3. Peggy's father takes the train to the city every morning. He buys a special ticket, good for a month, for $10.26. If he makes 54 trips on the ticket, how much does he pay for each trip? How much cheaper, for the month, is this than 54 single-trip tickets at $.28 each?

★4. A school needs 85 tons of coal this winter. The entire 85 tons can be bought for $1027.65. If one ton is bought at a time, the price is $13.60 per ton. How much per ton is saved by buying all the coal at one time?

★5. In the Emerson School, 48 children want to buy fountain pens. If the 48 pens are ordered together, they cost $62.40. If bought separately, each pen costs $1.49. How much is saved on each pen if they are ordered together?

6. Tickets to Woodlands usually cost $.25 each. Our class hired a bus which took 25 children there for $5.00. How much did we save on each fare?

7. If 6 doz. golf balls cost $39.60, how much does 1 golf ball cost?

DRILL IN LONG DIVISION

Divide and check.   Write R before remainders, if any:

1. 5612 ÷ 29	26. 2774 ÷ 88	51. $416.30 ÷ 78
2. 8712 ÷ 24	27. 8448 ÷ 44	52. $494.91 ÷ 81
3. 1763 ÷ 41	28. 8000 ÷ 23	53. $179.28 ÷ 83
4. 7695 ÷ 45	29. 9072 ÷ 14	54. $159.06 ÷ 22
5. 1197 ÷ 63	30. 3013 ÷ 26	55. $473.25 ÷ 75
6. 2080 ÷ 13	31. 4641 ÷ 36	56. $436.65 ÷ 68
7. 3008 ÷ 94	32. 6730 ÷ 23	57. $138.00 ÷ 15
8. 3008 ÷ 64	33. 7188 ÷ 28	58. $457.89 ÷ 87
9. 6963 ÷ 33	34. 1230 ÷ 39	59. $163.40 ÷ 43
10. 8184 ÷ 44	35. 8232 ÷ 24	60. $742.34 ÷ 86
11. 6995 ÷ 28	36. 8676 ÷ 37	61. $278.78 ÷ 53
12. 3330 ÷ 74	37. 9990 ÷ 74	62. $230.84 ÷ 27
13. 5002 ÷ 41	38. 6450 ÷ 86	63. $105.28 ÷ 47
14. 4810 ÷ 26	39. 7412 ÷ 17	64. $158.44 ÷ 17
15. 7344 ÷ 18	40. 8045 ÷ 39	65. $134.46 ÷ 55
16. 9431 ÷ 25	41. 8260 ÷ 59	66. $144.90 ÷ 45
17. 4947 ÷ 28	42. 5928 ÷ 52	67. $261.12 ÷ 64
18. 3536 ÷ 68	43. 9945 ÷ 45	68. $208.02 ÷ 36
19. 8075 ÷ 25	44. 6880 ÷ 16	69. $269.99 ÷ 29
20. 8340 ÷ 15	45. 4991 ÷ 37	70. $269.94 ÷ 33
21. 4028 ÷ 53	46. 3577 ÷ 49	71. $154.80 ÷ 18
22. 2170 ÷ 35	47. 8059 ÷ 25	72. $237.12 ÷ 39
23. 7657 ÷ 19	48. 5494 ÷ 41	73. $176.80 ÷ 34
24. 8375 ÷ 25	49. 5688 ÷ 72	74. $447.44 ÷ 47
25. 7347 ÷ 93	50. 1216 ÷ 19	75. $359.70 ÷ 55

STORE PROBLEMS

1. Jack Brown's father has a grocery store and sometimes Jack works in the store. To-day he sold Mrs. Lee 2 lb. of butter at $.28 a pound and 3 boxes of cookies at $.15 a box. What was Mrs. Lee's bill?

2. Saturday Mr. Brown had a sale of soap. The kind that he regularly sells at $.09 a bar was sold at $.85 for a dozen bars. How much less did a dozen bars cost at the sale price than at the regular price?

3. Twelve girls bought some food for a picnic. They bought 2 doz. oranges at $.39 a dozen, sandwich material for $1.25, and ginger ale for $.85. If the 12 girls divided the expense equally, how much did each one pay?

4. Mrs. Case bought fresh vegetables for $.69 and groceries for $2.13. She gave the grocer, Mr. Brown, $5.00. How much change did she get?

5. Jack earned $3.70 last week and $4.20 this week by helping his father in the store. How much more did he earn this week than last week?

DIVISORS OF THREE FIGURES

For a pageant our school made 216 costumes at a total cost of $36.85. Find the cost of each costume.

1. You have to divide $36.85 by 216.

2. To divide by 216, use the same method as for a 2-figure divisor like 21. To estimate each quotient figure, divide by 2. Since 3 ÷ 2 gives 1, try 1 as the first quotient figure. Why is 1 right?

$$\begin{array}{r} \$.17 \\ 216)\overline{\$36.85} \\ 21\ 6 \\ \hline 15\ 25 \\ 15\ 12 \\ \hline 13 \end{array}$$

3. Explain how you find the second quotient figure. The cost of each costume was a little over $.17.

Check the work by multiplying the quotient and the divisor and adding the remainder.

If the second figure of any divisor is 5 or less, divide by the first figure of the divisor to estimate the quotient figures.

Exercises

Divide and check. Write R before remainders, if any:

1. 9763 ÷ 751
2. 9112 ÷ 536
3. 9888 ÷ 412
4. 8132 ÷ 428
5. 9697 ÷ 418
6. 8427 ÷ 351
7. 9288 ÷ 344
8. 5808 ÷ 242
9. 7667 ÷ 451
10. 6929 ÷ 533
11. 5248 ÷ 328
12. 9430 ÷ 409
13. 91,437 ÷ 431
14. 75,969 ÷ 207
15. 72,127 ÷ 913
16. 96,959 ÷ 453
17. 26,008 ÷ 627
18. 55,590 ÷ 654
19. 40,888 ÷ 538
20. 22,631 ÷ 427
21. 16,198 ÷ 623
22. 41,361 ÷ 811
23. 38,626 ÷ 623
24. 37,592 ÷ 508
25. 32,028 ÷ 628
26. 49,197 ÷ 713
27. 23,692 ÷ 324
28. 21,518 ÷ 406
29. 13,099 ÷ 319
30. 39,888 ÷ 554
31. 52,984 ÷ 716
32. 224,991 ÷ 641
33. 100,492 ÷ 518
34. 114,704 ÷ 536
35. 269,892 ÷ 612
36. 234,171 ÷ 441

WATCHING ZEROS IN THE QUOTIENT

Study these examples carefully :

$$
\begin{array}{r}
207 \\
(a) \ 335\overline{)69348} \\
670 \\
\hline
2348 \\
2345 \\
\hline
3
\end{array}
\qquad
\begin{array}{r}
340 \\
(b) \ 543\overline{)184627} \\
1629 \\
\hline
2172 \\
2172 \\
\hline
7 \\
0 \\
\hline
7
\end{array}
$$

Divide and check. Write R before remainders, if any:

1. $64{,}262 \div 127$
2. $17{,}368 \div 334$
3. $11{,}544 \div 226$
4. $63{,}342 \div 207$
5. $35{,}990 \div 719$
6. $66{,}768 \div 642$
7. $43{,}217 \div 815$
8. $70{,}455 \div 340$
9. $64{,}906 \div 801$
10. $72{,}523 \div 347$
11. $62{,}833 \div 251$
12. $27{,}892 \div 442$
13. $96{,}370 \div 318$
14. $74{,}338 \div 225$
15. $46{,}329 \div 386$
16. $83{,}616 \div 416$
17. $48{,}270 \div 409$

18. $\$6511.47 \div 921$
19. $\$1962.52 \div 326$
20. $\$6042.20 \div 915$
21. $\$3749.78 \div 741$
22. $\$5630.30 \div 923$
23. $\$6871.20 \div 818$
24. $\$2184.72 \div 429$
25. $\$2224.80 \div 618$
26. $\$2210.08 \div 727$
27. $\$2640.00 \div 550$
28. $\$1911.52 \div 919$
29. $\$3547.50 \div 825$
30. $\$3493.80 \div 647$
31. $\$2604.70 \div 427$
32. $\$1156.32 \div 144$
33. $\$2764.84 \div 285$
34. $\$1250.48 \div 308$

DIVISORS OF THREE FIGURES

Mr. Lane has a shoe store. He paid $763.20 for 288 pairs of boys' shoes. How much did he pay per pair for the shoes?

As the second figure of 288 is 8, divide by 3 to estimate each quotient figure. You do this because 288 is almost 300.

1. To get the first quotient figure, divide 7 by 3, which gives 2.

2. To get the second quotient figure, divide 18 by 3, which gives 6.

3. To get the third quotient figure, divide 14 by 3, which gives 4. When you multiply 288 by 4, you find that 4 is too small, because the remainder, 288, is as large as the divisor. Hence try 5.

```
        $2.65
288)$763.20
    576
    1872
    1728
     1440
     1440
```

If the second figure of the divisor is 6 or more, divide by 1 more than the first figure of the divisor to estimate each quotient figure.

Exercises

Divide and check. Write R before remainders, if any:

1. 8834 ÷ 398	**12.** 47,336 ÷ 776	**23.** 29,267 ÷ 791
2. 7176 ÷ 276	**13.** 80,496 ÷ 387	**24.** 91,695 ÷ 275
3. 7880 ÷ 394	**14.** 99,348 ÷ 487	**25.** 56,012 ÷ 268
4. 9743 ÷ 687	**15.** 19,397 ÷ 496	**26.** 43,776 ÷ 684
5. 9118 ÷ 375	**16.** 41,577 ÷ 585	**27.** 80,551 ÷ 193
6. 8928 ÷ 288	**17.** 34,424 ÷ 662	**28.** 99,750 ÷ 475
7. 9702 ÷ 462	**18.** 12,150 ÷ 485	**29.** 96,876 ÷ 897
8. 7332 ÷ 282	**19.** 87,712 ÷ 896	**30.** 50,422 ÷ 689
9. 6375 ÷ 265	**20.** 25,740 ÷ 468	**31.** 94,800 ÷ 395
10. 5968 ÷ 373	**21.** 57,571 ÷ 787	**32.** 32,912 ÷ 968
11. 8398 ÷ 494	**22.** 48,384 ÷ 576	**33.** 68,935 ÷ 279

PRACTICE IN LONG DIVISION

Divide and check. Write R before remainders, if any:

1. 105,570 ÷ 115
2. 252,167 ÷ 461
3. 481,985 ÷ 571
4. 101,031 ÷ 283
5. 275,184 ÷ 624
6. 107,187 ÷ 117
7. 225,781 ÷ 394
8. 167,170 ÷ 365
9. 220,547 ÷ 223
10. 212,232 ÷ 478
11. 263,907 ÷ 497
12. 118,988 ÷ 386
13. 167,856 ÷ 269
14. 157,025 ÷ 571
15. 254,718 ÷ 534
16. 204,712 ÷ 493
17. 147,828 ÷ 582
18. 118,038 ÷ 382
19. 414,687 ÷ 651
20. 264,038 ÷ 474
21. 408,280 ÷ 865
22. 164,979 ÷ 797
23. 219,024 ÷ 676
24. 256,531 ÷ 799
25. 404,624 ÷ 968

26. $1871.86 ÷ 346
27. $1555.20 ÷ 288
28. $7263.75 ÷ 975
29. $1283.28 ÷ 182
30. $6085.72 ÷ 862
31. $4863.04 ÷ 721
32. $4287.78 ÷ 581
33. $4141.74 ÷ 619
34. $1247.40 ÷ 297
35. $4381.50 ÷ 575
36. $3801.00 ÷ 420
37. $1335.90 ÷ 365
38. $1836.12 ÷ 194
39. $5254.20 ÷ 973
40. $3361.46 ÷ 447
41. $6050.52 ÷ 882
42. $2397.60 ÷ 666
43. $2355.01 ÷ 733
44. $2206.40 ÷ 985
45. $1817.64 ÷ 594
46. $2037.02 ÷ 273
47. $3302.40 ÷ 344
48. $7505.92 ÷ 882
49. $1077.09 ÷ 161
50. $1138.50 ÷ 225

DIAGNOSTIC TEST — LONG DIVISION

If you miss exercises in any row, you need more practice. The Help Pages tell you where to find it.

Divide the following and check the work:

			HELP PAGES
1. 21)6762	64)34048	55)36968	**39, 41**
2. 33)7734	42)32172	73)22946	**39, 41**
3. 86)5418	39)17355	67)31222	**40, 41**
4. 49)3350	97)25511	58)31872	**40, 41**
5. 32)7360	56)22805	89)41830	**42**
6. 44)9108	73)44457	67)36859	**42**
7. 217)13237	515)38110	851)54590	**46, 49**
8. 426)24282	242)79184	921)78285	**46, 49**
9. 354)14624	631)51111	343)91586	**46, 49**
10. 262)15196	573)37818	196)43431	**48, 49**
11. 388)24469	395)85926	781)67246	**48, 49**
12. 499)36427	974)90582	367)81841	**48, 49**
13. 213)87117	305)70150	434)46668	**47**

IMPROVEMENT TEST NO. 3

Test 3 A — Division (Time 4 min.)

1. 2)1428   2. 3)1674   3. 7)6342   4. 9)9027

5. 4)1964   6. 4)2667   7. 7)2205   8. 6)4003

9. 3)2892   10. 5)3717   11. 6)2934   12. 8)7139

13. 9)8532   14. 5)1346   15. 2)1786   16. 8)3565

Test 3 B — Multiplication (Time 5 min. after copying)

1. 637 76	2. 654 28	3. 643 93	4. 460 92
5. 708 48	6. 582 96	7. 632 75	8. 943 84

Test 3 C — Division (Time 4 min. after copying)

1. 63)1512   2. 42)3150   3. 59)2006

4. 71)4473   5. 39)3471   6. 78)4389

Test 3 D — Division (Time 4 min. after copying)

1. 74)4588   2. 41)3321   3. 25)1550

4. 39)2067   5. 53)4028   6. 87)5494

NOTE. For directions for taking the above tests, see page 18.

PROBLEMS

1. The DeWitt Boat Club has 37 members. They buy a second-hand motor boat for $203.50. What is each member's share of the cost?

2. Yesterday 234 children had lunch in our school lunchroom. To-day it rained and 281 children stayed for lunch. How many more children were there to-day than yesterday?

3. Mr. Fall went on a trip last summer. He traveled 481 mi. by airplane, 320 mi. by train, 215 mi. by boat, and 80 mi. by bus. How many miles did he travel all together on this trip?

*4. The Empire State Building in the city of New York is 1248 ft. high. The house that Jack lives in is 52 ft. high. How many times as high as Jack's house is the Empire State Building?

5. At $732 each, how many automobiles can a dealer buy for $15,000? How much will he have left over?

6. Bob Brown earns $1.50 a week. If he saves $\frac{1}{3}$ of it each week, how much will he save in 25 wk.?

7. How much will 42 arithmetics cost at $.48 each?

8. Three boys paid $1.50 to rent a boat, $.40 for fish-lines, $.25 for bait, and $.52 for food. If they shared the expense equally, how much did each boy pay?

9. Dick wants to buy a pair of skates that cost $4.75. He has earned $1.98 and his father has given him $1.25. How much more does he need to buy the skates?

10. Helen bought a pair of shoes for $4.75 and a pair of rubbers for $.95. If she gave the clerk a 10-dollar bill, how much change did she get?

★WORKING PROBLEMS MENTALLY

Alice sells 4 boxes of berries at 26¢ a box. About how much will she get for them?

You know that $4 \times 25¢ = \$1$. Since 26¢ is a little larger than 25¢, Alice will get a little more than $1 for 4 boxes of berries.

Exercises

Estimate the answers to these problems mentally:

1. If you think of 27¢ as about 25¢, about how much is $2 \times 27¢$? $3 \times 27¢$? $4 \times 27¢$?

2. Jean has 50¢. If she uses it to buy phonograph records at 23¢ each, how many records can she buy? Will she have any money left?

3. Jack sells 5 dozen eggs at 39¢ a dozen. Remembering that 39¢ is almost 40¢, tell about how much Jack receives for the eggs. Is the exact answer larger or smaller than the answer you estimated?

4. Edna, Frank, and Albert are each receiving a gift of a bicycle. Estimate the cost of the 3 bicycles at $19.75 each. How does your estimate compare with the exact cost?

In estimating, consider $19.75 as almost $20.

5. Our class is buying 30 geographies at 98¢ each. Fred estimates that they will cost about $3 in all. Betty estimates $30. Whose estimate is nearer correct?

6. How many new uniforms can the Bedford baseball team buy with $45 if the uniforms cost $8.95 each?

7. Carl and his 3 brothers are going to a football game. The tickets cost 55¢ each. Will $2 pay for them?

★TESTING ANSWERS

A Scout troop was buying 6 flashlights at $1.12 each. Bill thought that they would cost $67.20. Henry said that this was impossible; for since 1 flashlight would cost a little more than $1, 6 flashlights would cost a little more than $6. Bill did the problem again and found the exact cost to be $6.72. Was Henry's estimate helpful?

Always make a rough mental estimate of the answer before you work the problem on paper. This will tell you whether your final answer is sensible.

Exercises

1. Tony sells Mr. Carr a basket of cherries for 98¢, a basket of peaches for 89¢, and a basket of apples for 85¢. Should he be paid more or less than $3? Find exactly how much more or less.

2. Dolly is buying a new dress for $7.98 and a hat for $2.98. Will a 10-dollar bill pay for both? Estimate how much change she will receive if she gives the clerk $15. Then find the exact amount of change.

In problems 3 to 5, first estimate the answer roughly. Then find the exact answer.

3. In a parade there were 15 groups of 102 children each. How many children marched?

4. John spent $19.79 for seed and fertilizer for his garden. He grew flowers and vegetables which he sold for $40.26. How much did he make on his garden?

5. Agnes is going from Washington, D. C., to Chicago, a distance of 817 mi. The train travels 43 mi. an hour. How long will it take Agnes to reach Chicago?

FINDING AVERAGES

1. Tom earned $1.38 one week, $1.66 the next week, and $1.58 the third week. What was the average amount he earned each week?

If you add $1.38, $1.66, and $1.58, you find that Tom earned $4.62 in 3 wk. Tom earned *different* amounts each week. If he had earned *the same* amount each week, he would have earned $\frac{1}{3}$ of $4.62, or $1.54, a week. We call $1.54 the **average amount** he earned each week. If you multiply $1.54 by 3, you get $4.62, which is the same total for 3 wk. as the one obtained above.

$$\begin{array}{r} \$1.38 \\ 1.66 \\ 1.58 \\ \hline 3)\overline{\$4.62} \\ \hline \$1.54 \end{array}$$

To find the average amount, you see that you add $1.38, $1.66, and $1.58 and then divide the sum by 3. This is a two-step problem because *first* you add and *then* you divide.

2. Mr. Hall drove 344 mi. on Monday, 256 mi. on Tuesday, and 285 mi. on Wednesday. What is the average number of miles he drove each day?

3. At the Lincoln School to-day the pupils were weighed. Ann weighs 78 lb., Mary weighs 82 lb., Betty weighs 75 lb., and Alice weighs 81 lb. Find the average weight of each girl.

You divide by 4 because you add 4 numbers.

4. Mary earned $4.89 in 3 wk. What was the average amount she earned each week?

There are no numbers to add in this problem because you are told that Mary earned $4.89 in all in 3 wk. Divide $4.89 by 3 to find the average amount Mary earned each week. This is a one-step problem.

5. An airplane went 1232 mi. in 11 hr. Find the average speed of the plane per hour.

6. Mr. Brown saved $336 in 12 mo. What was the average amount he saved each month?

PROBLEMS WITHOUT NUMBERS

1. If you know the distance you traveled on a train and the number of hours the trip took, how do you find the average speed of the train per hour?

2. If you know the cost of each of several articles you are buying, how do you find the amount of your change from a bill you give in payment?

3. If you know the number of sheets of paper in one box, how do you find the number of sheets of paper in several boxes of the same kind?

4. If you know the time you left home and the time you arrived at school, how do you tell the time it took you to walk from home to school?

5. If you know the weights of each of several boxes of books, how do you find the average weight of one box?

6. If you know the number of pupils in each room of the George Washington School, how do you find the total number of pupils in the school?

7. If you know the cost of one gallon of gasoline and the number of gallons your car holds, how do you tell the cost of filling the tank with gasoline?

★8. If you know the number of miles the speedometer on your car registered before you started on a trip and the number of miles it registered at the end of the trip, how do you tell how far you went on the trip?

9. If you know the number of people going on a picnic and the number of sandwiches that you think are needed for each person, how do you tell the total number of sandwiches that must be made?

ARE YOU A GOOD THINKER?

First tell what the problem asks you to find. Then decide how to find it. When possible, estimate the answer roughly in advance.

1. Walter buys a can of peas for 21¢, a pound of butter for 33¢, and a dozen eggs for 39¢. He gives the clerk $2. How much change should he get?

2. Father picked 924 peaches. He sold 108 of them. The rest mother preserved in jars containing 8 peaches each. How many jars did that make?

3. The boys in our school made 40 bird houses at a cost of $.48 each. They sold them at $1 each. What was their total profit on all the bird houses?

4. Ben's allowance is 25¢ a week. When his father went away on a business trip, he gave Ben a nickel, 2 dimes, a quarter, a half dollar, and a 1-dollar bill. How many weeks' allowance was that?

*5. Lena is saving to buy her mother an electric iron costing $3.95 for Christmas, which is 13 weeks off. If she saves 10¢ a week on moving pictures and 20¢ a week on candy, how much more will she need to buy the iron?

*6. The girls in our school are dressing dolls for Christmas. We buy 48 dolls at $1.06 each, 15 yd. of cloth at 39¢ a yard, and 25 yd. of ribbon at 19¢ a yard. How much do the dolls and their dresses cost in all?

*7. If our school orders 48 school pins at a time, they will cost $31.20 in all. If only 27 pins are ordered, they will cost $19.98. How much less will each pin cost if the larger order is given?

MIXED PRACTICE

Subtract	*Multiply*	*Divide*	*Add*
1. $119.50 73.86	**2.** 1806 37	**3.** 32)9984	**4.** 577 289 370

Divide	*Add*	*Subtract*	947
5. 46)21,050	**6.** $17.93 8.07	**7.** 2538 1598	715 925

Read these exercises carefully. Then do them:

8. How many times is 793 contained in 38,064?

9. Find the average of these numbers: 29, 37, 49, 41.

10. Divide 1287 by 9 and add 67 to the quotient.

11. Find one eighth of 1000 and subtract 87 from the quotient. Then multiply the remainder by 2.

12. Multiply 83 by 15. Add 355 to the product.

13. Subtract $9.38 from $12.00. Then multiply the remainder by 2.

14. Add $15.31, $7.68, $3.95, $10.15, and $2.46. Then divide the sum by 5.

15. What is the difference between 1807 and 3015?

16. Tom multiplied 167 by 70 and said that the answer was 11,690. Was he right? Which number is the multiplier? Which number is the product? What numbers are the factors of 11,690?

17. How do you check an example in subtraction? How do you check an example in long division if it has a remainder?

PROBLEM TEST A 2

1. There are 35 members of the Pine Lake Club. They bought a new boat for $490 and shared the expense equally. How much did each member have to pay?

2. Jane bought $1\frac{1}{2}$ doz. nut cookies at the bakery. How many cookies did she get?

3. Harry spends 10¢ a week for candy and 25¢ a week to go to the moving pictures. How much will he spend in this way in 9 wk.?

4. A Champion bicycle costs $27.65 and a Star bicycle costs $19.90. How much less does the Star bicycle cost than the Champion?

5. Joe put $1.78 in the school bank in April, $2.34 in May, and $1.25 in June. How much money did he put in the school bank in those three months?

6. Alice has a piece of ribbon 38 in. long. If she cuts it into badges each 3 in. long, how many badges will she get? How many inches of ribbon will be left over?

7. Miss White bought a sweater for $3.75 and a hat for $2.39. How much did she have left from $10.00?

8. A farmer sold 3 lb. of butter at $.33 a pound and 2 doz. eggs at $.35 a dozen. How much money did he get in all for these farm products?

Standards	Excellent 8 right	Good 6 or 7	Fair 5	Poor 0 to 4

This test is like Test A1 on page 37. Unless you had all the problems right on Test A1, you should do better this time. Keep your mark on this test.

LEARNING WHAT NUMBERS MEAN

1. It is important to understand what each figure in a number like 2643 means.

2643 means 2 *thousands*, 6 *hundreds*, 4 *tens*, and 3 *units*.

The *position*, or *place*, that a figure occupies tells whether the figure stands for *units* or *tens* or *hundreds* or *thousands*. The names of the places are shown at the right.

Thousands	Hundreds	Tens	Units
2	6	4	3

In the number 8709, the 9 stands for 9 *units*. The 0 stands for 0 *tens*, which means *no tens*. What does each of the other figures stand for?

In these numbers tell what each figure stands for :

2. 6457   2073   6003   2700   168   304

READING LARGE NUMBERS

1. John read that one year there were 986,771,116 acres of farm land in the United States. John read this large number like this : 986 *million*, 771 *thousand*, 116.

A large number like this is divided by commas into groups, or **periods,** of three figures each, beginning at the right. The first group is the *units' period*, the second is the *thousands' period*, and the third is the *millions' period.*

MILLIONS THOUSANDS UNITS

986,   771,   116

Read each of these large numbers :

2. 2,678,500   122,618,417   58,601,005

3. 4,065,715   320,200,065   40,160,720

READING ROMAN NUMERALS

The Romans wrote numbers by means of the following letters, whose values were as indicated below:

I	V	X	L	C	D	M
1	5	10	50	100	500	1000

When two Roman numerals stand side by side, read them according to these rules:

1. If the letters are alike or if the first letter has a greater value than the second, add them.

Thus, XX = 10 + 10, or 20; DC = 500 + 100, or 600.

2. If the first letter has a smaller value than the second, subtract the first from the second.

Thus, XL = 50 − 10, or 40. CD = 500 − 100, or 400. 900 may be written as CM or as DCCCC.

Exercises

1. The first page of the preface of a large dictionary is numbered I and the last page of the preface is numbered LXXXV. How many pages are there in the preface?

Read these numbers:

2. XXV   5. LXIV   8. CCCIII   11. MCDXCII

3. XIX   6. LXXI   9. CDLVI   12. MDCCCCV

4. XLV   7. XCIX   10. MDCCC   13. MCMXXIX

14. What Roman numeral is seen on some nickels?

15. The cornerstone of the Capitol building in Washington was laid in MDCCXCIII. What year was that?

16. Look for Roman numerals in the chapter headings of books and on the cornerstones of churches and public buildings and tell the class about them.

FRACTIONS

Finding Parts of One Thing

1. Arthur divides an apple into 4 equal parts. What do you call 1 part of the apple? 3 parts?

Write three fourths like this: $\frac{3}{4}$.

2. This pie is divided into 6 equal parts. What do you call 1 part? 5 parts?

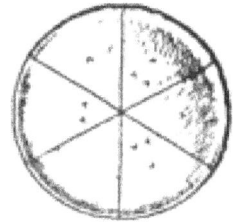

Five sixths is written like this: $\frac{5}{6}$.

3. Below is shown $\frac{3}{4}$ of an apple. What part of a pie is shown? what part of a cake?

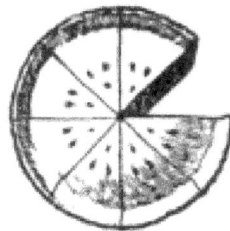

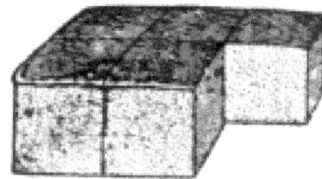

4. In the fraction $\frac{5}{8}$, 5 is the **numerator** and 8 is the **denominator**. 5 and 8 are the **terms** of the fraction.

$$\frac{5 = \text{numerator}}{8 = \text{denominator}}$$

The denominator 8 shows that 1 whole thing has been divided into 8 equal parts. The numerator 5 shows that 5 of these parts have been taken.

Tell what each numerator and each denominator means:

5. $\frac{1}{2}$ of a pie $\frac{3}{4}$ of a foot $\frac{5}{6}$ of a melon

6. $\frac{2}{3}$ of a cake $\frac{4}{5}$ of a garden $\frac{3}{8}$ of a yard

FINDING PARTS OF A GROUP OF THINGS

1. Ida has 15 daisies. She divides them into 5 equal bunches. What part of all the daisies is 1 bunch? 2 bunches? 3 bunches?

2. You see that $\frac{1}{5}$ of 15 is 3. How many are $\frac{2}{5}$ of 15? $\frac{3}{5}$ of 15? $\frac{4}{5}$ of 15? $\frac{5}{5}$ of 15?

3. There are 28 children in Mary's class. The teacher divides them into 4 equal teams. What part of the class is 1 team? 2 teams? 3 teams?

4. On page 62 you saw that $\frac{3}{4}$ can stand for a *part of one thing*, like $\frac{3}{4}$ of an apple. $\frac{3}{4}$ can also stand for a *part of a group of things*, like $\frac{3}{4}$ of 28 boys.

5. To find how many $\frac{3}{4}$ of 28 boys are, think:

$\frac{1}{4}$ of 28 boys = 7 boys

$\frac{3}{4}$ of 28 boys = 3×7 boys, or 21 boys

Exercises

1. There are 16 oz. in 1 lb. How many ounces are there in $\frac{1}{4}$ lb.? in $\frac{3}{4}$ lb.? in $\frac{1}{8}$ lb.? in $\frac{5}{8}$ lb.? in $\frac{8}{8}$ lb.?

2. How much will $\frac{3}{4}$ lb. of tea cost at 60¢ a pound?

3. How many inches are there in $\frac{1}{4}$ yd.? in $\frac{3}{4}$ yd.?

4. How much will $\frac{3}{4}$ yd. of ribbon cost at 48¢ a yard?

Find the following:

5. $\frac{1}{3}$ of 18	**6.** $\frac{1}{4}$ of 32	**7.** $\frac{1}{6}$ of 24	**8.** $\frac{1}{8}$ of $1.60
$\frac{2}{3}$ of 18	$\frac{3}{4}$ of 32	$\frac{5}{6}$ of 24	$\frac{3}{8}$ of $1.60
9. $\frac{1}{5}$ of 35	**10.** $\frac{1}{9}$ of 63	**11.** $\frac{1}{8}$ of 72	**12.** $\frac{1}{3}$ of $1.20
$\frac{2}{5}$ of 35	$\frac{2}{9}$ of 63	$\frac{5}{8}$ of 72	$\frac{2}{3}$ of $1.20
$\frac{3}{5}$ of 35	$\frac{5}{9}$ of 63	$\frac{7}{8}$ of 72	$\frac{3}{4}$ of $1.20

BARGAINS AT THE TOY SHOP

MURRAY'S TOY STORE

IMPORTANT AFTER-CHRISTMAS SALE

REDUCTIONS FROM REGULAR PRICES

½ Off on All Sleds and Skates

⅓ Off on All Books

¼ Off on All Other Things

---

1. Tom read the above advertisement in a newspaper and said that it was a good chance to buy things cheap. Before Christmas he had seen a sailboat marked $4.80. At ¼ off, what is its price now?

¼ of $4.80 is $1.20. Hence $1.20 is taken off the regular price. Subtracting $1.20 from $4.80 without rewriting the numbers, you get $3.60 as the price now.

$$\begin{array}{r} 4)\overline{\$4.80} \\ \$1.20 \\ \hline \$3.60 \end{array}$$

2. An electric train was marked $9.60 before Christmas. How much does it cost now? Read the advertisement to find out how much to take off.

3. Before Christmas Clara had seen a girl's bicycle marked $24.80. For how much can she buy it now?

Find the prices after ½ is taken off each price:

4. Hockey Skates . . $4.00 **5.** Boy's Sled . . $5.00

Find the prices after ¼ is taken off each price:

6. Sailboat . . . . $5.00 **7.** Dolls' Bed . . $2.40

Find the prices after ⅓ is taken off each price:

8. Poems for Girls . $1.35 **9.** Boys' Handbook $2.25

CAN YOU DIVIDE 3 APPLES AMONG 4 BOYS?

Alice is dividing 3 apples equally among 4 boys. What part of an apple does each boy get?

You must find what $3 \div 4$ means. If Alice had only 1 apple to divide among 4 boys, each boy $\qquad 3 \div 4 = \frac{3}{4}$ would get $\frac{1}{4}$ of an apple. Since she has 3 apples, each boy gets 3 times as much, or $\frac{3}{4}$ of an apple.

This shows that if 3 *things* are divided into 4 equal parts, each part equals $\frac{3}{4}$ of *one* thing. Thus, $3 \div 4 = \frac{3}{4}$. When you write $3 \div 4$ as $\frac{3}{4}$, the line between the numerator and the denominator means "divided by."

You now have a new use for a fraction.

A fraction can be used to indicate division. It then shows that its numerator is to be divided by its denominator.

Thus, $\frac{5}{6} = 5 \div 6$, $\frac{18}{5} = 18 \div 5$, $\frac{2}{3} = 2 \div 3$, $\frac{4}{4} = 4 \div 4$.

Exercises

Tell what part of a cake each child gets:

1. If 1 cake is divided equally among 3 boys.

2. If 2 cakes are divided equally among 3 boys.

3. If 1 cake is divided equally among 6 girls.

4. If 5 cakes are divided equally among 6 girls.

5. If 2 cakes are divided equally among 5 girls.

6. Since $6 \div 1 = 6$, you can also write 6 in the form of a fraction, thus: $\frac{6}{1}$. Likewise $15 = \frac{15}{1}$ and $1 = \frac{1}{1}$.

Write each of the following as a fraction:

7. $7 \div 8$	**10.** $7 \div 1$	**13.** $16 \div 5$	**16.** 5
8. $2 \div 3$	**11.** $20 \div 5$	**14.** $27 \div 9$	**17.** 8
9. $1 \div 2$	**12.** $10 \div 2$	**15.** $18 \div 1$	**18.** 2

FOUR WAYS OF EXPRESSING DIVISION

1. Uncle Ben was dividing 95 by 5. He asked Edna in how many different ways she could write this problem. This is what Edna wrote. Was she right?

$95 \div 5$ $5)\overline{95}$ $\frac{1}{5}$ of 95 $\frac{95}{5}$ (new way)

Write each of the following in three other ways:

2. $27 \div 4$ **4.** $3)\overline{18}$ **6.** $\frac{1}{7}$ of 56   **8.** $\frac{81}{9}$

3. $18 \div 5$ **5.** $7)\overline{25}$ **7.** $\frac{1}{9}$ of 75   **9.** $\frac{16}{4}$

10. Ruth says that any number divided by itself is always equal to 1. Is Ruth right? Does $\frac{5}{5} = 1$?

11. Tell what each of these equals: $\frac{7}{7}$; $\frac{3}{3}$; $\frac{4}{4}$; $\frac{9}{9}$.

WRITING THE REMAINDER AS A FRACTION

1. Edward has 55 in. of felt with which to make 4 school banners. How long does he make each?

Dividing 55 by 4, you get a quotient of 13, with a remainder of 3. Hence there are 3 in. still to be divided $4)\overline{55}$
by 4. Since you learned on page **65** that $3 \div 4 = \frac{3}{4}$, you $13\frac{3}{4}$
may write $\frac{3}{4}$ after 13.

Each banner is $13\frac{3}{4}$ in. long.

Whenever you have a remainder in a division problem, you can write the remainder over the divisor, thus making a fraction in the quotient.

2. Divide 14 yd. of ribbon equally among 3 girls. How many yards does each girl get?

Divide. Write the remainder over the divisor so as to make a fraction in the quotient:

3. $2)\overline{27}$ **5.** $3)\overline{43}$ **7.** $8)\overline{95}$ **9.** $5)\overline{323}$ **11.** $4)\overline{159}$

4. $4)\overline{33}$ **6.** $4)\overline{63}$ **8.** $6)\overline{83}$ **10.** $8)\overline{435}$ **12.** $3)\overline{224}$

PROPER AND IMPROPER FRACTIONS

1. A whole thing, like a whole cake, is 1 *unit*, or 1.

2. This cake is divided into quarters. Since 4 quarters make a whole cake, $\frac{4}{4} = 1$. How does the numerator of $\frac{4}{4}$ compare with its denominator?

You can also tell that $\frac{4}{4} = 1$ because $4 \div 4 = 1$.

3. Here you have 3 quarters of a cake. Is $\frac{3}{4}$ more or less than 1? Is the numerator of $\frac{3}{4}$ more or less than its denominator?

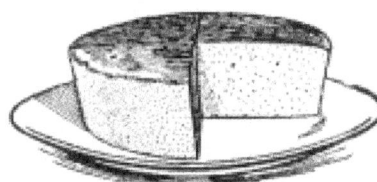

4. In the problems above, you have a whole cake divided into 4 quarters, and 3 quarters of another cake. How many quarters of a cake have you in all? Is $\frac{7}{4}$ more or less than 1? Is the numerator of $\frac{7}{4}$ more or less than its denominator?

5. Draw a line $\frac{7}{8}$ in. long. Also draw one $\frac{9}{8}$ in. long. Which is smaller than 1 in.? Which is larger than 1 in.?

Fractions like $\frac{3}{4}$ and $\frac{7}{8}$, in which the numerator is smaller than the denominator, are called **proper fractions.**

Fractions like $\frac{4}{4}$ and $\frac{9}{8}$, in which the numerator is equal to or larger than the denominator, are called **improper fractions.**

A proper fraction is always smaller than 1. An improper fraction equals 1 if the numerator equals the denominator, as in $\frac{4}{4}$. It is larger than 1 if the numerator is larger than the denominator, as in $\frac{9}{8}$.

6. Name the proper and the improper fractions below:

$$\frac{3}{5} \qquad \frac{8}{9} \qquad \frac{7}{3} \qquad \frac{14}{2} \qquad \frac{5}{1} \qquad \frac{8}{8} \qquad \frac{1}{4} \qquad \frac{10}{10}$$

REDUCING IMPROPER FRACTIONS

1. Dan's mother gives him 5 half oranges to share with his friends. The 5 half oranges make 2 whole oranges and $\frac{1}{2}$ of another orange, or $2\frac{1}{2}$ oranges.

Since $\frac{5}{2} = 5 \div 2$, you can also find that $\frac{5}{2} = 2\frac{1}{2}$ by dividing 5 by 2 and writing the remainder as a fraction in the quotient.

2. Kate has 21 quarters in her bank. Remembering that $\frac{21}{4} = 21 \div 4$, show that she has $5\frac{1}{4}$ dollars.

A number like 2 or 5 is a **whole number.**

A number like $2\frac{1}{2}$ or $5\frac{1}{4}$, consisting of a whole number and a fraction, is a **mixed number.**

To reduce an improper fraction to a whole number or to a mixed number, divide its numerator by its denominator.

Exercises

Reduce to whole numbers or to mixed numbers:

1. $\frac{9}{2}$	5. $\frac{15}{2}$	9. $\frac{19}{4}$	13. $\frac{41}{4}$	17. $\frac{31}{6}$	21. $\frac{26}{5}$
2. $\frac{5}{5}$	6. $\frac{17}{8}$	10. $\frac{21}{8}$	14. $\frac{50}{5}$	18. $\frac{25}{6}$	22. $\frac{45}{9}$
3. $\frac{7}{4}$	7. $\frac{30}{2}$	11. $\frac{16}{5}$	15. $\frac{37}{10}$	19. $\frac{25}{8}$	23. $\frac{37}{8}$
4. $\frac{14}{3}$	8. $\frac{23}{4}$	12. $\frac{32}{16}$	16. $\frac{41}{8}$	20. $\frac{21}{2}$	24. $\frac{75}{25}$

25. Jane made 7 boxes of fudge, each containing $\frac{1}{2}$ lb. How many pounds of fudge did she make?

26. Fred has 5 $\frac{1}{2}$-hour periods of arithmetic every week. How many hours of arithmetic per week has he?

27. Tom has 37 quarters. How many dollars is that?

ADDING FRACTIONS WITH THE SAME NAME

1. You can add things only if they have the same name. You can add 3 *balls* and 6 *balls*, but you cannot add 3 *balls* and 6 *tables*, because they are things with different names.

Can you add 5 cents and 7 cents? 8 fish and 4 fish? 6 dogs and 2 pens? 4 roses and 1 book?

2. A fraction has a name like any other thing. The denominator tells its name. Thus, the name of $\frac{5}{8}$ is *eighths*. The numerator, 5, shows that there are 5 *eighths*, just as the 5 in "5 cats" shows how many cats there are.

3. Since 5 eighths and 2 eighths have the same name, you can add $\frac{5}{8}$ and $\frac{2}{8}$, as shown at the right. Thus, $\frac{5}{8} + \frac{2}{8} = \frac{7}{8}$.

	Think this:	*Write this:*
	5 eighths = $\frac{5}{8}$	
	2 eighths = $\frac{2}{8}$	
	7 eighths	$\frac{7}{8}$

4. Add the following:

2 fourths	$\frac{2}{4}$	3 eighths	$\frac{3}{8}$	1 third	$\frac{1}{3}$
1 fourth	$\frac{1}{4}$	4 eighths	$\frac{4}{8}$	1 third	$\frac{1}{3}$

Give the name of each fraction and add:

5. $\frac{3}{8}$ **6.** $\frac{2}{4}$ **7.** $\frac{2}{5}$ **8.** $\frac{2}{8}$ **9.** $\frac{3}{16}$ **10.** $\frac{1}{10}$
$\frac{2}{8}$ $\frac{2}{4}$ $\frac{2}{5}$ $\frac{1}{8}$ $\frac{6}{16}$ $\frac{8}{10}$

11. John has 3 quarters in one pocket and 2 quarters in another. How much money has John in both pockets?

Adding $\$\frac{3}{4}$ and $\$\frac{2}{4}$, you get $\$\frac{5}{4}$. What mixed number does the improper fraction $\frac{5}{4}$ equal?

Add. Change the answers to whole or to mixed numbers:

12. $\frac{5}{8}$ **13.** $\frac{3}{4}$ **14.** $\frac{7}{8}$ **15.** $\frac{2}{3}$ **16.** $\frac{1}{2}$ **17.** $\frac{1}{8}$
$\frac{4}{8}$ $\frac{1}{4}$ $\frac{4}{8}$ $\frac{2}{3}$ $\frac{1}{2}$ $\frac{7}{8}$

WHAT BILLY DID AT CAMP

1. Last summer Billy went to High Hills Camp. One day he walked $3\frac{1}{4}$ mi. to Clover Lake; then he walked $1\frac{3}{4}$ mi. around the lake and $3\frac{1}{4}$ mi. back to camp. How many miles did he walk in all?

$3\frac{1}{4}$

Write the numbers as shown here.

$1\frac{3}{4}$

Think "$\frac{1}{4} + \frac{3}{4} + \frac{1}{4} = \frac{5}{4}$, or $1\frac{1}{4}$." Write $\frac{1}{4}$ and carry 1 to the whole numbers. Then think "$1 + 3 + 1 + 3 = 8$." Write 8.

$3\frac{1}{4}$

Billy walked $8\frac{1}{4}$ mi. in all.

$8\frac{1}{4}$

2. Another day Billy climbed $1\frac{1}{2}$ mi. up Wolf Mountain. He came back along a road $2\frac{1}{2}$ mi. long. How far did he travel that day?

$1\frac{1}{2}$

Think "$\frac{1}{2} + \frac{1}{2} = 1$." Carry the 1 to the whole numbers.
Billy walked 4 mi. that day.

$2\frac{1}{2}$

4

3. Billy rowed $4\frac{3}{4}$ mi. around Twin Lake, $2\frac{1}{4}$ mi. across the lake, and $2\frac{1}{4}$ mi. back. How far did he row?

Add the following:

4.	5.	6.	7.	8.
3	$2\frac{2}{4}$	$1\frac{1}{2}$	$2\frac{3}{4}$	$10\frac{1}{2}$
$2\frac{1}{4}$	$1\frac{1}{4}$	$\frac{1}{2}$	$1\frac{1}{4}$	$2\frac{1}{2}$

9.	10.	11.	12.	13.
$2\frac{1}{2}$	$8\frac{1}{4}$	$3\frac{2}{4}$	$5\frac{2}{8}$	$8\frac{1}{2}$
$3\frac{1}{2}$	$2\frac{3}{4}$	$3\frac{3}{4}$	$1\frac{1}{8}$	5

14.	15.	16.	17.	18.
$9\frac{1}{4}$	$6\frac{1}{8}$	$8\frac{1}{2}$	$2\frac{3}{8}$	$2\frac{1}{4}$
$3\frac{3}{4}$	$4\frac{3}{8}$	8	$2\frac{1}{8}$	$3\frac{3}{4}$
7	$5\frac{1}{8}$	$4\frac{1}{2}$	$5\frac{3}{8}$	$1\frac{1}{4}$

19.	20.	21.	22.	23.
$2\frac{1}{4}$	$9\frac{3}{4}$	$3\frac{2}{8}$	$2\frac{1}{2}$	$7\frac{1}{8}$
$1\frac{1}{4}$	$2\frac{1}{4}$	$6\frac{1}{8}$	$3\frac{1}{2}$	$3\frac{4}{8}$
$5\frac{1}{4}$	$7\frac{3}{4}$	$4\frac{5}{8}$	$2\frac{1}{2}$	$8\frac{6}{8}$

COMPARING HALVES AND FOURTHS

1. Jim earns a half dollar and Sam earns 2 quarters. Do they both earn the same amount? Does $\$\frac{1}{2} = \$\frac{2}{4}$?

2. How many halves of this circle are shaded? Show on this circle that $\frac{1}{2} = \frac{2}{4}$.

3. You see that $\frac{1}{2}$ and $\frac{2}{4}$ are always equal; that is, they have the same value. Hence *you can always change $\frac{1}{2}$ to $\frac{2}{4}$ or $\frac{2}{4}$ to $\frac{1}{2}$ to help you in working a problem.*

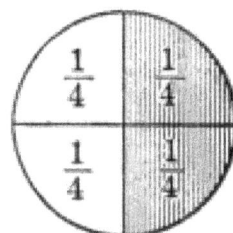

4. Remember these: $\qquad \frac{1}{2} = \frac{2}{4} \qquad \frac{2}{4} = \frac{1}{2}$

ADDING HALVES AND FOURTHS

1. Ellen had $\frac{1}{2}$ yd. of gingham. Her mother gave her $\frac{3}{4}$ yd. more. How much had she then?

The fractions must have the same name before you can add them. Change $\frac{1}{2}$ to $\frac{2}{4}$ and think "$\frac{2}{4} + \frac{3}{4} = \frac{5}{4}$." Then change $\frac{5}{4}$ to $1\frac{1}{4}$.

Ellen had $1\frac{1}{4}$ yd. of gingham in all.

$$\begin{aligned} \frac{3}{4} &= \frac{3}{4} \\ \frac{1}{2} &= \frac{2}{4} \\ \hline \frac{5}{4} &= 1\frac{1}{4} \end{aligned}$$

2. Eva used $1\frac{1}{2}$ lb. of almonds and $1\frac{3}{4}$ lb. of walnuts for candy. How many pounds of nuts did she use in all?

Explain the work.

$$\begin{aligned} 1\frac{1}{2} &= 1\frac{2}{4} \\ 1\frac{3}{4} &= 1\frac{3}{4} \\ \hline &\quad 3\frac{1}{4} \end{aligned}$$

Add. Check the work by going over it again:

3. $\frac{5}{4}$ $\frac{1}{2}$	**4.** $4\frac{3}{4}$ $5\frac{1}{2}$	**5.** $9\frac{1}{4}$ $8\frac{1}{2}$	**6.** $1\frac{1}{2}$ $2\frac{1}{4}$	**7.** $3\frac{1}{2}$ $2\frac{3}{4}$

8. $5\frac{1}{4}$ $4\frac{1}{2}$ $7\frac{1}{4}$	**9.** $8\frac{1}{4}$ $7\frac{1}{2}$ $5\frac{1}{2}$	**10.** $6\frac{3}{4}$ $2\frac{1}{2}$ $2\frac{1}{2}$	**11.** $5\frac{3}{4}$ $6\frac{3}{4}$ $2\frac{1}{2}$	**12.** $7\frac{1}{2}$ $3\frac{3}{4}$ $4\frac{1}{2}$

13. Count by $\frac{1}{4}$'s to 8, like this: $\frac{1}{4}, \frac{1}{2}, \frac{3}{4}, 1, 1\frac{1}{4}, 1\frac{1}{2}$, etc.

COMPARING HALVES, FOURTHS, AND EIGHTHS

1. Circle A is divided into eighths. How many eighths of a circle are there in a whole circle?

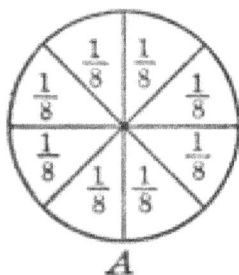

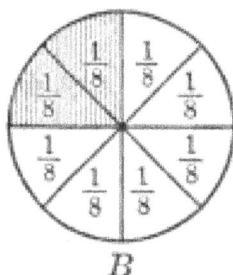

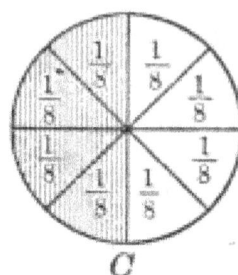

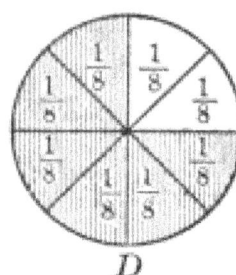

A   B   C   D

2. Study circle B. How many eighths of a circle make $\frac{1}{4}$ of a circle? This shows that $\frac{2}{8} = \frac{1}{4}$.

3. Study circle C. How many eighths of a circle make $\frac{1}{2}$ of a circle? This shows that $\frac{4}{8} = \frac{1}{2}$.

4. Study circle D. How many eighths of a circle make $\frac{3}{4}$ of a circle? This shows that $\frac{6}{8} = \frac{3}{4}$.

5. Since $\frac{1}{2}$ equals $\frac{4}{8}$, you can always change $\frac{1}{2}$ to $\frac{4}{8}$ or $\frac{4}{8}$ to $\frac{1}{2}$. You can also change $\frac{1}{4}$ to $\frac{2}{8}$ and $\frac{3}{4}$ to $\frac{6}{8}$.

6. Remember these because you will use them often:

$$\frac{1}{2} = \frac{4}{8} \qquad\qquad \frac{1}{4} = \frac{2}{8} \qquad\qquad \frac{3}{4} = \frac{6}{8}$$

$$\frac{4}{8} = \frac{1}{2} \qquad\qquad \frac{2}{8} = \frac{1}{4} \qquad\qquad \frac{6}{8} = \frac{3}{4}$$

COMPARING FOURTHS AND SIXTEENTHS

1. Draw line A, 1 in. long. Divide it into $\frac{1}{16}$'s of an inch.

2. Shade $\frac{1}{4}$ in., as in B. Show that $\frac{1}{4}$ in. $= \frac{4}{16}$ in.

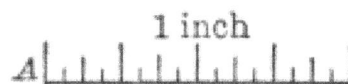

3. Shade $\frac{1}{2}$ in., as in C. Show that $\frac{1}{2}$ in. $= \frac{8}{16}$ in.

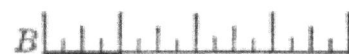

4. Shade $\frac{3}{4}$ in., as in D. Show that $\frac{3}{4}$ in. $= \frac{12}{16}$ in.

1 inch

A

B

C

D

REDUCING FRACTIONS TO LOWEST TERMS

1. You know that you can change $\frac{4}{8}$ to $\frac{1}{2}$ because $\frac{4}{8}$ and $\frac{1}{2}$ have the same value. A quick way to change $\frac{4}{8}$ to $\frac{1}{2}$ is to divide both terms of $\frac{4}{8}$ by 4, as shown in A.

$$A. \quad \frac{4 \div 4}{8 \div 4} = \frac{1}{2} \qquad\qquad B. \quad \frac{10 \div 2}{16 \div 2} = \frac{5}{8}$$

2. To change $\frac{10}{16}$ to $\frac{5}{8}$, divide its terms by 2, as in B.

If you divide both terms of a fraction by the same number, you get another fraction having the same value.

In changing $\frac{4}{8}$ to $\frac{1}{2}$, you reduce $\frac{4}{8}$ to its **lowest terms,** because the terms of $\frac{1}{2}$ cannot be made smaller without changing its value. If you change $\frac{4}{8}$ to $\frac{2}{4}$, you reduce $\frac{4}{8}$ to *lower* terms, but not to *lowest* terms, because $\frac{2}{4}$ can be further reduced to $\frac{1}{2}$.

To reduce a fraction to lowest terms, divide both terms by the largest number that divides both exactly.

Exercises

Reduce each of these fractions to lowest terms:

1. $\frac{8}{16}$ 3. $\frac{4}{16}$ 5. $\frac{2}{16}$ 7. $\frac{10}{16}$ 9. $\frac{14}{16}$

2. $\frac{2}{8}$ 4. $\frac{2}{4}$ 6. $\frac{6}{16}$ 8. $\frac{6}{8}$ 10. $\frac{16}{16}$

11. Harry had a board 8 in., or $\frac{8}{12}$ ft., wide. He said that it was $\frac{3}{4}$ ft. wide. What answer would you give?

12. In changing $\frac{8}{16}$ to lowest terms, Ben gave $\frac{4}{8}$ as an answer. Would you give that answer?

13. Tell which of these fractions are not reduced to their lowest terms:

$$\frac{4}{16} = \frac{2}{8} \qquad \frac{4}{8} = \frac{1}{2} \qquad \frac{10}{16} = \frac{5}{8} \qquad \frac{12}{16} = \frac{6}{8}$$

BETTY SHOPS FOR HER DOGS

1. Betty bought $\frac{5}{8}$ yd. of flannel for a coat for her dog Bubbles and $\frac{5}{8}$ yd. for Fluffy. How much flannel did she buy?

$$\frac{5}{8}$$
$$\frac{5}{8}$$
$$\overline{\frac{10}{8}} = 1\frac{1}{4}$$

The sum is $\frac{10}{8}$, or $1\frac{2}{8}$. Reduce $\frac{2}{8}$ to $\frac{1}{4}$.
Betty bought $1\frac{1}{4}$ yd. of flannel.

Always reduce fractions in the answer to lowest terms.

2. Betty bought $\frac{5}{8}$ yd. of ribbon for Bubbles and $\frac{7}{8}$ yd. for Fluffy. How much ribbon did she buy?

3. She bought $1\frac{1}{4}$ yd. of leather for each dog's lead. How many yards of leather did she get in all? Explain the work.

$$1\frac{1}{4}$$
$$1\frac{1}{4}$$
$$\overline{2\frac{2}{4}} = 2\frac{1}{2}$$

4. She bought $2\frac{1}{4}$ yd. of cotton blanket cloth for Bubbles and $1\frac{1}{4}$ yd. for Fluffy. How much blanket cloth did she buy?

Exercises

Add. Reduce fractions in sums to lowest terms:

1. $\frac{2}{8}$ $\frac{4}{8}$	2. $\frac{5}{8}$ $\frac{1}{8}$	3. $\frac{5}{16}$ $\frac{3}{16}$	4. $2\frac{1}{4}$ $2\frac{1}{4}$	5. $5\frac{5}{8}$ $6\frac{1}{8}$
6. $\frac{2}{8}$ $\frac{2}{8}$	7. $\frac{7}{8}$ $\frac{3}{8}$	8. $\frac{9}{16}$ $\frac{9}{16}$	9. $5\frac{1}{8}$ $2\frac{1}{8}$	10. $6\frac{3}{8}$ $9\frac{3}{8}$
11. $\frac{1}{8}$ $\frac{3}{8}$	12. $\frac{7}{8}$ $\frac{7}{8}$	13. $\frac{1}{16}$ $\frac{7}{16}$	14. $5\frac{7}{16}$ $7\frac{3}{16}$	15. $6\frac{7}{16}$ $2\frac{1}{16}$
16. $\frac{1}{4}$ $\frac{1}{4}$	17. $\frac{3}{8}$ $\frac{3}{8}$	18. $\frac{7}{16}$ $\frac{5}{16}$	19. $9\frac{3}{8}$ $4\frac{1}{8}$	20. $2\frac{9}{16}$ $5\frac{1}{16}$

ORDERING BY MAIL

1. John is ordering by mail articles whose shipping weight is $2\frac{9}{16}$ lb., $1\frac{11}{16}$ lb., and 3 lb. He needs to find their total weight so that he will know how much postage to send. How much do they all weigh?

Adding the fractions, you get $\frac{20}{16}$, which equals $1\frac{4}{16}$, or $1\frac{1}{4}$. Write $\frac{1}{4}$ under the line and carry the 1 to the whole numbers. Then add the whole numbers.

The three articles weigh $7\frac{1}{4}$ lb. in all.

$$2\frac{9}{16}$$
$$1\frac{11}{16}$$
$$\underline{3}$$
$$7\frac{1}{4}$$

2. David orders a bat whose shipping weight is $2\frac{1}{2}$ lb., a catcher's mitt weighing $1\frac{1}{4}$ lb., and a fielder's glove weighing $1\frac{1}{2}$ lb. Find the total weight.

3. Mr. Reed orders some things by mail. The catalogue gives their weights as $2\frac{1}{8}$ lb., $1\frac{7}{8}$ lb., $1\frac{5}{8}$ lb., and $3\frac{1}{8}$ lb. How much do they weigh in all?

Exercises

Add. Check the work by going over it again:

1. $2\frac{1}{2}$	**2.** $7\frac{3}{4}$	**3.** $5\frac{7}{8}$	**4.** $9\frac{5}{8}$	**5.** $7\frac{7}{8}$
$\underline{4\frac{1}{2}}$	$\underline{9\frac{1}{4}}$	$\underline{4\frac{5}{8}}$	$\underline{2\frac{3}{8}}$	$\underline{5\frac{3}{8}}$
6. $4\frac{3}{16}$	**7.** $4\frac{3}{8}$	**8.** $5\frac{15}{16}$	**9.** $9\frac{1}{4}$	**10.** $1\frac{7}{8}$
$\underline{5\frac{11}{16}}$	$\underline{7\frac{5}{8}}$	$\underline{4\frac{1}{16}}$	$\underline{7\frac{1}{4}}$	$\underline{5\frac{7}{8}}$
11. $8\frac{1}{8}$	**12.** $9\frac{1}{8}$	**13.** $2\frac{3}{16}$	**14.** $5\frac{2}{4}$	**15.** $8\frac{1}{2}$
7	$5\frac{7}{8}$	$9\frac{3}{16}$	$4\frac{1}{4}$	7
$\underline{5\frac{7}{8}}$	$\underline{7\frac{3}{8}}$	$\underline{8\frac{12}{16}}$	$\underline{9\frac{3}{4}}$	$\underline{3\frac{1}{2}}$
16. $9\frac{1}{4}$	**17.** $4\frac{7}{8}$	**18.** $2\frac{5}{16}$	**19.** $8\frac{3}{4}$	**20.** $1\frac{5}{16}$
2	$8\frac{5}{8}$	9	$4\frac{3}{4}$	$8\frac{7}{16}$
$5\frac{3}{4}$	2	$5\frac{4}{16}$	7	$8\frac{10}{16}$
$\underline{3\frac{1}{4}}$	$\underline{7\frac{3}{8}}$	$\underline{6\frac{11}{16}}$	$\underline{9\phantom{\frac{1}{1}}}$	$\underline{9\phantom{\frac{1}{1}}}$

A QUICK WAY TO CHANGE $\frac{1}{2}$ TO $\frac{4}{8}$

1. On page 73 you learned how to change $\frac{4}{8}$ to $\frac{1}{2}$ by *dividing* both terms of $\frac{4}{8}$ by 4. A quick way to change $\frac{1}{2}$ back to $\frac{4}{8}$ is to *multiply* both terms of $\frac{1}{2}$ by 4, as shown below in *A*.

$$A. \quad \frac{1 \times 4}{2 \times 4} = \frac{4}{8} \qquad\qquad B. \quad \frac{3 \times 2}{4 \times 2} = \frac{6}{8}$$

2. In the same way, you can change $\frac{3}{4}$ to $\frac{6}{8}$ by multiplying both terms of $\frac{3}{4}$ by 2, as shown in *B*.

If you multiply both terms of a fraction by the same number, you get another fraction with the same value.

Exercises

1. The quick way to change $\frac{3}{4}$ to $\frac{12}{16}$ is shown here. By what number do you multiply both terms of $\frac{3}{4}$ to get $\frac{12}{16}$? Have $\frac{3}{4}$ and $\frac{12}{16}$ the same value?

$$\frac{3 \times 4}{4 \times 4} = \frac{12}{16}$$

2. By what number do you multiply both terms of $\frac{1}{2}$ to get $\frac{8}{16}$? Have $\frac{1}{2}$ and $\frac{8}{16}$ the same value?

3. Joe says that $\frac{1}{4} = \frac{2}{16}$. Tell why he is wrong.

In each example tell what number should be put in place of the star so that the fractions will be equal:

4. $\frac{1}{8} = \frac{\ast}{16}$ **9.** $\frac{1}{4} = \frac{\ast}{8}$ **14.** $\frac{3}{4} = \frac{\ast}{16}$ **19.** $\frac{4}{4} = \frac{\ast}{16}$

5. $\frac{1}{2} = \frac{\ast}{8}$ **10.** $\frac{1}{4} = \frac{\ast}{16}$ **15.** $\frac{3}{4} = \frac{\ast}{8}$ **20.** $\frac{1}{2} = \frac{\ast}{4}$

6. $\frac{3}{8} = \frac{\ast}{16}$ **11.** $\frac{5}{8} = \frac{\ast}{16}$ **16.** $\frac{7}{8} = \frac{\ast}{16}$ **21.** $\frac{1}{2} = \frac{\ast}{16}$

7. $\frac{1}{2} = \frac{\ast}{32}$ **12.** $\frac{8}{8} = \frac{\ast}{16}$ **17.** $\frac{2}{4} = \frac{\ast}{8}$ **22.** $\frac{5}{8} = \frac{\ast}{32}$

8. $\frac{1}{4} = \frac{\ast}{32}$ **13.** $\frac{4}{8} = \frac{\ast}{16}$ **18.** $\frac{2}{8} = \frac{\ast}{16}$ **23.** $\frac{1}{8} = \frac{\ast}{32}$

ADDING FRACTIONS WITH DIFFERENT DENOMINATORS

1. You have learned that you can add only things that have the *same name*. Thus, you know at once that 4 *cents* and 5 *cents* are 9 *cents;* but before you can add 4 *cents*

$$4 \text{ cents} = 4 \text{ cents}$$
$$5 \text{ nickels} = 25 \text{ cents}$$
$$\overline{\phantom{5 \text{ nickels} =} 29 \text{ cents}}$$

and 5 *nickels*, which have different names, you must change the 5 *nickels* to 25 *cents*, as shown at the right. Then you can add 4 cents and 25 cents, which gives 29 cents.

2. Fred buys $\frac{3}{4}$ lb. of American cheese and $\frac{5}{8}$ lb. of Swiss cheese. How many pounds of cheese is that?

You see that $\frac{3}{4}$ and $\frac{5}{8}$ have different names, one being *fourths* and the other *eighths*. If you change $\frac{3}{4}$ to $\frac{6}{8}$, however, you can add $\frac{6}{8}$ and $\frac{5}{8}$ because they will then have the same name, or the same denominator. The sum is $\frac{11}{8}$, or $1\frac{3}{8}$.

$$\frac{3}{4} = \frac{6}{8}$$
$$\frac{5}{8} = \frac{5}{8}$$
$$\overline{} \quad \frac{11}{8} = 1\frac{3}{8}$$

Fred buys $1\frac{3}{8}$ lb. of cheese in all.

To add fractions having different denominators, first change them to fractions having the same denominator.

Exercises

1. Ann's mother bought two remnants of the same kind of cloth, one containing $3\frac{1}{4}$ yd. and the other, $2\frac{5}{8}$ yd. How many yards of cloth did she get?

Change the fractions to eighths and add. Check the work by going over it again:

2. $\frac{3}{4}$ $\frac{1}{8}$	4. $\frac{3}{8}$ $\frac{1}{2}$	6. $\frac{3}{8}$ $\frac{1}{4}$	8. $\frac{1}{2}$ $\frac{5}{8}$	10. $\frac{7}{8}$ $\frac{1}{4}$	12. $\frac{1}{2}$ $\frac{7}{8}$
3. $\frac{1}{2}$ $\frac{1}{8}$	5. $\frac{1}{8}$ $\frac{1}{4}$	7. $\frac{3}{4}$ $\frac{5}{8}$	9. $\frac{3}{8}$ $\frac{3}{4}$	11. $\frac{1}{4}$ $\frac{5}{8}$	13. $\frac{7}{8}$ $\frac{3}{4}$

HOW LARGE ARE THESE ORCHARDS?

1. Mr. Scott has $5\frac{1}{2}$ acres of apple trees, $3\frac{1}{4}$ acres of pear trees, and $\frac{3}{8}$ acre of cherry trees. This makes an orchard of how many acres?

$$5\frac{1}{2}=5\frac{4}{8}$$
$$3\frac{1}{4}=3\frac{2}{8}$$

Since the largest denominator is 8, change $\frac{1}{2}$ to $\frac{4}{8}$ and $\frac{1}{4}$ to $\frac{2}{8}$. $\frac{4}{8}+\frac{2}{8}+\frac{3}{8}=\frac{9}{8}$, or $1\frac{1}{8}$. Write $\frac{1}{8}$ and carry the 1 to the whole numbers.

$$\frac{3}{8}=\frac{3}{8}$$
$$\overline{9\frac{1}{8}}$$

Mr. Scott has an orchard of $9\frac{1}{8}$ acres.

2. Mr. Scott's neighbor has $1\frac{3}{4}$ acres of apple trees, $10\frac{1}{2}$ acres of peach trees, and $1\frac{5}{8}$ acres of pear trees. How large is his orchard?

3. How many acres do $12\frac{1}{4}$ acres of pear trees, $\frac{1}{2}$ acre of peach trees, and $\frac{5}{8}$ acre of cherry trees make?

Graded Exercises

Change the fractions to eighths and add. Check by going over the work again:

1.	2.	3.	4.	5.
$9\frac{1}{2}$	$2\frac{1}{8}$	$7\frac{3}{4}$	$7\frac{5}{8}$	$8\frac{7}{8}$
$6\frac{1}{2}$	$2\frac{1}{4}$	$5\frac{5}{8}$	$4\frac{1}{4}$	$4\frac{5}{8}$
$5\frac{7}{8}$	$2\frac{1}{2}$	$9\frac{1}{2}$	$5\frac{1}{2}$	$9\frac{1}{2}$

6.	7.	8.	9.	10.
$1\frac{3}{8}$	$8\frac{7}{8}$	$7\frac{3}{8}$	$6\frac{1}{2}$	$3\frac{3}{8}$
$2\frac{1}{4}$	$2\frac{1}{4}$	$5\frac{1}{2}$	$7\frac{1}{8}$	$2\frac{1}{2}$
$7\frac{3}{4}$	$6\frac{1}{2}$	$2\frac{1}{8}$	$9\frac{3}{4}$	$6\frac{5}{8}$

Change the fractions to sixteenths and add:

11.	12.	13.	14.	15.
$2\frac{1}{8}$	$6\frac{3}{8}$	$4\frac{7}{8}$	$2\frac{1}{4}$	$4\frac{1}{2}$
$1\frac{3}{16}$	$4\frac{5}{16}$	$3\frac{5}{16}$	$8\frac{1}{16}$	$3\frac{1}{16}$

16.	17.	18.	19.	20.
$4\frac{3}{8}$	$2\frac{1}{16}$	$3\frac{1}{16}$	$5\frac{1}{8}$	$5\frac{3}{4}$
$2\frac{1}{16}$	$2\frac{1}{4}$	$5\frac{1}{8}$	$5\frac{7}{16}$	$7\frac{5}{16}$

DIAGNOSTIC TEST

*If you miss exercises in any row, you need more practice.
The Help Pages tell you where to find it.*

Add.   Check the work by going over it:

						HELP PAGES
1.	$\dfrac{1}{3}$ $\dfrac{1}{3}$	$\dfrac{1}{8}$ $\dfrac{4}{8}$	$\dfrac{3}{8}$ $\dfrac{5}{8}$	$\dfrac{7}{10}$ $\dfrac{4}{10}$	$\dfrac{5}{8}$ $\dfrac{6}{8}$	**69**
2.	$8\frac{1}{4}$ $4\frac{2}{4}$	9 $5\frac{7}{8}$	$3\frac{1}{4}$ $7\frac{3}{4}$	$4\frac{6}{8}$ $3\frac{7}{8}$	$8\frac{1}{2}$ $8\frac{1}{2}$	**70**
3.	$3\frac{3}{4}$ $3\frac{1}{2}$	$2\frac{1}{2}$ $8\frac{1}{4}$	$6\frac{3}{4}$ $7\frac{1}{4}$	$5\frac{1}{4}$ $8\frac{1}{2}$	$9\frac{1}{2}$ $3\frac{3}{4}$	**71**
4.	$\dfrac{5}{8}$ $\dfrac{1}{2}$	$\dfrac{1}{2}$ $\dfrac{1}{8}$	$\dfrac{3}{4}$ $\dfrac{1}{8}$	$\dfrac{1}{4}$ $\dfrac{7}{8}$	$\dfrac{5}{8}$ $\dfrac{3}{4}$	**77**
5.	$\dfrac{7}{16}$ $\dfrac{3}{16}$	$\dfrac{5}{8}$ $\dfrac{5}{8}$	$4\frac{1}{4}$ $9\frac{1}{4}$	$1\frac{9}{16}$ $5\frac{5}{16}$	$6\frac{7}{16}$ $6\frac{13}{16}$	**74**
6.	$\dfrac{1}{16}$ $\dfrac{5}{16}$	$\dfrac{3}{8}$ $\dfrac{3}{8}$	$8\frac{1}{8}$ $3\frac{5}{8}$	$9\frac{9}{16}$ $1\frac{9}{16}$	$2\frac{3}{8}$ $7\frac{1}{8}$	**74**
7.	$9\frac{1}{2}$ $6\frac{5}{16}$	$7\frac{1}{4}$ $8\frac{9}{16}$	$5\frac{5}{8}$ $6\frac{7}{16}$	$4\frac{3}{4}$ $5\frac{9}{16}$	$8\frac{7}{8}$ $9\frac{7}{16}$	**78**
8.	$1\frac{3}{4}$ $6\frac{3}{8}$ $3\frac{1}{2}$	$2\frac{1}{2}$ $8\frac{3}{8}$ $7\frac{1}{2}$	$4\frac{7}{8}$ $1\frac{3}{4}$ $6\frac{3}{8}$	$2\frac{1}{8}$ $3\frac{3}{4}$ $8\frac{7}{8}$	$6\frac{1}{4}$ $1\frac{1}{2}$ $1\frac{1}{8}$	**78**

CATCHING VERY LARGE FISH

The well-known American writer, Mr. Zane Grey, enjoys catching big fish. From 1924 to 1930 he caught the following big fish with rod and reel:

NAME OF FISH	WEIGHT	YEAR CAUGHT	WHERE CAUGHT
Tuna fish . . .	758 lb.	1924	Nova Scotia
Yellowtail . . .	111 lb.	1926	New Zealand
Dolphin	63 lb.	1930	Tahiti
Swordfish . . .	1040 lb.	1930	Tahiti

1. What was the total weight of the four big fish caught by Mr. Grey from 1924 to 1930?

2. How much less than the swordfish did the tuna fish, yellowtail, and dolphin together weigh?

3. About how many dolphins, each weighing 63 lb., would it have taken to equal the weight of the tuna fish?

4. The largest tuna fish that has been caught weighed about 1500 lb. About how many times the weight of the tuna fish that Mr. Grey caught was the weight of this large fish?

5. The largest of all living fish to-day is the whale shark, since the whale itself is not a true fish. In 1912 a whale shark weighing 26,594 lb. was caught off the coast of Florida. This fish weighed about how many times as much as Mr. Grey's tuna fish? as Mr. Grey's swordfish?

MIXED PRACTICE

Find the answers:

1. $219 \times 750 = ?$

2. $3420 \div 45 = ?$

3. $1806 - 1293 = ?$

4. $\$8.75 + \$1.25 = ?$

5. $\frac{6}{5} = ?$

6. $\frac{10}{3} = ?$

7. $\frac{3}{8} = \frac{?}{16}$

8. $\frac{9}{12} = \frac{?}{4}$

9. $\frac{7}{8} + \frac{3}{4} = ?$

10. $\frac{1}{2}$ of $38 = ?$

11. $\frac{3}{4} + \frac{5}{16} = ?$

12. $\frac{3}{4}$ of $24 = ?$

Read each exercise carefully. Then do it:

13. Write each of these numbers in Roman numerals: 42, 57, 98, 148, 862, 1934.

14. Add these numbers: $2\frac{3}{4}$, $1\frac{1}{2}$, $4\frac{5}{8}$, and 3.

15. Reduce the fraction $\frac{24}{36}$ to lowest terms.

16. Write a fraction equal to $\frac{3}{4}$ that will have 12 for its denominator.

17. Find the sum of $1\frac{1}{4} + 2 + 3\frac{7}{16} + 5$.

18. From the product of 28 and 47 subtract 728.

19. Is the fraction $\frac{11}{12}$ equal to the fraction $\frac{5}{6}$?

20. Beginning with $\frac{1}{4}$, count by $\frac{1}{4}$'s to 3.

21. Reduce each of these fractions to a whole number or to a mixed number: $\frac{17}{4}$, $\frac{35}{5}$, $\frac{19}{8}$, $\frac{12}{6}$, $\frac{15}{6}$, $\frac{25}{8}$, $\frac{8}{8}$.

22. How do you check an example in column addition?

23. How much less is 450 than 609?

24. If you multiply 754 by 203, how would you check the work to make sure that it is correct?

25. Find the difference between 145 and 263.

26. Beginning with 1, count by 6's to 73.

PROBLEM TEST A3

1. Miss Lee is making a dress. She bought 4 yd. of silk at $.89 a yard and 3 yd. of lace at $.37 a yard. How much did all this cost her?

2. Anna spent $5.35 for school lunches one month, $4.95 the next month, and $5.12 the third month. How much in all did her lunches cost for those three months?

3. Ned spent $3.75 for a tennis racket and $1.10 for some tennis balls. He gave the clerk $5.00. How much change did Ned get?

4. There are 235 children in our school. If we march by 4's, how many rows do we make? Will there be any children left over? If so, how many?

5. The pupils in the 12 rooms of the Oak Park School made a profit of $288 when they gave the school fair. If the rooms shared the profit equally, how much did each room get?

6. There are 2173 pupils in the Lennox schools this year and there were 1897 pupils in the schools last year. How many more pupils are there in the Lennox schools this year than last year?

7. James puts 25¢ a week in the school bank and 40¢ a week in his dime bank. How much will he save in 7 wk.?

8. Helen Ford practiced on the piano 1 hr. 10 min. yesterday. How many minutes did she practice in all?

Standards	Excellent	Good	Fair	Poor
	8 right	6 or 7	5	0 to 4

This test is like Tests A1 and A2, pages 37 and 59. You should have all the problems right on this test.

IMPROVEMENT TEST No. 4

Test 4 A — Addition   (Time 4 min.)

1.	2.	3.	4.	5.
748	155	686	984	953
696	372	998	948	155
971	681	743	849	130
753	945	715	150	443
462	937	460	885	542
319	368	737	210	226
638	694	279	564	178
823	287	943	798	675

Test 4 B — Subtraction   (Time 4 min.)

1.	2.	3.
$484.94	$840.56	$860.50
357.85	127.89	166.59

4.	5.	6.
$683.46	$313.58	$833.36
393.08	126.72	199.16

7.	8.	9.
$630.30	$835.19	$997.04
134.08	340.79	594.50

10.	11.	12.
$885.20	$868.41	$846.11
677.80	270.42	490.61

Test 4 C — Multiplication   (Time 4 min. after copying)

1.	2.	3.	4.	5.
2358	4628	7692	9084	4673
36	95	27	54	38

Test 4 D — Division   (Time 5 min. after copying)

1. 93)69099   2. 85)64855   3. 48)23280

4. 57)45903   5. 82)51865

SUBTRACTING FRACTIONS WITH THE SAME NAME

You know that you can add fractions that have the same denominator. You can also subtract fractions that have the same denominator.

Suppose that you have $\frac{7}{8}$ yd. of cloth and use $\frac{3}{8}$ yd. To find how much is left, subtract $\frac{3}{8}$ from $\frac{7}{8}$.

Think of $\frac{7}{8}$ as 7 *eighths* and of $\frac{3}{8}$ as 3 *eighths*. You see that 7 *eighths* less 3 *eighths* are 4 *eighths*, just as 7 *balls* less 3 *balls* are 4 *balls*. Hence $\frac{7}{8} - \frac{3}{8} = \frac{4}{8}$, which equals $\frac{1}{2}$.

You find that $\frac{1}{2}$ yd. of cloth is left.

Think this: Write this:

$$7 \text{ eighths} = \frac{7}{8}$$
$$3 \text{ eighths} = \frac{3}{8}$$
$$4 \text{ eighths} = \frac{4}{8} = \frac{1}{2}$$

Exercises

1. Dick had $\frac{3}{4}$ lb. of copper wire. He sold $\frac{1}{4}$ lb. of it to Sam. How much wire had Dick left?

2. Bert can walk $3\frac{3}{4}$ mi. in an hour. Bob can walk $3\frac{1}{4}$ mi. in the same time. How much farther can Bert walk in an hour than Bob can walk?

3. Anna weighs $68\frac{5}{8}$ lb. Her sister May weighs $74\frac{7}{8}$ lb. How much heavier is May than Anna?

Subtract. Reduce the answers to lowest terms:

4. $\frac{7}{8}$
$\frac{5}{8}$

6. $\frac{1}{2}$
$\frac{1}{2}$

8. $\frac{5}{16}$
$\frac{1}{16}$

10. $\frac{15}{16}$
$\frac{4}{16}$

12. $\frac{11}{16}$
$\frac{1}{16}$

14. $\frac{9}{8}$
$\frac{3}{8}$

5. $\frac{3}{8}$
$\frac{1}{8}$

7. $\frac{5}{8}$
$\frac{2}{8}$

9. $\frac{15}{16}$
$\frac{3}{16}$

11. $\frac{7}{8}$
$\frac{1}{8}$

13. $\frac{11}{8}$
$\frac{5}{8}$

15. $\frac{5}{4}$
$\frac{3}{4}$

16. How much must you add to each fraction to make 1? Think of 1 as $\frac{2}{2}$ or $\frac{4}{4}$ or $\frac{8}{8}$ or $\frac{16}{16}$.

$\frac{7}{8}$ $\frac{1}{4}$ $\frac{3}{4}$ $\frac{1}{2}$ $\frac{3}{8}$ $\frac{1}{16}$ $\frac{5}{16}$

HOW HEAVY ARE YOUR SCHOOLBOOKS?

1. When Jane weighs herself with her schoolbooks, the scale registers $96\frac{3}{4}$ lb. Without her books she weighs $91\frac{1}{8}$ lb. How much do the books weigh?

Since $\frac{1}{8}$ and $\frac{3}{4}$ have different denominators, you cannot subtract them as they stand. Change $\frac{3}{4}$ to $\frac{6}{8}$. Then subtract $\frac{1}{8}$ from $\frac{6}{8}$, which leaves $\frac{5}{8}$.

You see that Jane's books weigh $5\frac{5}{8}$ lb.

$$96\frac{3}{4} = 96\frac{6}{8}$$
$$91\frac{1}{8} = 91\frac{1}{8}$$
$$5\frac{5}{8}$$

To subtract fractions with different denominators, first change them to fractions having the same denominator.

2. Philip with his schoolbooks weighs $87\frac{5}{8}$ lb. Philip alone weighs $84\frac{1}{2}$ lb. How heavy are Philip's books? Are his books as heavy as Jane's?

3. Little Dora weighs $47\frac{1}{4}$ lb. With her schoolbooks she weighs $48\frac{7}{8}$ lb. How heavy are her books?

Other Problems

1. John swam across the pool in $44\frac{1}{2}$ sec. Ed did it in $50\frac{3}{4}$ sec. By how many seconds did John beat Ed?

2. A train usually takes $3\frac{1}{4}$ hr. to go from Omaha to the city where Ann lives. Last Sunday the train took $4\frac{1}{2}$ hr. to make this trip. How many hours late was it?

Subtract. Check by going over the work again:

3. $5\frac{1}{2}$ $\;\;4\frac{1}{4}$	4. $6\frac{1}{2}$ $\;\;2\frac{1}{8}$	5. $8\frac{7}{8}$ $\;\;7\frac{1}{4}$	6. $6\frac{3}{4}$ $\;\;4\frac{3}{8}$	7. $5\frac{1}{2}$ $\;\;2\frac{1}{16}$
8. $9\frac{1}{4}$ $\;\;7\frac{1}{8}$	9. $8\frac{3}{4}$ $\;\;3\frac{1}{2}$	10. $5\frac{5}{8}$ $\;\;1\frac{1}{2}$	11. $7\frac{3}{8}$ $\;\;5\frac{1}{16}$	12. $9\frac{3}{16}$ $\;\;8\frac{1}{8}$
13. $5\frac{1}{2}$ $\;\;3\frac{3}{8}$	14. $6\frac{7}{8}$ $\;\;2\frac{1}{2}$	15. $9\frac{3}{8}$ $\;\;5\frac{1}{4}$	16. $9\frac{7}{8}$ $\;\;3\frac{3}{4}$	17. $7\frac{1}{2}$ $\;\;4\frac{5}{16}$

CHANGING MONEY

1. Mr. Jones wanted to give Fred a quarter. He had only a 5-dollar bill, which he changed to 4 dollars and 4 quarters; that is, he changed $5 to 4\frac{4}{4}$. After giving $\$\frac{1}{4}$ to Fred, he had $\$4\frac{3}{4}$ left, because $4\frac{4}{4} - \frac{1}{4} = 4\frac{3}{4}$.

2. Mr. Baker has 4 whole dollars and 1 quarter. He wants to change one of the dollars into quarters. Dora says that he will then have 3 dollars and 5 quarters. Is she right? Does $\$4\frac{1}{4} = \$3\frac{5}{4}$?

Tell what numbers should be put in place of the stars:

3. $10 equals $9 and * quarters. Hence $10 = 9\frac{*}{4}$.

4. $5 equals $4 and * half dollars. Hence $5 = 4\frac{*}{2}$.

5. 7\frac{1}{4}$ equals $6 and * quarters. Hence $7\frac{1}{4} = 6\frac{*}{4}$.

6. 8\frac{1}{2}$ equals $7 and * half dollars. Hence $8\frac{1}{2} = 7\frac{*}{2}$.

7. 5\frac{1}{4}$ equals $4 and * quarters. Hence $5\frac{1}{4} = 4\frac{*}{4}$.

8. 6\frac{1}{4}$ equals $5 and * quarters. Hence $6\frac{1}{4} = 5\frac{*}{4}$.

9. A dime is * of a dollar. A nickel is * of a dollar.

10. $5 equals $4 and * dimes. Hence $5 = 4\frac{*}{10}$.

11. $3 equals $2 and * nickels. Hence $3 = 2\frac{*}{20}$.

12. 4\frac{1}{10}$ equals $3 and * dimes. Hence $4\frac{1}{10} = 3\frac{*}{10}$.

What numbers should be put in place of the stars?

13. $7 = 6\frac{*}{4}$

14. $7 = 6\frac{*}{8}$

15. $9 = 8\frac{*}{2}$

16. $9 = 8\frac{*}{8}$

17. $3 = 2\frac{*}{4}$

18. $3 = 2\frac{*}{16}$

19. $9\frac{1}{2} = 8\frac{*}{2}$

20. $8\frac{1}{4} = 7\frac{*}{4}$

21. $5\frac{3}{4} = 4\frac{*}{4}$

22. $9\frac{3}{8} = 8\frac{*}{8}$

23. $5\frac{1}{8} = 4\frac{*}{8}$

24. $3\frac{3}{16} = 2\frac{*}{16}$

25. $5\frac{1}{4} = 5\frac{2}{8} = 4\frac{*}{8}$

26. $8\frac{1}{2} = 8\frac{*}{8} = 7\frac{*}{8}$

27. $6\frac{1}{2} = 6\frac{*}{4} = 5\frac{*}{4}$

28. $4\frac{1}{4} = 4\frac{*}{8} = 3\frac{*}{8}$

29. $7\frac{3}{4} = 7\frac{*}{8} = 6\frac{*}{8}$

30. $3\frac{1}{8} = 3\frac{2}{16} = 2\frac{*}{16}$

★GAMES WITH FRACTIONS

Divide the class into two teams, the Reds and the Blues, and play these games. *Do all the work mentally.* If you give an incorrect answer, you must take your seat. The team with the most children standing at the end wins.

1. *Game of 1's.* Fred, the leader, gives the fraction $\frac{2}{3}$. The first child of the Blue team tells how much is added to $\frac{2}{3}$ to make 1. Then Fred gives the fraction $\frac{3}{16}$, and the first Red tells what is added to $\frac{3}{16}$ to make 1. Then Fred tries other fractions.

2. *Changing Money Game.* Mary, the leader, gives a number like $3\frac{1}{2}$, which must be changed to $2\frac{3}{2}$. Then she gives $3\frac{3}{4}$, which must be changed to $2\frac{7}{4}$, and so on.

3. *Reduction Match.* The leader gives a fraction like $\frac{3}{4}$ and asks the teams to keep changing it to other fractions having the same value by always multiplying both terms by 2. A Red changes it to $\frac{6}{8}$. Then a Blue changes it to $\frac{12}{16}$. If the next Red changes it to $\frac{24}{30}$, which is wrong, he must sit down. When the terms of the fraction get large, as in $\frac{24}{32}$, the teams start reducing the fraction to lower terms again until they get back to $\frac{3}{4}$. Then they start with another fraction, like $\frac{1}{2}$, and choose a different multiplier, like 3.

Another form of this game is for the leader to say " Change $\frac{3}{4}$ to twelfths " or " Change $\frac{5}{8}$ to sixteenths."

4. *Mental Addition Match.* Make some flash cards each 8 in. long and 6 in. wide. Write one of these fractions on each card : $\frac{1}{2}, \frac{1}{4}, \frac{3}{4}, \frac{1}{8}, \frac{3}{8}, \frac{5}{8}, \frac{7}{8}$. The leader holds up two of these cards, like $\frac{1}{2}$ and $\frac{3}{4}$, and asks the child whose turn it is to give the sum mentally. Then he shows two other cards.

A CLASS PARTY

1. The children in our class made candy for a party. From a 7-pound package of sugar they used $4\frac{5}{8}$ lb. How much sugar was left?

Since there is no fraction in the minuend 7, you must change 7 to $6\frac{8}{8}$ before you can subtract. Can you subtract $4\frac{5}{8}$ from $6\frac{8}{8}$?

$$7 \;= 6\tfrac{8}{8}$$
$$4\tfrac{5}{8} = 4\tfrac{5}{8}$$
$$\overline{\phantom{4\tfrac{5}{8}} 2\tfrac{3}{8}}$$

The children had $2\frac{3}{8}$ lb. of sugar left.

2. The children had $3\frac{1}{4}$ lb. of butter. They used $\frac{3}{4}$ lb. of it for the candy. How much butter had they then?

Since you cannot take $\frac{3}{4}$ from $\frac{1}{4}$, change $3\frac{1}{4}$ to $2\frac{5}{4}$. Then subtract $\frac{3}{4}$ from $2\frac{5}{4}$, which leaves $2\frac{2}{4}$, or $2\frac{1}{2}$.

$$3\tfrac{1}{4} = 2\tfrac{5}{4}$$
$$\tfrac{3}{4} = \tfrac{3}{4}$$
$$\overline{2\tfrac{2}{4} = 2\tfrac{1}{2}}$$

The children had $2\frac{1}{2}$ lb. of butter left.

3. If the children had $2\frac{3}{8}$ lb. of sugar and used $1\frac{5}{8}$ lb. of it for cocoa, how much sugar was left?

4. If they used $3\frac{1}{2}$ lb. of flour from a 5-pound bag, how much flour was left?

Other Problems

1. May does the 50-yard dash in $8\frac{3}{4}$ sec. and Lucy in $10\frac{1}{4}$ sec. How much longer does Lucy take than May?

2. Ted caught a $3\frac{1}{8}$-pound fish. After it was cleaned, it weighed $2\frac{3}{8}$ lb. How much weight was lost in cleaning?

Subtract. Check the work by going over it again:

3. 10	**4.** 7	**5.** 4	**6.** $8\frac{1}{8}$	**7.** $5\frac{1}{8}$
$\underline{5\frac{1}{2}}$	$\underline{4\frac{3}{4}}$	$\underline{2\frac{1}{8}}$	$\underline{2\frac{5}{8}}$	$\underline{2\frac{7}{8}}$
8. 9	**9.** 6	**10.** $7\frac{1}{4}$	**11.** $6\frac{3}{8}$	**12.** $6\frac{3}{16}$
$\underline{6\frac{1}{4}}$	$\underline{3\frac{7}{8}}$	$\underline{4\frac{3}{4}}$	$\underline{4\frac{7}{8}}$	$\underline{3\frac{7}{16}}$

COMPARING WEIGHTS

1. Alice weighs $65\frac{1}{2}$ lb. Her little sister Peggy weighs $29\frac{3}{4}$ lb. How much more does Alice weigh than Peggy?

Since you cannot subtract *fourths* from *halves*, change $65\frac{1}{2}$ to $65\frac{2}{4}$. Since you cannot take $\frac{3}{4}$ from $\frac{2}{4}$, change $65\frac{2}{4}$ to $64\frac{6}{4}$. How many are $64\frac{6}{4} - 29\frac{3}{4}$?

$$65\frac{1}{2} = 65\frac{2}{4} = 64\frac{6}{4}$$
$$29\frac{3}{4} = 29\frac{3}{4} = 29\frac{3}{4}$$
$$\overline{35\frac{3}{4}}$$

Alice weighs $35\frac{3}{4}$ lb. more than Peggy.

2. Stanley weighs $85\frac{1}{2}$ lb. His brother Fred weighs $6\frac{3}{4}$ lb. less. How heavy is Fred?

Exercises

Subtract. Check by going over the work carefully. Arrange the work as in ex. 1 above:

1. $8\frac{1}{4}$ $5\frac{1}{2}$	**2.** $6\frac{1}{8}$ $1\frac{1}{2}$	**3.** $9\frac{1}{4}$ $5\frac{7}{8}$	**4.** $9\frac{1}{2}$ $1\frac{3}{8}$	**5.** $5\frac{1}{2}$ $3\frac{7}{8}$
6. $7\frac{1}{8}$ $4\frac{1}{4}$	**7.** $7\frac{1}{8}$ $5\frac{3}{4}$	**8.** $9\frac{3}{4}$ $2\frac{7}{8}$	**9.** $8\frac{1}{2}$ $2\frac{3}{4}$	**10.** $8\frac{1}{4}$ $7\frac{5}{8}$

PROBLEMS AND PRACTICE

1. The average weight of the girls in Betty's class is $72\frac{3}{8}$ lb. Betty's weight is $67\frac{1}{2}$ lb. How much below the average is her weight?

2. Frank weighs $86\frac{1}{4}$ lb. This is $9\frac{1}{2}$ lb. more than the average weight of the children in his class. Find the average weight of the children in Frank's class.

3. John weighs $78\frac{1}{4}$ lb. Harry weighs 82 lb. What is the difference in their weights?

4. Ann weighed $58\frac{3}{4}$ lb. last fall. Now she weighs 63 lb. How many pounds has she gained?

Exercises

Subtract. Check the work by going over it again:

1. $9\frac{5}{8}$	6	$9\frac{1}{4}$	$7\frac{5}{8}$	$8\frac{1}{8}$	$32\frac{5}{16}$
$3\frac{1}{8}$	$4\frac{3}{4}$	$2\frac{3}{4}$	$7\frac{1}{4}$	$6\frac{1}{4}$	$24\frac{9}{16}$
2. 6	$8\frac{3}{8}$	$8\frac{1}{16}$	$8\frac{3}{4}$	$5\frac{1}{4}$	$24\frac{1}{2}$
$3\frac{1}{2}$	$4\frac{7}{16}$	$7\frac{3}{8}$	$3\frac{1}{4}$	$2\frac{5}{8}$	$12\frac{11}{16}$
3. $7\frac{3}{8}$	$9\frac{1}{4}$	$7\frac{13}{16}$	$9\frac{1}{8}$	9	$12\frac{1}{16}$
2	$6\frac{7}{16}$	$3\frac{5}{16}$	$1\frac{1}{2}$	$5\frac{3}{8}$	$6\frac{1}{4}$
4. $8\frac{1}{2}$	$5\frac{3}{8}$	$6\frac{3}{4}$	$8\frac{1}{8}$	$7\frac{7}{8}$	$15\frac{7}{16}$
$3\frac{7}{8}$	$4\frac{5}{8}$	$2\frac{7}{8}$	$2\frac{5}{16}$	$4\frac{1}{2}$	$6\frac{1}{16}$
5. $6\frac{3}{4}$	$8\frac{1}{8}$	$5\frac{7}{8}$	$7\frac{1}{2}$	$6\frac{5}{8}$	$16\frac{1}{4}$
$1\frac{1}{4}$	$5\frac{9}{16}$	$1\frac{15}{16}$	$5\frac{3}{8}$	5	$7\frac{11}{16}$

DIAGNOSTIC TEST

If you miss exercises in any row, you need more practice
The Help Pages tell you where to find it.

Subtract.   Check the work by going over it again:

1. $\dfrac{3}{4}$ $\dfrac{15}{16}$ $\dfrac{7}{8}$ $\dfrac{11}{16}$ $\dfrac{11}{8}$ **84**
  $\dfrac{1}{4}$ $\dfrac{7}{16}$ $\dfrac{3}{8}$ $\dfrac{6}{16}$ $\dfrac{7}{8}$

2. $6\frac{1}{2}$ $5\frac{3}{8}$ $7\frac{3}{4}$ $9\frac{5}{8}$ $8\frac{5}{16}$ **85**
  $2\frac{3}{16}$ $1\frac{1}{4}$ $3\frac{7}{16}$ $2\frac{1}{2}$ $4\frac{1}{8}$

3. $7\frac{7}{8}$ $9\frac{9}{16}$ $6\frac{1}{2}$ $8\frac{1}{4}$ $3\frac{7}{16}$ **85**
  $5\frac{1}{4}$ $4\frac{1}{2}$ $1\frac{1}{16}$ $5\frac{1}{8}$ $1\frac{1}{8}$

4. 7 4 $9\frac{7}{16}$ $7\frac{3}{16}$ $8\frac{5}{8}$ **88**
  $2\frac{5}{8}$ $1\frac{7}{8}$ $5\frac{11}{16}$ $6\frac{15}{16}$ $3\frac{7}{8}$

5. 6 $7\frac{1}{8}$ $6\frac{1}{4}$ $9\frac{5}{16}$ $7\frac{1}{16}$ **88**
  $5\frac{1}{4}$ $4\frac{5}{8}$ $4\frac{3}{4}$ $6\frac{11}{16}$ $1\frac{13}{16}$

6. $2\frac{3}{4}$ $9\frac{1}{2}$ $8\frac{5}{8}$ $4\frac{1}{4}$ $6\frac{3}{16}$ **89**
  $1\frac{7}{8}$ $3\frac{11}{16}$ $6\frac{3}{4}$ $2\frac{7}{16}$ $3\frac{7}{8}$

7. $5\frac{1}{8}$ $8\frac{1}{16}$ $9\frac{3}{8}$ $5\frac{5}{16}$ $9\frac{3}{4}$ **89**
  $3\frac{1}{2}$ $2\frac{1}{4}$ $1\frac{1}{2}$ $2\frac{3}{4}$ $7\frac{15}{16}$

What numbers should be put in place of the stars?

8. $9 = 8\frac{*}{4}$ $7\frac{5}{8} = 6\frac{*}{8}$ $9\frac{3}{8} = 8\frac{*}{16}$ **86**

HALVES, THIRDS, AND SIXTHS

1. How many inches are there in $\frac{1}{2}$ yd.? in $\frac{3}{6}$ yd.? This shows that $\frac{1}{2}$ yd. $= \frac{3}{6}$ yd.

2. How many inches are there in $\frac{1}{3}$ yd.? in $\frac{2}{6}$ yd.? This shows that $\frac{1}{3}$ yd. $= \frac{2}{6}$ yd.

3. How many inches are there in $\frac{2}{3}$ yd.? in $\frac{4}{6}$ yd.? This shows that $\frac{2}{3}$ yd. $= \frac{4}{6}$ yd. By what number do you multiply both terms of $\frac{2}{3}$ to show quickly that $\frac{2}{3} = \frac{4}{6}$?

4. How many eggs are there in $\frac{2}{3}$ doz.? in $\frac{8}{12}$ doz.? This shows that $\frac{2}{3}$ doz. $= \frac{8}{12}$ doz. How can you change $\frac{2}{3}$ to $\frac{8}{12}$ quickly without finding parts of a dozen?

Exercises

In ex. 1 to 8, by what do you multiply both terms of the first fraction to change it to the second fraction?

1. $\frac{1}{3} = \frac{2}{6}$ **3.** $\frac{1}{2} = \frac{3}{6}$ **5.** $\frac{2}{3} = \frac{8}{12}$ **7.** $\frac{1}{6} = \frac{2}{12}$

2. $\frac{2}{3} = \frac{4}{6}$ **4.** $\frac{1}{3} = \frac{4}{12}$ **6.** $\frac{1}{2} = \frac{6}{12}$ **8.** $\frac{5}{6} = \frac{10}{12}$

9. Mr. Thomas keeps a clothing store. If he wants part of a dozen pairs of gloves, he writes the order like this: " Send me $\frac{3}{12}$ doz. gloves." Write $\frac{3}{12}$ another way. How would Mr. Thomas write $\frac{1}{2}$ doz. caps? $\frac{1}{3}$ doz.? $\frac{2}{3}$ doz.? $\frac{1}{6}$ doz.? $\frac{5}{6}$ doz.? $\frac{3}{4}$ doz.?

10. What part of a foot is 4 in.? 10 in.? 6 in.?

Reduce the fractions that are not in lowest terms:

11. $\frac{2}{6}$ $\frac{10}{12}$ $\frac{3}{6}$ $\frac{3}{12}$ $\frac{4}{6}$ $\frac{6}{12}$ $\frac{11}{12}$

12. $\frac{5}{6}$ $\frac{8}{12}$ $\frac{1}{6}$ $\frac{9}{12}$ $\frac{2}{3}$ $\frac{4}{12}$ $\frac{5}{12}$

13. Count by $\frac{1}{6}$'s to 5, thus: $\frac{1}{6}, \frac{1}{3}, \frac{1}{2}, \frac{2}{3}, \frac{5}{6}, 1, 1\frac{1}{6}$, etc.

14. Remember these: $\frac{2}{6} = \frac{1}{3}$ $\frac{3}{6} = \frac{1}{2}$ $\frac{4}{6} = \frac{2}{3}$

ADDING HALVES, THIRDS, AND SIXTHS

Arthur works at Mr. Ball's store. Yesterday he sold $6\frac{1}{2}$ doz. black pencils, $3\frac{1}{6}$ doz. red pencils, and $1\frac{2}{3}$ doz. blue pencils. How many dozen pencils was that?

Since $\frac{1}{2}$, $\frac{1}{6}$, and $\frac{2}{3}$ have different denominators, change them to fractions with the same denominator.

$\frac{4}{6} + \frac{1}{6} + \frac{3}{6} = \frac{8}{6}$, which equals $1\frac{2}{6}$. Write $\frac{2}{6}$ and carry 1 to the whole numbers. The result is $11\frac{2}{6}$, which equals $11\frac{1}{3}$.

Arthur sold $11\frac{1}{3}$ doz. pencils in all.

$$6\frac{1}{2} = 6\frac{3}{6}$$
$$3\frac{1}{6} = 3\frac{1}{6}$$
$$1\frac{2}{3} = 1\frac{4}{6}$$
$$11\frac{2}{6} = 11\frac{1}{3}$$

Exercises

1. Jane kept this record of the time she practiced on the piano last week: $1\frac{1}{2}$ hr., $1\frac{2}{3}$ hr., $\frac{5}{6}$ hr., $1\frac{1}{2}$ hr., $1\frac{1}{6}$ hr. How many hours was that in all?

2. Last week Jim helped at the drug store $2\frac{1}{2}$ hr. on Monday, $1\frac{1}{6}$ hr. on Tuesday, and $4\frac{2}{3}$ hr. on Friday. How many hours did he work last week?

Add. Check the work by going over it again:

3. $4\frac{1}{6}$ $5\frac{1}{3}$ **4.** $3\frac{1}{2}$ $2\frac{1}{6}$ **5.** $6\frac{2}{3}$ $4\frac{1}{6}$ **6.** $9\frac{5}{6}$ $8\frac{1}{3}$ **7.** $7\frac{1}{2}$ $7\frac{5}{6}$

8. $7\frac{1}{6}$ $5\frac{1}{2}$ **9.** $4\frac{1}{6}$ $9\frac{2}{3}$ **10.** $2\frac{1}{2}$ $5\frac{2}{3}$ **11.** $8\frac{2}{3}$ $4\frac{5}{6}$ **12.** $9\frac{1}{3}$ $7\frac{1}{2}$

13. $9\frac{1}{6}$ $2\frac{1}{6}$ $4\frac{2}{3}$ **14.** $8\frac{1}{2}$ $5\frac{1}{2}$ $3\frac{1}{6}$ **15.** $7\frac{2}{3}$ $6\frac{1}{6}$ $2\frac{5}{6}$ **16.** $8\frac{5}{6}$ $9\frac{1}{3}$ $4\frac{1}{3}$ **17.** $9\frac{1}{2}$ $7\frac{1}{3}$ $1\frac{1}{6}$

18. $7\frac{1}{2}$ $8\frac{5}{6}$ $2\frac{1}{3}$ **19.** $1\frac{2}{3}$ $4\frac{5}{6}$ $8\frac{1}{2}$ **20.** $3\frac{1}{3}$ $2\frac{1}{2}$ $5\frac{1}{6}$ **21.** $8\frac{1}{3}$ $5\frac{1}{6}$ $6\frac{2}{3}$ **22.** $9\frac{1}{3}$ $7\frac{2}{3}$ $5\frac{1}{2}$

COMPARING RECORDS IN JUMPING

1. In the running broad jump Rose can jump $6\frac{1}{2}$ ft. Little Doris can jump only $4\frac{2}{3}$ ft. How much farther can Rose jump than Doris?

Since you cannot change $\frac{1}{2}$ to *thirds*, change both $\frac{1}{2}$ and $\frac{2}{3}$ to *sixths*.

You find that Rose can jump $1\frac{5}{6}$ ft. farther than Doris.

Check by going over the work carefully.

$$6\frac{1}{2} = 6\frac{3}{6} = 5\frac{9}{6}$$
$$4\frac{2}{3} = 4\frac{4}{6} = 4\frac{4}{6}$$
$$\overline{1\frac{5}{6}}$$

2. The world's champion in the running broad jump jumped $26\frac{1}{6}$ ft. Arthur can jump $11\frac{1}{3}$ ft. How much longer was the champion's jump than Arthur's?

3. In the standing high jump, the champion record is $5\frac{1}{2}$ ft., while in the running high jump it is $6\frac{2}{3}$ ft. Which record is higher, and how much higher?

Exercises in Subtraction

Subtract. Check by going over the work again:

1. $8\frac{5}{6}$ $3\frac{1}{6}$	**2.** $9\frac{5}{6}$ $7\frac{1}{2}$	**3.** $9\frac{1}{6}$ $1\frac{1}{2}$	**4.** $9\frac{2}{3}$ $5\frac{1}{2}$	**5.** $8\frac{1}{6}$ $4\frac{2}{3}$
6. $7\frac{1}{3}$ $1\frac{2}{3}$	**7.** $8\frac{1}{2}$ $4\frac{1}{6}$	**8.** $7\frac{1}{6}$ $5\frac{1}{3}$	**9.** $6\frac{1}{3}$ $3\frac{1}{2}$	**10.** 8 $4\frac{1}{6}$
11. $9\frac{1}{6}$ $8\frac{5}{6}$	**12.** $7\frac{5}{6}$ $6\frac{1}{3}$	**13.** $8\frac{1}{2}$ $2\frac{1}{3}$	**14.** $4\frac{1}{2}$ $2\frac{2}{3}$	**15.** $4\frac{5}{6}$ $3\frac{1}{6}$
16. 4 $2\frac{5}{6}$	**17.** $5\frac{5}{6}$ $3\frac{2}{3}$	**18.** 7 $2\frac{2}{3}$	**19.** 4 $3\frac{5}{6}$	**20.** $2\frac{2}{3}$ $1\frac{5}{6}$

HALVES, FIFTHS, AND TENTHS

1. This cake of chocolate is divided into 10 squares. Copy the picture. Show by shading that $\frac{1}{5} = \frac{2}{10}$; that $\frac{1}{2} = \frac{5}{10}$; that $\frac{3}{5} = \frac{6}{10}$. What does $\frac{4}{5}$ equal?

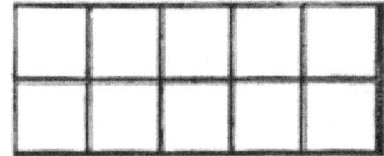

2. How many minutes are there in $\frac{3}{5}$ hr.? in $\frac{6}{10}$ hr.? Does $\frac{3}{5} = \frac{6}{10}$?

3. By what number do you multiply both terms of $\frac{1}{5}$ to show that $\frac{1}{5} = \frac{2}{10}$? How do you change $\frac{3}{5}$ to $\frac{6}{10}$?

Exercises

Tell how the first fraction is changed to the second fraction:

1. $\frac{1}{2} = \frac{5}{10}$ 3. $\frac{1}{6} = \frac{2}{12}$ 5. $\frac{3}{5} = \frac{6}{10}$ 7. $\frac{1}{2} = \frac{10}{20}$

2. $\frac{4}{5} = \frac{8}{10}$ 4. $\frac{1}{4} = \frac{5}{20}$ 6. $\frac{2}{5} = \frac{8}{20}$ 8. $\frac{3}{5} = \frac{60}{100}$

9. Mr. Day's speedometer registers $148\frac{6}{10}$ mi. Sam says that this is equal to $148\frac{1}{2}$ mi. Is Sam right?

10. Will says that 5¢ is $\frac{5}{100}$ of a dollar. Say this in another way by changing $\frac{5}{100}$ to a small fraction.

What word or number should be put in each blank space?

11. To change $\frac{8}{10}$ to $\frac{4}{5}$, ······ both terms of $\frac{8}{10}$ by ···

12. To change $\frac{1}{2}$ to $\frac{50}{100}$, ······ both terms of $\frac{1}{2}$ by ···

13. To change $\frac{6}{10}$ to $\frac{3}{5}$, ······ both terms of $\frac{6}{10}$ by ···

14. To change $\frac{4}{5}$ to $\frac{8}{10}$, ······ both terms of $\frac{4}{5}$ by ···

15. To change $\frac{5}{10}$ to $\frac{1}{2}$, ······ both terms of $\frac{5}{10}$ by ···

Reduce the fractions that are not in lowest terms:

16. $\frac{3}{10}$ $\frac{8}{12}$ $\frac{4}{6}$ $\frac{7}{12}$ $\frac{20}{50}$ $\frac{8}{20}$ $\frac{4}{5}$

17. $\frac{16}{100}$ $\frac{6}{8}$ $\frac{9}{20}$ $\frac{10}{20}$ $\frac{5}{6}$ $\frac{1}{2}$ $\frac{12}{16}$

NOTE TO TEACHER. Caution pupils never to write in their books to fill in blank spaces.

A RELAY RACE

In a track meet, four teams ran in the relay race. Each team had four boys on it.

1. The times of the boys on the Dalton team were $7\frac{3}{5}$ sec., $8\frac{4}{5}$ sec., $7\frac{1}{2}$ sec., $8\frac{2}{5}$ sec. What was their total time?

$$7\frac{3}{5} = 7\frac{6}{10}$$
$$8\frac{4}{5} = 8\frac{8}{10}$$
$$7\frac{1}{2} = 7\frac{5}{10}$$
$$8\frac{2}{5} = 8\frac{4}{10}$$
$$\overline{\phantom{8\frac{4}{10}}32\frac{3}{10}}$$

The common denominator of halves and fifths is tenths. Hence change each fraction to tenths. $\frac{4}{10} + \frac{5}{10} + \frac{8}{10} + \frac{6}{10} = \frac{23}{10}$, or $2\frac{3}{10}$. Write $\frac{3}{10}$ and carry 2.

The total time was $32\frac{3}{10}$ sec.

2. The times of the four boys on the Westfield team were $7\frac{4}{5}$ sec., $8\frac{1}{5}$ sec., $8\frac{1}{10}$ sec., $7\frac{1}{2}$ sec. What was their total time?

3. The runners on the Midget team made these times: $7\frac{2}{5}$ sec., $8\frac{1}{10}$ sec., $8\frac{1}{2}$ sec., $7\frac{3}{10}$ sec. How long did they take for the race?

4. The times of the Stanwich boys were $7\frac{4}{5}$ sec., $7\frac{7}{10}$ sec., $8\frac{1}{2}$ sec., $8\frac{3}{5}$ sec. Find their total time.

5. Which of the teams in ex. 1 to 4 won the race?

Exercises

Add. Check the work by going over it again:

1. $4\frac{1}{5}$ $9\frac{1}{10}$

2. $2\frac{1}{2}$ $8\frac{3}{10}$

3. $7\frac{4}{5}$ $6\frac{1}{10}$

4. $5\frac{7}{10}$ $3\frac{2}{5}$

5. $2\frac{1}{2}$ $4\frac{1}{10}$

6. $7\frac{1}{2}$ $4\frac{1}{5}$

7. $8\frac{4}{5}$ $8\frac{1}{2}$

8. $9\frac{3}{5}$ $5\frac{1}{2}$

9. $8\frac{1}{2}$ $3\frac{2}{5}$

10. $4\frac{1}{2}$ $6\frac{4}{5}$

11. $2\frac{2}{5}$ $9\frac{1}{5}$ $5\frac{7}{10}$

12. $7\frac{9}{10}$ $9\frac{3}{10}$ $7\frac{4}{5}$

13. $7\frac{1}{5}$ $5\frac{1}{2}$ $3\frac{9}{10}$

14. $2\frac{3}{5}$ $9\frac{1}{2}$ $1\frac{3}{10}$

15. $8\frac{1}{10}$ $3\frac{4}{5}$ $6\frac{1}{2}$

HALVES, FIFTHS, AND TENTHS

1. Mr. Wood's speedometer read $96\frac{1}{10}$ mi. when he started his trip. After an hour it read $118\frac{1}{2}$ mi. How far did he travel in the hour?

The common denominator is 10. To what fraction do you change $\frac{1}{2}$?

Mr. Wood traveled $22\frac{2}{5}$ mi. in 1 hr.

Check the work by going over it.

$$118\frac{1}{2} = 118\frac{5}{10}$$
$$96\frac{1}{10} = 96\frac{1}{10}$$
$$22\frac{4}{10} = 22\frac{2}{5}$$

2. Dick drives a delivery car. His speedometer registered $89\frac{3}{10}$ mi. on Monday morning and $192\frac{1}{5}$ mi. on Saturday night. How many miles in all did he drive the car during the week?

3. Jim's time for the 100-yard dash is $16\frac{1}{5}$ sec. Roy's time is $15\frac{7}{10}$ sec. Roy runs how much faster than Jim?

4. When Tom first got his bicycle he rode it at $10\frac{1}{5}$ mi. an hour. Now his speed is $14\frac{1}{2}$ mi. an hour. How much has his speed increased?

Subtract the following. Check the work by going over each step again carefully:

5. $6\frac{4}{5}$
$\underline{4\frac{1}{10}}$

6. $8\frac{1}{10}$
$\underline{6\frac{2}{5}}$

7. $8\frac{3}{10}$
$\underline{5\frac{1}{2}}$

8. $7\frac{2}{5}$
$\underline{2\frac{1}{2}}$

9. $6\frac{1}{2}$
$\underline{1\frac{1}{5}}$

10. $8\frac{9}{10}$
$\underline{3\frac{1}{5}}$

11. 9
$\underline{4\frac{1}{5}}$

12. 7
$\underline{4\frac{7}{10}}$

13. $5\frac{3}{5}$
$\underline{3\frac{1}{2}}$

14. $9\frac{1}{2}$
$\underline{3\frac{3}{5}}$

15. $9\frac{1}{10}$
$\underline{7\frac{1}{5}}$

16. $9\frac{1}{5}$
$\underline{7\frac{1}{10}}$

17. $8\frac{1}{2}$
$\underline{7\frac{2}{5}}$

18. $8\frac{4}{5}$
$\underline{4\frac{1}{2}}$

19. $7\frac{1}{2}$
$\underline{1\frac{4}{5}}$

20. In a class of boys, the best time in the 50-yard dash was $7\frac{3}{10}$ sec.; the poorest time was 9 sec. How much faster was the best record than the poorest one?

PROBLEMS WITHOUT NUMBERS

Tell whether you add, subtract, multiply, or divide to get the answer. If the problem has two steps, tell what you do in each step:

1. How do you find the difference between two numbers?

2. How do you find the product of two numbers?

3. How do you find how much larger one number is than another?

4. How do you find how many times one number is contained in another number?

5. When several people share a number of things equally, how do you find each one's share?

6. How do you find the sum of several different numbers?

7. How do you find the average of several numbers?

★8. If you know the amount of money you can save in a week, the number of weeks for which you will save that amount, and the cost of a bicycle you want, how do you find how much you will have left after you buy the bicycle?

★9. If you know the cost of a box of paints and also the cost of a paint brush and the number of pupils in the class, how do you find the cost of enough paint boxes and brushes for the whole class?

★10. If you know the cost of a second-hand boat, the amount of money you spent to repair it, and also the amount for which you sold the boat, how do you find the amount of money you made when you sold it?

AREA AND POPULATION OF THE UNITED STATES

1. The area of a state tells how large it is. The area of Texas is 265,896 sq. mi. The areas of ten important states along the Atlantic coast are as follows:

	Sq. Mi.		Sq. Mi.
Maine	33,040	Maryland	12,327
New Hampshire	9,341	Virginia	42,627
Massachusetts	8,266	North Carolina	52,426
Connecticut	4,965	South Carolina	30,989
New Jersey	8,224	Georgia	59,265

Is the area of Texas larger or smaller than the total area of these ten states together? Tell how much larger or smaller the area of Texas is.

2. California has an area of 158,297 sq. mi., Oregon has 96,699 sq. mi., and Washington has 69,127 sq. mi. The states bordering the Atlantic Ocean have a total area of 372,958 sq. mi. Which group has the greater area, the states on the Pacific or those on the Atlantic, and how much greater?

★3. The population of each of the ten largest cities in the United States in 1930 was as follows:

Baltimore	804,874	Los Angeles	1,238,048
Boston	781,188	New York	6,930,446
Chicago	3,376,438	Philadelphia	1,950,961
Cleveland	900,429	Pittsburgh	669,817
Detroit	1,568,662	St. Louis	821,960

The population of the United States in 1930 was 122,775,046. Is it correct to say that almost $\frac{1}{7}$ of the total population of the United States lived in the ten largest cities in 1930, or would it be more nearly correct to make the fraction $\frac{1}{6}$ instead of $\frac{1}{7}$?

FINDING A COMMON DENOMINATOR

When you add $\frac{1}{2}$ and $\frac{5}{8}$, the common denominator, 8, is also the denominator of one of the fractions; but when you add $\frac{1}{2}$ and $\frac{2}{5}$, the common denominator is 10. This denominator is different from the denominator of either fraction. It is a number large enough to contain each of the other denominators, 2 and 5, without a remainder.

$$\frac{1}{2} = \frac{5}{10}$$
$$\frac{2}{5} = \frac{4}{10}$$
$$\frac{9}{10}$$

Notice in this example that the common denominator, 10, is the product of 2 and 5.

If you cannot see the common denominator of two fractions quickly, you can always get a common denominator by multiplying the two denominators together.

Exercises

1. Ella bought $\frac{3}{4}$ doz. red roses and $\frac{2}{3}$ doz. white roses. How many dozen roses did she buy?

The common denominator is 12 because 12 contains both 4 and 3. You can get 12 by multiplying 4 by 3.

To change $\frac{3}{4}$ to *twelfths*, multiply both terms of $\frac{3}{4}$ by 3. How do you change $\frac{2}{3}$ to twelfths?

Ella bought $1\frac{5}{12}$ doz. roses.

Check the work by going over each step.

$$\frac{3}{4} = \frac{9}{12}$$
$$\frac{2}{3} = \frac{8}{12}$$
$$\frac{17}{12} = 1\frac{5}{12}$$

Add. Check the work by going over it again:

2. $\frac{1}{3}$ $\frac{1}{2}$	**3.** $\frac{1}{3}$ $\frac{2}{5}$	**4.** $\frac{1}{6}$ $\frac{3}{5}$	**5.** $\frac{1}{4}$ $\frac{2}{5}$	**6.** $\frac{3}{4}$ $\frac{1}{5}$	**7.** $\frac{1}{2}$ $\frac{1}{9}$
8. $\frac{2}{3}$ $\frac{1}{4}$	**9.** $\frac{1}{3}$ $\frac{3}{4}$	**10.** $\frac{2}{3}$ $\frac{1}{2}$	**11.** $\frac{1}{6}$ $\frac{1}{5}$	**12.** $\frac{2}{3}$ $\frac{2}{5}$	**13.** $\frac{3}{8}$ $\frac{1}{3}$
14. $\frac{3}{5}$ $\frac{1}{2}$	**15.** $\frac{3}{10}$ $\frac{1}{3}$	**16.** $\frac{1}{3}$ $\frac{1}{4}$	**17.** $\frac{2}{3}$ $\frac{1}{8}$	**18.** $\frac{5}{8}$ $\frac{2}{3}$	**19.** $\frac{4}{5}$ $\frac{1}{3}$

USING FRACTIONS

1. Albert weighs 90 lb. Margaret weighs $82\frac{1}{4}$ lb. How much less than Albert does Margaret weigh?

Subtract. Check the work by going over it again:

2. $8\frac{1}{8}$ $6\frac{1}{3}$

3. $9\frac{1}{5}$ $2\frac{3}{4}$

4. $8\frac{2}{3}$ $6\frac{9}{10}$

5. $4\frac{5}{6}$ $2\frac{4}{5}$

6. $6\frac{1}{2}$ $\frac{3}{5}$

7. $5\frac{2}{3}$ $3\frac{3}{10}$

8. $5\frac{4}{5}$ $3\frac{1}{2}$

9. $7\frac{3}{8}$ $3\frac{1}{5}$

10. $9\frac{5}{8}$ $7\frac{1}{3}$

11. $9\frac{4}{5}$ $5\frac{1}{3}$

12. $8\frac{1}{5}$ $2\frac{5}{6}$

13. $7\frac{2}{3}$ $4\frac{4}{5}$

14. $8\frac{3}{5}$ $6\frac{2}{3}$

15. $8\frac{4}{5}$ $3\frac{3}{4}$

16. $7\frac{3}{4}$ $\frac{1}{3}$

HOW FAST CAN YOU WORK?

Can you add ex. 1 to 10 in 8 minutes (after copying)?

1. $7\frac{1}{2}$ $3\frac{1}{4}$ $4\frac{3}{8}$

2. $6\frac{3}{4}$ $4\frac{1}{2}$ $5\frac{7}{8}$

3. $4\frac{1}{5}$ $7\frac{1}{10}$ $5\frac{1}{2}$

4. $4\frac{3}{4}$ $3\frac{1}{4}$ $7\frac{7}{8}$

5. $6\frac{9}{16}$ $3\frac{3}{4}$ $5\frac{7}{8}$

6. $6\frac{1}{2}$ $7\frac{1}{3}$ $5\frac{1}{6}$

7. $8\frac{1}{3}$ $9\frac{1}{2}$ $2\frac{5}{6}$

8. $4\frac{5}{16}$ $3\frac{3}{8}$ $2\frac{1}{2}$

9. $9\frac{9}{10}$ $1\frac{1}{2}$ $4\frac{2}{5}$

10. $8\frac{1}{6}$ $9\frac{2}{3}$ $9\frac{1}{2}$

Can you subtract ex. 11 to 20 in 4 minutes (after copying)?

11. $8\frac{1}{2}$ $5\frac{5}{8}$

12. $9\frac{3}{4}$ $4\frac{3}{8}$

13. $7\frac{3}{4}$ $4\frac{1}{3}$

14. $7\frac{7}{10}$ $5\frac{4}{5}$

15. $8\frac{5}{8}$ $2\frac{3}{4}$

16. $7\frac{2}{3}$ $3\frac{1}{6}$

17. $3\frac{2}{5}$ $1\frac{7}{10}$

18. $8\frac{5}{8}$ $2\frac{5}{16}$

19. $9\frac{1}{3}$ $3\frac{5}{6}$

20. $6\frac{1}{3}$ $3\frac{1}{5}$

FINDING THE LEAST COMMON DENOMINATOR

The teacher asked Larry and Tom to add $\frac{1}{6}$ and $\frac{3}{4}$. This is the way each of them did it:

Larry's work

$$\frac{1}{6} = \frac{1\times4}{6\times4} = \frac{4}{24}$$

$$\frac{3}{4} = \frac{3\times6}{4\times6} = \frac{18}{24}$$

$$\frac{22}{24} = \frac{11}{12}$$

Tom's work

$$\frac{1}{6} = \frac{1\times2}{6\times2} = \frac{2}{12}$$

$$\frac{3}{4} = \frac{3\times3}{4\times3} = \frac{9}{12}$$

$$\frac{11}{12}$$

Larry got a common denominator of 24 by multiplying the denominators together. To change $\frac{1}{6}$ and $\frac{3}{4}$ to 24ths, he multiplied both terms of $\frac{1}{6}$ by 4 and both terms of $\frac{3}{4}$ by 6. He reduced $\frac{22}{24}$, the sum, to $\frac{11}{12}$.

Tom used a smaller common denominator, 12, which also contains both 6 and 4. He did the work as shown at the right above, and got the same answer as Larry. Tom did not have to reduce his answer to lowest terms as Larry did.

Both Larry and Tom worked the problem correctly; but it is better to use 12 as the common denominator, because small numbers are easier to work with. 12 is the **least common denominator** of 6 and 4 because it is the *smallest* number containing both 6 and 4. In this example the least common denominator is *smaller* than the product of the denominators.

Exercises

Add. Try to find the least common denominator:

1. $\frac{5}{6}$ 3. $\frac{5}{6}$ 5. $\frac{5}{8}$ 7. $9\frac{7}{8}$ 9. $7\frac{1}{4}$
   $\frac{1}{4}$ $\frac{1}{10}$ $\frac{1}{10}$ $2\frac{1}{20}$ $4\frac{1}{6}$

2. $\frac{1}{8}$ 4. $\frac{1}{9}$ 6. $8\frac{3}{8}$ 8. $4\frac{3}{8}$ 10. $6\frac{1}{6}$
   $\frac{1}{6}$ $\frac{1}{6}$ $3\frac{1}{6}$ $5\frac{1}{6}$ $3\frac{9}{10}$

A RULE FOR FINDING COMMON DENOMINATORS

In adding fractions such as $\frac{2}{3}$, $\frac{5}{6}$, and $\frac{3}{8}$, you must first find the *least* common denominator, which is the *smallest* number that will contain 3, 6, and 8 exactly. An easy way to do this is shown below.

$$\frac{2}{3} = \frac{16}{24}$$
$$\frac{5}{6} = \frac{20}{24}$$
$$\frac{3}{8} = \frac{9}{24}$$
$$\frac{45}{24} = 1\frac{21}{24} = 1\frac{7}{8}$$

First try the largest denominator, which is 8, and see if it contains both 6 and 3. You find that it *does not* contain both numbers. Then multiply 8 by 2, which gives 16, and see if 16 contains both 6 and 3. You still find that it *does not* contain them. Then multiply 8 by 3, which gives 24, and see if 24 contains both 6 and 3. You find that 24 *does* contain both 6 and 3, hence 24 is the least common denominator. Therefore change $\frac{2}{3}$, $\frac{5}{6}$, and $\frac{3}{8}$ each to 24ths, as shown above, and add the fractions. Then reduce $1\frac{21}{24}$ to $1\frac{7}{8}$.

To find the least common denominator, see if the largest denominator contains the other denominators. If not, multiply it in turn by 2, 3, 4, etc., until you get a number that exactly contains each denominator.

Exercises

Add. Find the least common denominator by the rule:

1. $5\frac{3}{10}$ $3\frac{1}{15}$
2. $4\frac{5}{6}$ $8\frac{3}{4}$
3. $9\frac{7}{8}$ $7\frac{5}{6}$
4. $6\frac{5}{6}$ $5\frac{7}{16}$
5. $5\frac{1}{12}$ $9\frac{5}{6}$

6. $8\frac{7}{10}$ $6\frac{5}{6}$
7. $2\frac{3}{10}$ $3\frac{7}{8}$
8. $7\frac{5}{8}$ $4\frac{5}{6}$
9. $9\frac{5}{8}$ $9\frac{7}{12}$
10. $5\frac{3}{4}$ $3\frac{5}{6}$

11. $7\frac{1}{2}$ $5\frac{2}{3}$ $3\frac{5}{6}$
12. $4\frac{2}{3}$ $6\frac{1}{2}$ $2\frac{1}{4}$
13. $8\frac{1}{2}$ $7\frac{5}{6}$ $9\frac{5}{12}$
14. $5\frac{1}{2}$ $4\frac{4}{5}$ $8\frac{7}{10}$
15. $3\frac{2}{3}$ $2\frac{3}{8}$ $6\frac{1}{2}$

EXERCISES IN FINDING COMMON DENOMINATORS

Add the following and check the work. Use the rule on page 103 *for finding the least common denominator:*

1. $1\frac{7}{8}$
   $\frac{1}{2}$
   $9\frac{5}{16}$

2. $1\frac{2}{3}$
   $8\frac{11}{12}$
   $9\frac{1}{2}$

3. $3\frac{3}{4}$
   $8\frac{1}{6}$
   $8\frac{1}{2}$

4. $9\frac{9}{10}$
   $5\frac{2}{5}$
   $4\frac{1}{4}$

5. $5\frac{2}{3}$
   $\frac{3}{4}$
   $6\frac{7}{12}$

6. $8\frac{1}{2}$
   $5\frac{2}{3}$
   $9\frac{4}{5}$

7. $7\frac{1}{3}$
   $7\frac{5}{6}$
   $3\frac{1}{9}$

8. $3\frac{1}{2}$
   $2\frac{4}{5}$
   $5\frac{4}{15}$

9. $7\frac{5}{6}$
   $4\frac{1}{3}$
   $9\frac{3}{8}$

10. $9\frac{1}{12}$
    $5\frac{5}{8}$
    $4\frac{1}{6}$

11. $7\frac{1}{2}$
    $4\frac{2}{3}$
    $6\frac{3}{4}$
    $5\frac{11}{12}$

12. $9\frac{1}{2}$
    $4\frac{2}{3}$
    $3\frac{1}{4}$
    $2\frac{5}{6}$

13. $7\frac{1}{3}$
    $\frac{7}{8}$
    $5\frac{1}{6}$
    $4\frac{5}{12}$

14. $8\frac{2}{9}$
    $6\frac{1}{3}$
    $\frac{3}{4}$
    $5\frac{5}{6}$

15. $1\frac{3}{8}$
    $2\frac{1}{16}$
    $9\frac{5}{12}$
    $8\frac{1}{6}$

★16. Fred weighed $96\frac{9}{10}$ lb. on one scale that registered tenths of a pound, and $96\frac{3}{4}$ lb. on another that registered fourths of a pound. On which scale did he weigh more? how much more?

★17. In making furniture, thin layers of mahogany or other expensive woods are often glued over cheaper woods. These thin layers are called *veneering*. To a board $\frac{3}{8}$ in. thick, three layers of veneering are glued. Two of the layers are each $\frac{3}{32}$ in. thick and one layer is $\frac{1}{16}$ in. thick. What is the total thickness of the veneered board?

★18. By using a stop watch, a foreman found that a lazy mechanic in his shop worked these lengths of time during one hour: $4\frac{2}{5}$ min., $6\frac{1}{2}$ min., $7\frac{3}{5}$ min., $4\frac{1}{10}$ min., $3\frac{3}{4}$ min., $4\frac{1}{3}$ min. How much time did the mechanic actually work?

IMPROVEMENT TEST No. 5

Test 5 A — Addition   (Time 4 min.)

1.	41550	2.	98856	3.	77668	4.	47589
	156		6368		46146		2455
	4198		579		18978		53297
	818		63795		4259		39

5.	99847	6.	36036	7.	65771	8.	14760
	95		4352		241		999
	873		4820		9512		36893
	28297		36809		94095		366

Test 5 B — Subtraction   (Time 4 min.)

1.	$586.06	2.	$675.20	3.	$760.87
	147.54		285.70		286.79

4.	$768.21	5.	$942.56	6.	$820.00
	591.32		568.47		284.19

7.	$952.41	8.	$861.27	9.	$526.64
	284.06		601.50		165.75

10.	$629.07	11.	$755.90	12.	$940.01
	213.59		195.81		172.90

Test 5 C — Multiplication   (Time 4 min. after copying)

1.	605	2.	598	3.	932	4.	458	5.	706
	346		602		158		298		907

Test 5 D — Division   (Time 4 min. after copying)

1. 82)52070   2. 39)19827   3. 295)75637

MAGIC SQUARES WITH FRACTIONS

1. Here is a kind of magic square. Follow the directions carefully and you will discover something very interesting.

Add the three fractions in the top row. How much is $\frac{7}{8} + \frac{3}{4} + \frac{3}{8}$? Then add the three fractions in the middle row. Next add the bottom row. What is the sum each time?

$\frac{7}{8}$	$\frac{3}{4}$	$\frac{3}{8}$
$\frac{1}{4}$	$\frac{5}{8}$	$\frac{9}{8}$
$\frac{7}{8}$	$\frac{5}{8}$	$\frac{1}{2}$

Now add the three fractions in the left-hand column running up and down. How much is $\frac{7}{8} + \frac{1}{4} + \frac{7}{8}$? Add the middle column. Add the right-hand column. If your work is right, the six sums are all alike.

Test the following squares by adding each row and each column. Are the six sums alike in each square? Which square is not a magic square?

2.

$\frac{1}{3}$	$\frac{5}{6}$	$\frac{5}{6}$
$\frac{4}{3}$	$\frac{1}{4}$	$\frac{5}{12}$
$\frac{1}{3}$	$\frac{11}{12}$	$\frac{3}{4}$

3.

$\frac{1}{4}$	$\frac{1}{8}$	$\frac{5}{8}$
$\frac{5}{16}$	$\frac{5}{8}$	$\frac{1}{16}$
$\frac{7}{16}$	$\frac{1}{4}$	$\frac{5}{16}$

4.

$\frac{1}{4}$	$\frac{1}{2}$	$\frac{1}{8}$
$\frac{3}{8}$	$\frac{1}{2}$	$\frac{5}{8}$
$\frac{1}{4}$	$\frac{1}{2}$	$\frac{1}{8}$

5.

$\frac{2}{3}$	$\frac{10}{9}$	$\frac{2}{9}$
$\frac{2}{3}$	0	$\frac{4}{3}$
$\frac{2}{3}$	$\frac{8}{9}$	$\frac{4}{9}$

*6. Complete this square so that the sum of each row and of each column is $1\frac{1}{2}$.

First put the right fraction in place of A so that the top row adds up to $1\frac{1}{2}$. After you find A, find the right fraction for B so that the right-hand column adds up to $1\frac{1}{2}$. Next find the right fraction for C so that the bottom row equals $1\frac{1}{2}$. Then find D so that the left-hand column equals $1\frac{1}{2}$. Finish by finding

$\frac{1}{2}$	$\frac{1}{4}$	A
D	E	$\frac{1}{8}$
C	$\frac{3}{8}$	B

the right fraction for E to make the middle row equal $1\frac{1}{2}$. Now test your work by adding each row and each column to make sure that the six sums are all $1\frac{1}{2}$.

★ MAKING MAGIC SQUARES

Complete these squares by finding A, then B, C, D, and E. The sum for each row is above the square.

1. sum = 2

$\frac{1}{2}$	$\frac{3}{4}$	A
D	E	$\frac{5}{8}$
C	$\frac{9}{8}$	B

2. sum = $\frac{7}{8}$

$\frac{3}{16}$	$\frac{1}{4}$	A
D	E	$\frac{1}{16}$
C	$\frac{3}{8}$	B

3. sum = $\frac{7}{8}$

$\frac{1}{4}$	$\frac{3}{8}$	A
D	E	$\frac{1}{2}$
C	$\frac{1}{4}$	B

4. sum = $1\frac{1}{2}$

$\frac{3}{5}$	$\frac{7}{10}$	A
D	E	$\frac{2}{5}$
C	$\frac{1}{2}$	B

5. sum = 1

$\frac{1}{6}$	$\frac{1}{3}$	A
D	E	$\frac{1}{12}$
C	$\frac{1}{3}$	B

6. sum = 2

$\frac{7}{8}$	$\frac{5}{8}$	A
D	E	$\frac{9}{8}$
C	$\frac{7}{8}$	B

7. sum = $\frac{1}{2}$

$\frac{1}{16}$	$\frac{1}{4}$	A
D	E	$\frac{1}{8}$
C	0	B

8. sum = 1

$\frac{1}{16}$	$\frac{1}{2}$	A
D	E	$\frac{1}{4}$
C	$\frac{1}{16}$	B

★ PLAYING TIT-TAT-TO WITH FRACTIONS

Helen and Tom play tit-tat-to on a magic square whose sum is 1 each time. Tom starts by putting $\frac{1}{5}$ in A. Helen puts $\frac{3}{10}$ in B. Then Helen and Tom each try to put a fraction in C that will make the top row add up to 1. As Helen gets $\frac{1}{2}$ first, she scores 1 point. Then Helen puts any small fraction, like $\frac{1}{10}$, in D. Tom finds $\frac{2}{5}$ for E first; he gets 1 point. Tom puts $\frac{1}{2}$ in F. If Helen fills G and H first and Tom fills J first, Helen wins because she has 3 points and Tom has only 2. Then they check the square to see if each sum is 1.

A $\frac{1}{5}$	B $\frac{3}{10}$	C $\frac{1}{2}$
H $\frac{7}{10}$	J $\frac{1}{5}$	D $\frac{1}{10}$
G $\frac{1}{10}$	F $\frac{1}{2}$	E $\frac{2}{5}$

Play this game. Make the sum any small number.

MIXED PRACTICE

1. Find the sum of $3\frac{2}{3}$, $8\frac{5}{6}$, and $4\frac{1}{2}$.

2. Multiply 75 by 42.   Then divide the product by **9.**

3. How much is two thirds of 27?

4. Find the quotient when 6426 is divided by 17.

5. How much more than 578 is 619?

6. How many 25's are there in 4000?

7. If you multiply 140 by 57, what is the product?

8. What is the difference between $9\frac{1}{2}$ and $7\frac{5}{8}$?

9. Reduce $\frac{25}{4}$ to a mixed number.

10. Which of these fractions are in their lowest terms: $\frac{3}{4}$, $\frac{11}{16}$, $\frac{2}{4}$, $\frac{4}{5}$, $\frac{3}{8}$, $\frac{6}{8}$, $\frac{5}{6}$, $\frac{7}{10}$, $\frac{3}{6}$?

11. What is the average of 2847 and 1029?

12. How much less than $10.00 is $8.72?

13. How many inches are there in 5 ft. 3 in.?

14. Which of these numbers is larger: XCVI or CXVI?   CXV or XCV?

15. Change the following fractions to fractions having a common denominator: $\frac{1}{2}$, $\frac{3}{4}$, $\frac{7}{8}$, $\frac{1}{4}$.

16. Which of these fractions is larger: $\frac{3}{4}$ or $\frac{7}{8}$?

Do these examples:

17. 79 minus 31 equals what?

18. 14 times 92 equals what?

19. 87 and 59 equals what?

20. 29 less 17 equals what?

21. 18 from 81 equals what?

22. $3\frac{1}{2} + 2\frac{1}{4} + 12\frac{3}{8} = ?$

23. $7\frac{1}{2} + 12\frac{1}{4} - 8\frac{3}{4} = ?$

24. $2\frac{1}{3} + 3\frac{1}{2} + 17\frac{5}{6} = ?$

25. $9\frac{5}{8} - 2\frac{1}{4} + 12\frac{1}{2} = ?$

26. $4\frac{3}{4} - 2\frac{1}{2} - 2\frac{1}{4} = ?$

DIAGNOSTIC TEST

If you miss exercises in any row, you need more practice. The Help Pages tell you where to find it.

Add. Check the work by going over it:

1. $2\frac{1}{6}$ $\quad 1\frac{2}{3}$ $\quad 7\frac{1}{2}$ $\quad 3\frac{1}{6}$ $\quad 8\frac{1}{3}$ $\qquad$ **93**

$6\frac{1}{2}$ $\quad 4\frac{1}{6}$ $\quad 2\frac{1}{3}$ $\quad 2\frac{2}{3}$ $\quad 1\frac{5}{6}$

$\underline{3\frac{5}{6}}$ $\quad \underline{2\frac{1}{3}}$ $\quad \underline{4\frac{5}{6}}$ $\quad \underline{4\frac{1}{2}}$ $\quad \underline{6\frac{1}{3}}$

2. $5\frac{3}{5}$ $\quad 1\frac{7}{10}$ $\quad 8\frac{1}{2}$ $\quad 4\frac{9}{10}$ $\quad 2\frac{1}{2}$ $\qquad$ **96**

$\underline{4\frac{3}{10}}$ $\quad \underline{3\frac{4}{5}}$ $\quad \underline{6\frac{7}{10}}$ $\quad \underline{4\frac{1}{5}}$ $\quad \underline{9\frac{2}{5}}$

3. $\frac{2}{3}$ $\quad \frac{3}{5}$ $\quad 5\frac{5}{8}$ $\quad 3\frac{1}{4}$ $\quad 4\frac{2}{5}$ $\qquad$ **100**

$\underline{\frac{1}{2}}$ $\quad \underline{\frac{1}{3}}$ $\quad \underline{1\frac{2}{3}}$ $\quad \underline{2\frac{1}{3}}$ $\quad \underline{7\frac{5}{6}}$

4. $3\frac{1}{2}$ $\quad 7\frac{2}{3}$ $\quad 4\frac{3}{16}$ $\quad 2\frac{3}{4}$ $\quad 4\frac{2}{3}$ $\qquad$ **103, 104**

$1\frac{3}{8}$ $\quad 2\frac{1}{2}$ $\quad 8\frac{5}{6}$ $\quad 3\frac{5}{6}$ $\quad 5\frac{4}{5}$

$\underline{2\frac{5}{6}}$ $\quad \underline{5\frac{3}{4}}$ $\quad \underline{1\frac{1}{2}}$ $\quad \underline{2\frac{1}{2}}$ $\quad \underline{1\frac{1}{2}}$

Subtract. Check the work by going over it:

5. $9\frac{2}{3}$ $\quad 5\frac{1}{2}$ $\quad 7\frac{2}{3}$ $\quad 8\frac{5}{6}$ $\quad 6\frac{1}{6}$ $\qquad$ **94**

$\underline{2\frac{1}{6}}$ $\quad \underline{1\frac{5}{6}}$ $\quad \underline{4\frac{1}{2}}$ $\quad \underline{5\frac{1}{6}}$ $\quad \underline{2\frac{1}{3}}$

6. $7\frac{3}{5}$ $\quad 8$ $\quad 6\frac{1}{5}$ $\quad 9\frac{1}{2}$ $\quad 4\frac{3}{10}$ $\qquad$ **97**

$\underline{7\frac{3}{10}}$ $\quad \underline{3\frac{4}{5}}$ $\quad \underline{4\frac{7}{10}}$ $\quad \underline{6\frac{1}{5}}$ $\quad \underline{1\frac{4}{5}}$

7. $5\frac{1}{2}$ $\quad 9\frac{3}{5}$ $\quad 8\frac{1}{2}$ $\quad 7\frac{5}{8}$ $\quad 6\frac{2}{3}$ $\qquad$ **101**

$\underline{3\frac{1}{3}}$ $\quad \underline{4\frac{7}{8}}$ $\quad \underline{2\frac{4}{5}}$ $\quad \underline{5\frac{2}{3}}$ $\quad \underline{3\frac{1}{5}}$

PROBLEM TEST B1

1. Yesterday the Scout troop went on a hike of $8\frac{1}{4}$ mi. to the top of Ash Mountain and to-day they went $6\frac{1}{2}$ mi. to Long Lake. How many miles all together did they walk in the two days?

2. Mr. Smith is paying for an automobile on the installment plan. He paid $100 down when he bought the car and has agreed to pay $37 each month for 20 mo. What is the total cost of the car?

3. Henry saved $.35 a week for 8 wk. and George saved $.30 a week for 9 wk. How much more did Henry save than George?

4. Mr. West is an agent for electric fans. Last year he earned $1116 in all in 12 mo. by selling them. How many dollars per month did his earnings average?

5. Last spring the baseball team for the fifth grade bought 8 baseballs at $.65 each and a baseball bat for $1.25. How much did these things cost?

6. The 14 girls in our sewing class went on a picnic. Sandwiches cost $.89, lemons and sugar cost $.40, and ice cream cost $.95. If the girls shared the expenses equally, how much did each one pay?

7. Susan bought a coat at a sale and got $\frac{1}{4}$ off the regular price. How much did she pay for the coat, if it was sold regularly for $13.00?

Standards	Excellent	Good	Fair	Poor
	7 right	5 or 6	4	0 to 3

Write down the number of problems you got right on this test. Try to do better on your next problem test.

DICK TELLS A SECRET ABOUT THE NUMBER 9

Dick asked Ella to find out if 9 would exactly divide 2651 or 1935. Ella did the work as shown here and said that 2651 is not divisible by 9 because there is a remainder of 5, but that 1935 is divisible by 9 because there is no remainder. To say that a number is *divisible* by 9 means that it is *exactly divisible* by 9, without a remainder.

$$9)\overline{2651} \qquad 9)\overline{1935}$$
$$294\tfrac{5}{9} \qquad\quad 215$$

Dick then showed Ella a way of finding if a number is divisible by 9 *without actually dividing*. He added each of the figures, or *digits*, of 2651 thus: $2 + 6 + 5 + 1 = 14$. Since 14 is *not* divisible by 9, the number 2651 is *not* divisible by 9. Then he added the digits of 1935 thus: $1 + 9 + 3 + 5 = 18$. Since 18 *is* divisible by 9, then 1935 is divisible by 9.

A number is divisible by 9 if the sum of its digits is divisible by 9.

This rule is called a **test of divisibility** because it shows when a number is divisible by 9.

Exercises

Use Dick's rule to tell which of these numbers are divisible by 9. Then divide each number by 9 to see if the rule always works:

1. 137	**4.** 738	**7.** 8109	**10.** 5688	**13.** 81005
2. 243	**5.** 251	**8.** 2654	**11.** 8298	**14.** 60003
3. 528	**6.** 648	**9.** 3519	**12.** 6660	**15.** 11223

16. Can Uncle Ben divide a collection of stamps equally among his 9 nephews, if it contains 1643 stamps? if it contains 2664 stamps? 1927 stamps? 1233 stamps?

DICK'S OTHER TESTS OF DIVISIBILITY

Dick also told Ella these simple rules:

A number is divisible by 3 if the sum of its digits is divisible by 3.

Thus, 114 is divisible by 3 because $1 + 1 + 4 = 6$, and 6 is divisible by 3; but 236 is not divisible by 3 because $2 + 3 + 6 = 11$, and 11 is not divisible by 3.

A number is divisible by 5 if it ends in 0 or 5.

Thus, 140 and 225 are divisible by 5, but 141 is not.

A number is divisible by 2 if it ends in 0, 2, 4, 6, or 8.

Thus, 458 is divisible by 2 because it ends in 8; but 359 is not divisible by 2 because it ends in 9.

A number like 8 or 42, which is exactly divisible by 2, is called an **even number.**

A number like 5 or 117, which is not divisible by 2, is called an **odd number.**

Exercises

1. Can you divide 75 boys into teams of 5 boys each so that there will be no boys left over? into teams of 3 boys each? of 9 boys each?

Which numbers are divisible by 2? by 3? by 5? by 9?

2. 745	**4.** 851	**6.** 276	**8.** 855	**10.** 1764
3. 879	**5.** 682	**7.** 105	**9.** 480	**11.** 4282

12. Are 765 and 1170 both divisible by 9? by 5? by 2?

13. Are 855 and 402 both divisible by 9? by 5? by 3?

Tell if both numbers are divisible by 2, 3, 5, or 9:

14. 78 and 42	**17.** 117 and 54	**20.** 270 and 315
15. 72 and 54	**18.** 165 and 75	**21.** 243 and 297
16. 70 and 130	**19.** 315 and 225	**22.** 450 and 270

A NEW WAY TO REDUCE FRACTIONS

1. You have learned that dividing both terms of a fraction by the *same* number does not change the value of the fraction. If you divide both terms of $\frac{12}{16}$ by 4, you get $\frac{3}{4}$, which has the *same value* as $\frac{12}{16}$.

$$\frac{12}{16} = \frac{12 \div 4}{16 \div 4} = \frac{3}{4}$$

2. Instead of writing the work as shown above, it may be done more quickly as follows:

Divide 12 by 4, which gives 3; cross out 12 to show that it has been divided and write the 3 above it. Divide 16 by 4, which gives 4. Cross out 16 and write the 4 below it. You have now reduced $\frac{12}{16}$ to lowest terms by dividing both its terms by 4. The result is $\frac{3}{4}$.

$$\frac{\overset{3}{\cancel{12}}}{\underset{4}{\cancel{16}}} = \frac{3}{4}$$

When you divide 12 and 16 each by 4, you sometimes say that you *cancel* 4. To *cancel* 4 means to *divide by* 4.

3. Reduce $\frac{8}{16}$ to lowest terms.

In dividing by 8, remember that $8 \div 8 = 1$. When you cross out 8, it is safer to write the 1 above it. If you do not write the 1, you must think of it as there. How did you get the 2 that is written below 16? What is the result?

$$\frac{\overset{1}{\cancel{8}}}{\underset{2}{\cancel{16}}} = \frac{1}{2}$$

4. Reduce $\frac{15}{75}$ to lowest terms.

In this example you must divide twice. First divide both terms of $\frac{15}{75}$ by 5, which gives $\frac{3}{15}$. How do you know that 5 exactly divides both 15 and 75? Then divide both terms of $\frac{3}{15}$ by 3, which gives $\frac{1}{5}$. Is $\frac{1}{5}$ the answer in the lowest terms? Tell why you cannot reduce $\frac{1}{5}$ further.

$$\frac{\overset{\overset{1}{3}}{\cancel{\cancel{15}}}}{\underset{\underset{5}{15}}{\cancel{\cancel{75}}}} = \frac{1}{5}$$

Reduce these fractions to lowest terms:

5. $\frac{9}{12}$ 8. $\frac{18}{20}$ 11. $\frac{18}{24}$ 14. $\frac{12}{30}$ 17. $\frac{16}{48}$ 20. $\frac{18}{96}$

6. $\frac{12}{15}$ 9. $\frac{40}{55}$ 12. $\frac{15}{30}$ 15. $\frac{11}{33}$ 18. $\frac{28}{35}$ 21. $\frac{40}{160}$

7. $\frac{24}{36}$ 10. $\frac{16}{32}$ 13. $\frac{20}{35}$ 16. $\frac{36}{64}$ 19. $\frac{25}{80}$ 22. $\frac{45}{120}$

REDUCING FRACTIONS IN LONG DIVISION

Maud is dividing 3960 by 225. Writing the remainder over the divisor to form a fraction, she gets a quotient of $17\frac{135}{225}$. She then reduces $\frac{135}{225}$ to lowest terms.

In reducing the fraction, Maud sees that both terms of $\frac{135}{225}$ are divisible by 5 because they both end in 5. Dividing both terms by 5, she gets $\frac{27}{45}$. How does she know that the terms of $\frac{27}{45}$ are not divisible by 2? that both terms are divisible by 9?

Maud's answer is $17\frac{3}{5}$. Why is $\frac{3}{5}$ an easier fraction to work with than $\frac{135}{225}$?

$$17\frac{135}{225}$$
$$225\overline{)3960}$$
$$\underline{225}$$
$$1710$$
$$\underline{1575}$$
$$135$$

$$\frac{135}{225} = \frac{3}{5}$$

Exercises

1. There are 396 girls and 405 boys in the Grant School. Can the girls alone march by 3's and have no girls left over? Can the boys alone march by 3's?

Can the girls march by 5's? by 2's? by 9's? Can the boys march by 5's? by 2's? by 9's?

These fractions occur in long division. Reduce them to lowest terms, using the tests of divisibility:

2. $\frac{45}{75}$ **5.** $\frac{108}{234}$ **8.** $\frac{120}{225}$ **11.** $\frac{111}{303}$ **14.** $\frac{180}{315}$

3. $\frac{42}{84}$ **6.** $\frac{210}{360}$ **9.** $\frac{126}{225}$ **12.** $\frac{132}{174}$ **15.** $\frac{104}{312}$

4. $\frac{32}{96}$ **7.** $\frac{170}{250}$ **10.** $\frac{315}{405}$ **13.** $\frac{42}{114}$ **16.** $\frac{75}{105}$

Divide. Reduce fractions in quotients to lowest terms:

17. $1410 \div 24$ **20.** $5715 \div 135$ **23.** $3088 \div 216$

18. $6396 \div 48$ **21.** $8037 \div 360$ **24.** $7074 \div 486$

19. $7944 \div 72$ **22.** $4590 \div 864$ **25.** $4245 \div 240$

ADDITION AND SUBTRACTION

Add the following and check the work :

	1.		2.		3.		4.		5.
	886		557		368		412		698
	195		637		237		176		919
	938		509		416		283		325
	427		738		370		445		995
	962		975		389		682		420
	540		481		740		521		143
	606		609		204		649		303
	173		520		297		917		546

	6.		7.		8.		9.		10.
	878		306		259		809		771
	603		844		123		388		581
	984		898		514		351		250
	159		765		416		137		708
	365		752		912		872		692
	836		240		572		348		977
	830		107		700		791		692
	768		989		645		849		372

Subtract the following and check the work :

	11.		12.		13.
	$866.17		$500.00		$855.43
	189.36		258.97		295.56

	14.		15.		16.
	$928.33		$817.75		$500.09
	479.99		499.86		147.60

	17.		18.		19.
	$487.54		$696.53		$260.00
	87.76		97.88		13.08

	20.		21.		22.
	$232.33		$500.33		$733.21
	76.87		95.64		45.85

MULTIPLYING A FRACTION BY A WHOLE NUMBER

1. How much is 5×1 apple? 5×1 third? $5 \times \frac{1}{3}$?

2. How much is 5×2 pears? 5×2 thirds? $5 \times \frac{2}{3}$?

3. If Laura practices on her violin $\frac{3}{4}$ hr. a day, how many hours does she spend at practicing in 6 days?

You must find what $6 \times \frac{3}{4}$ equals.

Just as 6×3 *dogs* $= 18$ *dogs*, so 6×3 *fourths* $= 18$ *fourths*. Hence $6 \times \frac{3}{4} = \frac{18}{4}$.

Change $\frac{18}{4}$ to $4\frac{2}{4}$, or $4\frac{1}{2}$.

Laura practices $4\frac{1}{2}$ hr. in 6 days.

$$6 \times \frac{3}{4} = \frac{6 \times 3}{4} = \frac{18}{4} = 4\frac{1}{2}$$

To multiply a fraction by a whole number, multiply the numerator by the whole number and divide the result by the denominator.

Oral Drill

Try to multiply mentally. Give results in lowest terms:

1. $3 \times \frac{1}{4}$	**10.** $9 \times \frac{1}{2}$	**19.** $9 \times \frac{2}{3}$	**28.** $5 \times \frac{1}{6}$
2. $2 \times \frac{1}{3}$	**11.** $8 \times \frac{1}{4}$	**20.** $2 \times \frac{1}{4}$	**29.** $4 \times \frac{1}{4}$
3. $4 \times \frac{1}{5}$	**12.** $6 \times \frac{2}{5}$	**21.** $3 \times \frac{1}{6}$	**30.** $9 \times \frac{1}{5}$
4. $5 \times \frac{2}{3}$	**13.** $4 \times \frac{3}{8}$	**22.** $6 \times \frac{3}{8}$	**31.** $2 \times \frac{3}{8}$
5. $3 \times \frac{1}{2}$	**14.** $5 \times \frac{7}{8}$	**23.** $3 \times \frac{4}{5}$	**32.** $4 \times \frac{2}{3}$
6. $6 \times \frac{1}{5}$	**15.** $8 \times \frac{1}{2}$	**24.** $2 \times \frac{1}{3}$	**33.** $6 \times \frac{3}{5}$
7. $5 \times \frac{1}{2}$	**16.** $6 \times \frac{2}{3}$	**25.** $4 \times \frac{3}{5}$	**34.** $4 \times \frac{5}{6}$
8. $4 \times \frac{1}{6}$	**17.** $9 \times \frac{1}{3}$	**26.** $2 \times \frac{7}{8}$	**35.** $7 \times \frac{1}{5}$
9. $8 \times \frac{3}{4}$	**18.** $2 \times \frac{5}{8}$	**27.** $6 \times \frac{1}{6}$	**36.** $8 \times \frac{2}{3}$

37. How many yards of silk does Mary Ann need for 6 sofa cushions, if she needs $\frac{7}{8}$ yd. for each cushion?

RIDING TO SCHOOL

1. Every day Ralph rides $12\frac{3}{4}$ mi. going to and from school.   How far does he ride in 23 school days?

First multiply $\frac{3}{4}$ by 23, which gives $17\frac{1}{4}$.   Then multiply 12 by 23, placing the products as shown at the right.   Add the products.

Check by going over the work.

Ralph rides $293\frac{1}{4}$ mi. in 23 school days.

$$
\begin{array}{r}
12\frac{3}{4} \\
23 \\
\hline
17\frac{1}{4} \\
36 \\
24 \\
\hline
293\frac{1}{4}
\end{array}
$$

$$23 \times \frac{3}{4} = \frac{69}{4} = 17\frac{1}{4}$$

2. Ann's daily ride to and from school covers $17\frac{1}{2}$ mi. How many miles does she ride in 22 days?

3. Billy travels $13\frac{3}{4}$ mi. a day in the school bus.   How many miles does he ride in a term of 98 days?

Exercises

Multiply.   Check your work by going over it:

1. $6\times3\frac{1}{2}$
2. $8\times5\frac{2}{3}$
3. $4\times3\frac{3}{4}$
4. $3\times3\frac{5}{8}$
5. $7\times6\frac{1}{2}$
6. $9\times6\frac{2}{3}$
7. $5\times9\frac{1}{4}$
8. $8\times7\frac{7}{8}$
9. $5\times8\frac{2}{3}$
10. $4\times9\frac{5}{8}$
11. $7\times2\frac{1}{4}$
12. $8\times5\frac{1}{2}$

13. $6\times14\frac{3}{8}$
14. $7\times14\frac{2}{5}$
15. $2\times17\frac{1}{2}$
16. $8\times11\frac{3}{4}$
17. $7\times15\frac{1}{2}$
18. $4\times16\frac{5}{6}$
19. $2\times25\frac{5}{6}$
20. $5\times18\frac{1}{4}$
21. $9\times13\frac{3}{5}$
22. $7\times10\frac{1}{2}$
23. $6\times27\frac{2}{3}$
24. $9\times19\frac{2}{3}$

25. $56\times14\frac{7}{8}$
26. $28\times13\frac{2}{3}$
27. $15\times28\frac{1}{2}$
28. $16\times19\frac{1}{8}$
29. $23\times18\frac{3}{8}$
30. $25\times13\frac{3}{5}$
31. $96\times11\frac{3}{4}$
32. $18\times13\frac{1}{2}$
33. $28\times11\frac{1}{4}$
34. $19\times12\frac{3}{8}$
35. $15\times19\frac{4}{5}$
36. $24\times16\frac{5}{12}$

MULTIPLYING A WHOLE NUMBER BY A FRACTION

1. How much will $\frac{3}{4}$ yd. of ribbon cost at 20¢ a yard?

You find that $\frac{3}{4}$ of 20¢ is 15¢, as in A below.

$A.$ $\frac{1}{4}$ of 20 = 5 $B.$ $\frac{1}{4} \times 20 = 5$

$\frac{3}{4}$ of 20 = 3×5, or 15 $\frac{3}{4} \times 20 = 3 \times 5$, or 15

Another way to write $\frac{3}{4}$ of 20 is $\frac{3}{4} \times 20$, as shown in B. The sign ✕ takes the place of the word " of " when written after a fraction.

Multiplying a number by a fraction is the same as taking a fractional part of it.

2. Find $\frac{1}{4}$ of 16. Find $\frac{3}{4}$ of 16. When you have found $\frac{1}{4}$ of a number, how do you find $\frac{3}{4}$ of the number?

3. Find $\frac{1}{4}$ of 24. Find $\frac{3}{4}$ of 24.

4. Find $\frac{1}{3} \times 36$; $\frac{2}{3} \times 36$; $\frac{1}{6} \times 36$; $\frac{5}{6} \times 36$.

5. If 1 lb. of tea costs 60¢, how much does $\frac{3}{4}$ lb. cost?

6. If Ruth sells candy at 48¢ a pound, how much does she charge for $\frac{5}{8}$ lb.? How much is $\frac{5}{8} \times 48$?

Multiply mentally:

7. $\frac{3}{8} \times 24$	**12.** $\frac{5}{6} \times 18$	**17.** $\frac{2}{3} \times 15$	**22.** $\frac{3}{4} \times 120$
8. $\frac{2}{3} \times 21$	**13.** $\frac{2}{7} \times 21$	**18.** $\frac{2}{9} \times 27$	**23.** $\frac{5}{9} \times 180$
9. $\frac{7}{8} \times 32$	**14.** $\frac{4}{5} \times 45$	**19.** $\frac{7}{8} \times 40$	**24.** $\frac{5}{6} \times 240$
10. $\frac{2}{3} \times 90$	**15.** $\frac{3}{5} \times 35$	**20.** $\frac{2}{3} \times 75$	**25.** $\frac{3}{5} \times 125$
11. $\frac{2}{5} \times 45$	**16.** $\frac{3}{8} \times 32$	**21.** $\frac{2}{3} \times 33$	**26.** $\frac{7}{8} \times 320$

In the above problems, the whole number is always exactly divisible by the denominator. In such problems you see that you multiply by using the following rule:

To multiply a whole number by a fraction, divide the whole number by the denominator, if it is exactly divisible; then multiply the result by the numerator.

MULTIPLYING A WHOLE NUMBER BY A FRACTION

A grocer charges 27¢ a pound for cookies. How much does he charge for $\frac{3}{4}$ lb.?

To find $\frac{3}{4} \times 27$ you may first divide 27 by 4 and then multiply by 3, as in A. But 4 does not divide 27 exactly; therefore it is better *first to multiply* 27 by 3 and *then to divide* the product by 4, as in B.

A. Here you divide first and then multiply.

$$4)\overline{27}$$
$$6\frac{3}{4}$$
$$3$$
$$2\frac{1}{4}$$
$$18$$
$$20\frac{1}{4}$$

B. Here you multiply first and then divide.

$$27$$
$$3$$
$$4)\overline{81}$$
$$20\frac{1}{4}$$

B is shorter than A because there are fewer fractions to handle.

The cookies cost $20\frac{1}{4}$¢. Since a fraction of a cent is usually counted as an extra cent, the charge is 21¢.

When the denominator of the fraction does not divide the whole number exactly, use this rule:

To multiply a whole number by a fraction, multiply the whole number by the numerator and divide by the denominator.

This is like the rule on page 118. In both rules you always divide by the denominator. To help your memory, notice that *divide* and *denominator* both begin with *d*.

Exercises

Multiply, using the above rule:

1. $\frac{2}{3} \times 8$	6. $\frac{1}{3} \times 10$	11. $\frac{2}{3} \times 10$	16. $\frac{3}{8} \times 30$
2. $\frac{3}{4} \times 6$	7. $\frac{4}{5} \times 12$	12. $\frac{5}{8} \times 45$	17. $\frac{3}{4} \times 25$
3. $\frac{5}{6} \times 8$	8. $\frac{5}{8} \times 36$	13. $\frac{3}{4} \times 75$	18. $\frac{7}{8} \times 124$
4. $\frac{3}{8} \times 9$	9. $\frac{4}{5} \times 14$	14. $\frac{7}{8} \times 50$	19. $\frac{4}{5} \times 164$
5. $\frac{2}{3} \times 5$	10. $\frac{3}{8} \times 36$	15. $\frac{5}{8} \times 25$	20. $\frac{3}{4} \times 125$

ADVERTISING IN A SCHOOL PAPER

Count a fraction of a cent as an extra cent.

1. The Ralston School paper charges $25 a page for advertising. Complete the table at the right, giving the price for each part of a page.

2. If a school paper charges $12\frac{1}{2}$¢ a line, how much does a 9-line advertisement cost?

3. At $15.50 a page, how much do you pay for an advertisement covering $\frac{3}{4}$ of a page?

RALSTON NEWS

ADVERTISING RATES

1 page	$25.00
$\frac{3}{4}$ page	
$\frac{5}{8}$ page	
$\frac{1}{2}$ page	
$\frac{3}{8}$ page	
$\frac{1}{4}$ page	
$\frac{1}{8}$ page	

4. How much do you pay for an 8-line advertisement in a school paper at $6\frac{1}{2}$¢ a line? at $6\frac{3}{4}$¢ a line?

Other Problems

1. Lucy needs $\frac{7}{8}$ yd. of linen for each of 6 towels which she is making. How much linen does she need?

2. Joseph spends $4\frac{3}{4}$ hr. a day in school. How many hours does he spend in school in 5 days?

Multiply mentally when possible. In each example tell whether you use the rule on page 118 or that on page 119:

3. $\frac{2}{3} \times 15$	**11.** $\frac{3}{4} \times 85$	**19.** $\frac{3}{8} \times 84$	**27.** $\frac{5}{6} \times 126$
4. $\frac{7}{8} \times 10$	**12.** $\frac{3}{8} \times 64$	**20.** $\frac{4}{5} \times 98$	**28.** $\frac{3}{4} \times 175$
5. $\frac{2}{3} \times 20$	**13.** $\frac{3}{8} \times 25$	**21.** $\frac{3}{4} \times 60$	**29.** $\frac{2}{3} \times 150$
6. $\frac{5}{8} \times 56$	**14.** $\frac{5}{8} \times 75$	**22.** $\frac{3}{8} \times 96$	**30.** $\frac{3}{4} \times 110$
7. $\frac{1}{4} \times 75$	**15.** $\frac{5}{9} \times 50$	**23.** $\frac{2}{3} \times 60$	**31.** $\frac{3}{4} \times 200$
8. $\frac{4}{5} \times 50$	**16.** $\frac{5}{6} \times 30$	**24.** $\frac{7}{8} \times 45$	**32.** $\frac{2}{5} \times 550$
9. $\frac{3}{4} \times 80$	**17.** $\frac{3}{4} \times 35$	**25.** $\frac{9}{10} \times 90$	**33.** $\frac{2}{3} \times 240$
10. $\frac{2}{3} \times 24$	**18.** $\frac{7}{8} \times 40$	**26.** $\frac{3}{10} \times 50$	**34.** $\frac{3}{16} \times 160$

MULTIPLYING BY A MIXED NUMBER

John earned $.25 an hour delivering groceries. Last week he worked $16\frac{3}{4}$ hr. How much did he earn?

You must multiply $.25 by $16\frac{3}{4}$.

First find what John earned for working $\frac{3}{4}$ hr. by multiplying $.25 by $\frac{3}{4}$. Next find what he earned for 16 hr. by multiplying $.25 by 16. Then add the products.

In the result, call $\frac{3}{4}$¢ another cent. John earned $4.19.

$$\begin{array}{r} \$.25 \\ 16\frac{3}{4} \\ \hline 18\frac{3}{4} \\ 150 \\ 25 \\ \hline \$4.18\frac{3}{4} \end{array}$$

To multiply a whole number by a mixed number, multiply first by the fraction and then by the whole number and add the products.

Exercises

Multiply. Check the work by going over it again:

1. $4\frac{1}{2} \times 56$
2. $3\frac{5}{6} \times 20$
3. $4\frac{3}{4} \times 60$
4. $5\frac{2}{5} \times 26$
5. $5\frac{3}{8} \times 40$
6. $4\frac{2}{7} \times 35$
7. $2\frac{7}{8} \times 15$
8. $3\frac{1}{4} \times 48$
9. $7\frac{1}{2} \times 36$
10. $4\frac{1}{3} \times 25$
11. $6\frac{3}{4} \times 30$
12. $9\frac{3}{8} \times 25$
13. $4\frac{1}{3} \times 47$
14. $5\frac{2}{5} \times 16$
15. $4\frac{3}{7} \times 28$

16. $6\frac{4}{5} \times 40$
17. $3\frac{5}{8} \times 24$
18. $4\frac{2}{3} \times 25$
19. $6\frac{2}{3} \times 39$
20. $5\frac{3}{4} \times 64$
21. $2\frac{5}{8} \times 45$
22. $7\frac{2}{5} \times 50$
23. $2\frac{1}{2} \times 15$
24. $4\frac{1}{4} \times 21$
25. $5\frac{2}{5} \times 36$
26. $4\frac{3}{8} \times 48$
27. $7\frac{2}{3} \times 33$
28. $5\frac{5}{16} \times 25$
29. $7\frac{7}{16} \times 32$
30. $4\frac{5}{12} \times 36$

31. $8\frac{4}{5} \times \$1.35$
32. $9\frac{2}{3} \times \$2.50$
33. $7\frac{3}{4} \times \$1.85$
34. $3\frac{3}{4} \times \$4.70$
35. $1\frac{5}{8} \times \$1.44$
36. $4\frac{3}{8} \times \$4.00$
37. $3\frac{1}{4} \times \$2.55$
38. $4\frac{1}{2} \times \$2.94$
39. $5\frac{3}{4} \times \$5.00$
40. $6\frac{1}{2} \times \$5.00$
41. $2\frac{1}{2} \times \$6.65$
42. $2\frac{3}{16} \times \$3.20$
43. $6\frac{1}{12} \times \$1.20$
44. $2\frac{2}{5} \times \$10.00$
45. $3\frac{1}{4} \times \$12.00$

★MRS. KING GOES SHOPPING

1. Last Saturday Mrs. King went shopping. She bought $2\frac{3}{4}$ yd. of muslin at 20¢ a yard and $2\frac{3}{8}$ yd. of gingham at 39¢ a yard. How much did both cost?

2. Mrs. King also bought $3\frac{1}{2}$ yd. of white satin at $1.45 a yard and $2\frac{3}{4}$ yd. of black silk at $1.88 a yard. How much did she spend for these things?

3. How much did she have to pay for $7\frac{3}{4}$ yd. of ribbon at 48¢ a yard?

4. Mrs. King bought $3\frac{3}{8}$ yd. of lace at $.64 a yard and 1 pair of gloves for $1.65. How much did she pay for the lace and the gloves?

5. At the baker's she ordered $\frac{3}{4}$ doz. rolls at 20¢ a dozen and $1\frac{1}{4}$ doz. buns at 30¢ a dozen. How much did this order cost?

6. Mrs. King placed this order with the Hilltop Dairy: $\frac{1}{2}$ lb. butter at 36¢ a pound, $1\frac{1}{4}$ lb. dates at 24¢ a pound, 2 lb. prunes at 28¢ a pound, $2\frac{1}{2}$ doz. eggs at 36¢ a dozen, $\frac{5}{8}$ lb. American cheese at 35¢ a pound. How much was her bill for this entire order?

7. At the grocer's she ordered $2\frac{1}{2}$ lb. string beans at 15¢ a pound, $\frac{1}{2}$ doz. bananas at 40¢ a dozen, $3\frac{1}{2}$ lb. apples at 8¢ a pound, a $1\frac{7}{8}$-pound cabbage at 8¢ a pound, $2\frac{3}{4}$ doz. lemons at 36¢ a dozen, and $\frac{1}{2}$ lb. tea at 96¢ a pound. How much did that order cost?

8. How much must Mrs. King pay at the fish store for some codfish weighing $2\frac{5}{8}$ lb. and costing 19¢ a pound?

9. For Jane's birthday she bought at the florist's $3\frac{1}{2}$ doz. carnations at $1.85 a dozen and $1\frac{1}{4}$ doz. roses at $2.25 a dozen. How much did they cost in all?

WATCHING THE NUMBER 1

The number 1 is a very interesting number, but unless you watch it, it will play tricks on you. In watching 1's, remember that a fraction may indicate division.

Thus, $\frac{5}{5}$ means $5 \div 5$, or 1. $\frac{5}{1}$ means $5 \div 1$, or 5.

1. Write the multiplication table of 1's like this: $1 \times 1 = 1$, $2 \times 1 = 2$, etc., up to 12×1. Then write it like this: $1 \times 1 = 1$, $1 \times 2 = 2$, $1 \times 3 = 3$, etc.

2. Write a table like this: $\frac{1}{1} = 1$, $\frac{2}{2} = 1$, etc.

3. Write a table like this: $\frac{1}{1} = 1$, $\frac{2}{1} = 2$, etc.

Tell what each of the following equals:

4. $\frac{1}{1}$ **8.** $1 \div 1$ **12.** $1\overline{)1}$ **16.** $\frac{5}{5} + \frac{5}{5}$

5. $\frac{2}{2}$ **9.** 1×1 **13.** $\frac{1}{3}$ of 3   **17.** $\frac{5}{1} + \frac{5}{1}$

6. $\frac{30}{1}$ **10.** $\frac{1}{4}$ of 4   **14.** $\frac{4}{4} + \frac{4}{1}$ **18.** $1 \times 1 \times 1$

7. $\frac{1 \times 4}{1 \times 1}$ **11.** $\frac{1 \times 1}{1 \times 1}$ **15.** $\frac{3 \times 1}{1}$ **19.** $\frac{1}{4 \times 1}$

20. What does $263 \div 263$ equal? What does $145\overline{)145}$ equal? What does any number divided by itself equal?

21. Warren asks the pupils in his class to write something equal to 2 by using four 1's.

Anna does it like this: $\frac{1}{1} + \frac{1}{1}$. Is she right?

Joe does it like this: $1 + 1 + 1 - 1$. Is he right?

Mary does it like this: $\frac{1 \times 1}{1} + 1$. Is she right?

22. Write something equal to 8 by using three 7's and one 1. Write something equal to 4 by using nine 1's.

23. Make up other tricks in which you use 1's.

★PROBLEMS OF THE SCHOOL LUNCHROOM

1. Miss Lane runs the school lunchroom. She served 127 boys, 156 girls, and 14 teachers to-day and took in $89.10. What was the average amount spent per person?

2. Harry ate his lunch at school to-day. He had soup for 7¢, a roll for 3¢, peas for 7¢, milk for 5¢, ice cream for 10¢, and a cookie for 3¢. How much change did he get from 50¢?

3. Jane eats lunch at school every school day. Last week she spent 25¢, 31¢, 28¢, 39¢, and 37¢ for her lunches. What was the average cost of her lunch per day?

4. Today Miss Lane served 213 dishes of ice cream at $.10 a dish. She paid $12.50 for the ice cream she sold. What was the profit on the ice cream?

5. Last week the receipts of the lunchroom were $421.15. If the cost of the food was $234.79 and the other expenses were $128.33, how much profit was made last week?

6. Yesterday Miss Lane bought 15 doz. eggs at $.26 a dozen, 19½ lb. of meat at $.28 a pound, and a crate of oranges for $4.50. How much did she spend in all?

PROBLEM TEST B2

1. Mrs. Dale bought $2\frac{1}{2}$ lb. of meat at $.32 a pound and a pound of butter for $.34. How much in all did these things cost her?

2. Last summer Ned earned $2.75 a week for 9 wk. and Will earned $2.50 a week for 11 wk. How much less did Ned earn than Will?

3. Mr. Case went fishing yesterday and brought home two fish. One weighed $2\frac{1}{2}$ lb. and the other weighed $3\frac{1}{4}$ lb. How much did the two fish weigh together?

4. Four men went on an automobile trip and shared the expenses. The gasoline and oil cost $17.23, repairs cost $4.50, and garage rent cost $3.75. What was each man's share of the expenses?

5. A train making the trip from Silver City to Brownville goes the 512 mi. in 16 hr. What is the average speed of the train per hour?

6. Mr. Davis bought a radio set at Brown's store. He paid $10 down and $2 a week for 20 wk. How much in all did the radio set cost him?

7. Fred got a white sweater for $\frac{1}{3}$ off the regular price because the sweater was soiled. If the regular price of the sweater was $4.50, how much did Fred pay for it?

Standards	Excellent	Good	Fair	Poor
	7 right	5 or 6	4	0 to 3

This test is like Test B1 on page 110. Unless you had all the problems right on Test B1, you should do better this time. Keep your mark on this test.

TAKING AN IMPROVEMENT TEST IN FRACTIONS

IMPROVEMENT TEST

Test A — Subtraction

1. $6\frac{7}{8}$	2. $7\frac{1}{8}$	3. $9\frac{1}{4}$	4. $5\frac{1}{2}$
$2\frac{1}{2}$	$5\frac{3}{8}$	$5\frac{7}{8}$	$3\frac{3}{8}$

① $6\frac{7}{8}$ ② $7\frac{7}{8}$ ③ $9\frac{2}{8} = 8\frac{10}{8}$ ④ $5\frac{4}{8}$

   $2\frac{4}{8}$ $5\frac{3}{8}$ $5\frac{7}{8} = 5\frac{7}{8}$ $3\frac{3}{8}$

   $4\frac{3}{8}$ $2\frac{4}{8} = 2\frac{1}{2}$ $3\frac{3}{8}$ $2\frac{1}{8}$

In taking an Improvement Test in the addition or subtraction of fractions, like Test 6 A or 6 B, first place the edge of your paper just under the top row of examples. Write ex. 1 on your paper under ex. 1 of the test; but, instead of copying the example exactly as it stands in the test, change the fractions, as you copy, to fractions having a common denominator. When you have worked the first example, slide your paper slightly to the left and copy ex. 2 in the same way. Write the number of each example in a circle, as shown in the illustration above.

When you have done all the examples in the first row of the test, fold under the examples on your paper and do the next row along the folded edge of the paper. After finishing the second row, fold your work under again, and so on.

The illustration at the top of this page shows how the first row of examples in a subtraction test similar to Test 6 B should look on your paper. Study it carefully and tell how each example was changed as it was copied.

NOTE. The time allowed for tests in the addition or subtraction of fractions includes the copying of each example in the new form, in which the fractions have a common denominator.

IMPROVEMENT TEST NO. 6

Test 6 A — Addition (Time 4 min.)

1. $4\frac{1}{8}$
   $1\frac{3}{8}$

2. $2\frac{3}{4}$
   $8\frac{3}{4}$

3. $5\frac{1}{8}$
   $8\frac{1}{4}$

4. $4\frac{5}{8}$
   $1\frac{3}{4}$

5. $5\frac{2}{5}$
   $4\frac{4}{5}$

6. $5\frac{1}{6}$
   $1\frac{1}{3}$

7. $6\frac{3}{4}$
   $3\frac{1}{2}$

8. $9\frac{11}{16}$
   $2\frac{1}{4}$

9. $5\frac{7}{8}$
   $2\frac{1}{2}$

10. $7\frac{2}{5}$
    $7\frac{1}{2}$

11. $6\frac{1}{2}$
    $4\frac{3}{10}$

12. $9\frac{3}{4}$
    $8\frac{1}{12}$

Test 6 B — Subtraction (Time 4 min.)

1. $7\frac{5}{8}$
   $6\frac{3}{8}$

2. $5\frac{5}{12}$
   $1\frac{5}{12}$

3. $6\frac{1}{2}$
   $5\frac{5}{8}$

4. $6\frac{3}{4}$
   $4\frac{5}{8}$

5. $4\frac{7}{8}$
   $3\frac{1}{2}$

6. $9\frac{1}{4}$
   $3\frac{3}{4}$

7. $6\frac{7}{10}$
   $6\frac{1}{2}$

8. $7\frac{1}{8}$
   $4\frac{7}{8}$

9. 8
   $2\frac{3}{8}$

10. $6\frac{9}{10}$
    $2\frac{1}{2}$

11. $7\frac{2}{3}$
    $4\frac{1}{6}$

12. $9\frac{5}{6}$
    $3\frac{1}{4}$

Test 6 C — Addition (Time 4 min.)

1. $4\frac{1}{2}$
   $6\frac{3}{4}$
   $8\frac{5}{16}$

2. $8\frac{1}{4}$
   $7\frac{5}{6}$
   $2\frac{11}{12}$

3. $6\frac{1}{2}$
   $4\frac{3}{5}$
   $1\frac{7}{10}$

4. $3\frac{3}{4}$
   $4\frac{1}{2}$
   $5\frac{3}{8}$

5. $3\frac{1}{2}$
   $2\frac{2}{3}$
   $7\frac{3}{4}$

MULTIPLYING A FRACTION BY A FRACTION

1. Bob cuts $\frac{1}{2}$ of a melon into 2 equal pieces. Then each piece is $\frac{1}{4}$ of a whole melon. What is $\frac{1}{2}$ of $\frac{1}{2}$?

Another way to write $\frac{1}{2}$ of $\frac{1}{2}$ is $\frac{1}{2}\times\frac{1}{2}$, since the sign $\times$ after a fraction takes the place of the word " of." How much is $\frac{1}{2}\times\frac{1}{2}$?

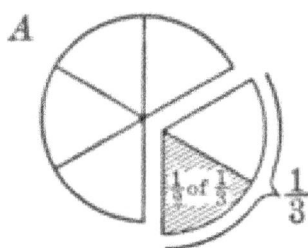

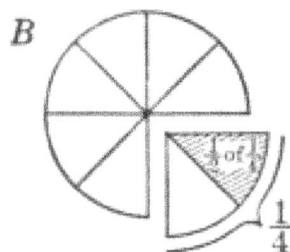

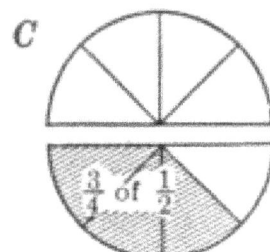

A   B   C

2. John buys $\frac{1}{3}$ of a pie and eats $\frac{1}{2}$ of it. Look at A above and tell what part of the whole pie he eats. What is $\frac{1}{2}$ of $\frac{1}{3}$? $\frac{1}{2}\times\frac{1}{3}$?

3. Ida has $\frac{1}{4}$ of a pie and gives $\frac{1}{2}$ of it to Ann. Look at B above and tell what part of a whole pie Ann gets. What is $\frac{1}{2}$ of $\frac{1}{4}$? $\frac{1}{2}\times\frac{1}{4}$?

4. Look at C above. $\frac{3}{4}$ of $\frac{1}{2}$ of a pie equals how many eighths of a whole pie? Hence $\frac{3}{4}\times\frac{1}{2}$ equals what?

5. Instead of finding the products by making drawings, you can get the results quickly like this:

$$\frac{1}{2}\times\frac{1}{3} = \frac{1\times1}{2\times3} = \frac{1}{6} \qquad \frac{3}{4}\times\frac{1}{2} = \frac{3\times1}{4\times2} = \frac{3}{8}$$

In each problem, you first multiplied the numerators together and then multiplied the denominators together.

To multiply a fraction by a fraction, multiply the numerators together for a new numerator and the denominators together for a new denominator.

PROBLEMS

1. A cream pitcher holds $\frac{3}{4}$ pt. of cream. When it is half full, what part of a pint does it hold?

2. Will picks $\frac{3}{4}$ bu. of berries for Mr. Cox. If he receives $\frac{1}{3}$ of all he picks, what part of a bushel of berries does he get? What is $\frac{1}{3} \times \frac{3}{4}$?

3. A recipe calls for $\frac{2}{3}$ cup of sugar. Nell makes $\frac{3}{4}$ the amount of the recipe. How much sugar does she need? What does $\frac{3}{4} \times \frac{2}{3}$ equal?

4. It takes James $\frac{2}{3}$ hr. to walk to school. His father says it would take him only $\frac{1}{4}$ as long to ride. How long would it take him to ride? What is $\frac{1}{4} \times \frac{2}{3}$?

5. Frank has $\frac{5}{8}$ lb. of candy. He gives Ted $\frac{1}{2}$ of it. What part of a pound does he give Ted?

6. Mary buys $\frac{3}{4}$ yd. of blue ribbon and divides it into 6 equal parts for badges. How long will each badge be? What does $\frac{1}{6}$ of $\frac{3}{4}$ equal? What is $\frac{1}{6} \times \frac{3}{4}$?

Multiply. Reduce the results when possible:

7. $\frac{1}{2} \times \frac{1}{4}$	**17.** $\frac{7}{8}$ of $\frac{1}{2}$	**27.** $\frac{2}{3} \times \frac{1}{2}$	**37.** $\frac{3}{5} \times \frac{1}{3}$
8. $\frac{1}{2} \times \frac{1}{2}$	**18.** $\frac{2}{3}$ of $\frac{1}{4}$	**28.** $\frac{3}{5} \times \frac{1}{2}$	**38.** $\frac{3}{4} \times \frac{1}{4}$
9. $\frac{1}{2} \times \frac{1}{3}$	**19.** $\frac{1}{3}$ of $\frac{3}{4}$	**29.** $\frac{3}{5} \times \frac{3}{4}$	**39.** $\frac{5}{8} \times \frac{3}{5}$
10. $\frac{3}{4} \times \frac{1}{2}$	**20.** $\frac{2}{3}$ of $\frac{1}{5}$	**30.** $\frac{2}{3} \times \frac{4}{5}$	**40.** $\frac{1}{3} \times \frac{1}{3}$
11. $\frac{1}{4} \times \frac{1}{2}$	**21.** $\frac{1}{2}$ of $\frac{1}{5}$	**31.** $\frac{5}{8} \times \frac{1}{2}$	**41.** $\frac{3}{4} \times \frac{2}{5}$
12. $\frac{1}{2} \times \frac{3}{8}$	**22.** $\frac{1}{3}$ of $\frac{1}{8}$	**32.** $\frac{2}{5} \times \frac{1}{3}$	**42.** $\frac{1}{5} \times \frac{2}{5}$
13. $\frac{1}{2} \times \frac{3}{5}$	**23.** $\frac{3}{8}$ of $\frac{1}{2}$	**33.** $\frac{1}{2} \times \frac{2}{3}$	**43.** $\frac{4}{5} \times \frac{5}{8}$
14. $\frac{1}{4} \times \frac{1}{3}$	**24.** $\frac{1}{2}$ of $\frac{2}{5}$	**34.** $\frac{2}{3} \times \frac{3}{4}$	**44.** $\frac{3}{4} \times \frac{4}{5}$
15. $\frac{1}{4} \times \frac{4}{5}$	**25.** $\frac{1}{4}$ of $\frac{3}{4}$	**35.** $\frac{2}{3} \times \frac{5}{8}$	**45.** $\frac{7}{8} \times \frac{2}{3}$
16. $\frac{2}{3} \times \frac{2}{5}$	**26.** $\frac{1}{5}$ of $\frac{1}{3}$	**36.** $\frac{1}{4} \times \frac{1}{4}$	**46.** $\frac{2}{3} \times \frac{3}{5}$

SAVING TIME IN MULTIPLYING FRACTIONS

1. Harry rode $\frac{4}{5}$ mi. on his bicycle in 6 min. What part of a mile did he ride in 1 min.?

You can find $\frac{1}{6}$ of $\frac{4}{5}$ either as shown in A or as in B.

In A you first multiply the numerators together and the denominators together and get $\frac{4}{30}$; then you reduce $\frac{4}{30}$ to $\frac{2}{15}$ by dividing both terms by 2. Here you reduce the result to lowest terms *after multiplying*.

$$A.\ \frac{1}{6} \times \frac{4}{5} = \frac{1 \times 4}{6 \times 5} = \frac{4}{30} = \frac{2}{15}$$

Think the step in the dotted square. Do not write it.

In B you first divide both 4 and 6 by 2. Then you multiply as shown in the dotted square. You get $\frac{2}{15}$ as a result. This result is already reduced to lowest terms because you did the reducing *before multiplying* when you divided both 4 and 6 by 2.

$$B.\ \frac{1}{\underset{3}{6}} \times \frac{\overset{2}{4}}{5} = \frac{1 \times 2}{3 \times 5} = \frac{2}{15}$$

You see that it is shorter to do the work as shown in B.

2. Multiply $\frac{2}{3}$ by $\frac{5}{6}$.

In dividing both 2 and 6 by 2, think "$2 \div 2 = 1$" and write 1 over 2; then think "$6 \div 2 = 3$" and write 3 under 6.

$$\frac{5}{\underset{3}{6}} \times \frac{\overset{1}{2}}{3} = \frac{5 \times 1}{3 \times 3} = \frac{5}{9}$$

Explain each step in the following problems. **In** ex. 4 notice that you cancel twice.

3. Find $\frac{7}{16}$ of 24.

$$\frac{7}{16} \times 24 = \frac{7 \times \overset{3}{24}}{\underset{2}{16}} = \frac{21}{2} = 10\frac{1}{2}$$

4. Find $\frac{5}{6} \times \frac{9}{10}$.

$$\frac{\overset{1}{5}}{\underset{2}{6}} \times \frac{\overset{3}{9}}{\underset{2}{10}} = \frac{3}{4}$$

When you cancel in multiplying fractions, you divide a numerator and a denominator by the same number.

GRADED EXERCISES

Multiply the following.   Cancel when you can:

GROUP

A. 1. $\frac{3}{8} \times \frac{4}{5}$ 2. $\frac{5}{6} \times \frac{2}{3}$ 3. $\frac{7}{8} \times \frac{2}{3}$

     4. $\frac{2}{5} \times \frac{3}{4}$ 5. $\frac{2}{3} \times \frac{5}{8}$ 6. $\frac{3}{4} \times \frac{5}{6}$

B. 7. $\frac{2}{3} \times \frac{6}{7}$ 8. $\frac{3}{5} \times \frac{15}{16}$ 9. $\frac{2}{7} \times \frac{14}{15}$

   10. $\frac{4}{5} \times \frac{10}{3}$ 11. $\frac{5}{2} \times \frac{8}{9}$ 12. $\frac{7}{8} \times \frac{16}{3}$

C. 13. $\frac{1}{3} \times \frac{9}{10}$ 14. $\frac{1}{5} \times \frac{10}{11}$ 15. $\frac{1}{2} \times \frac{4}{5}$

   16. $\frac{1}{4} \times \frac{8}{9}$ 17. $\frac{1}{3} \times \frac{6}{7}$ 18. $\frac{1}{2} \times \frac{8}{9}$

   19. $\frac{3}{5} \times \frac{5}{8}$ 20. $\frac{5}{7} \times \frac{7}{12}$ 21. $\frac{3}{4} \times \frac{4}{5}$

D. 22. $\frac{3}{4} \times \frac{6}{7}$ 23. $\frac{1}{4} \times \frac{3}{5}$ 24. $\frac{3}{4} \times \frac{6}{5}$

   25. $\frac{1}{6} \times \frac{4}{5}$ 26. $\frac{1}{6} \times \frac{9}{16}$ 27. $9 \times \frac{5}{6}$

   28. $\frac{1}{4} \times \frac{10}{3}$ 29. $\frac{5}{6} \times \frac{9}{2}$ 30. $\frac{5}{8} \times \frac{10}{3}$

   31. $10 \times \frac{3}{8}$ 32. $18 \times \frac{5}{12}$ 33. $\frac{1}{6} \times \frac{9}{10}$

   34. $15 \times \frac{8}{9}$ 35. $15 \times \frac{3}{10}$ 36. $24 \times \frac{3}{16}$

E. 37. $24 \times \frac{7}{8}$ 38. $24 \times \frac{1}{4}$ 39. $27 \times \frac{2}{3}$

   40. $\frac{3}{4} \times 16$ 41. $\frac{5}{6} \times 18$ 42. $\frac{2}{3} \times 21$

F. 43. $\frac{3}{4} \times \frac{8}{15}$ 44. $\frac{2}{3} \times \frac{15}{16}$ 45. $\frac{2}{3} \times \frac{9}{8}$

   46. $\frac{2}{3} \times \frac{9}{10}$ 47. $\frac{4}{5} \times \frac{15}{8}$ 48. $\frac{5}{3} \times \frac{9}{10}$

G. 49. $\frac{5}{6} \times \frac{9}{10}$ 50. $\frac{3}{4} \times \frac{10}{3}$ 51. $\frac{8}{9} \times \frac{15}{4}$

   52. $\frac{7}{8} \times \frac{10}{7}$ 53. $\frac{5}{6} \times \frac{4}{5}$ 54. $\frac{15}{16} \times \frac{12}{25}$

NOTE. The above examples are graded according to types of difficulty.

THE NUMBER 1 PLAYS HIDE AND SEEK

The number 1 often causes trouble when we multiply fractions because it seems to hide behind other numbers.

1. Find $\frac{1}{4}$ of $\frac{4}{5}$.

When you divide the numerator 4 by 4, think "$4 \div 4 = 1$" and write 1 *over* the 4. In the denominator also think "$4 \div 4 = 1$" and write 1 *under* the 4. How much is 1×1? How much is 1×5?

$$\frac{1}{4} \times \frac{\overset{1}{\cancel{4}}}{5} = \frac{1 \times 1}{1 \times 5} = \frac{1}{5}$$

2. Multiply $\frac{3}{4}$ by $\frac{2}{9}$.

In this example you must cancel twice. What do you think when you divide 3 and 9 by 3? What do you think when you divide 2 and 4 by 2? In the answer, $\frac{1}{6}$, how did you get the 1? How did you get the 6?

$$\frac{\overset{1}{\cancel{2}}}{\underset{3}{\cancel{9}}} \times \frac{\overset{1}{\cancel{3}}}{\underset{2}{\cancel{4}}} = \frac{1}{6}$$

3. Multiply $\frac{3}{2}$ by $\frac{2}{3}$.

Elizabeth worked this problem as shown in *A*, writing the 1's when she canceled. She said that the answer is 1.

$$A. \quad \frac{\overset{1}{\cancel{2}}}{\underset{3}{\cancel{3}}} \times \frac{\overset{1}{\cancel{3}}}{\underset{2}{\cancel{2}}} = \frac{1 \times 1}{1 \times 1} = 1$$

Bert did the work as in *B*, without writing the 1's when he canceled. He said that the answer is nothing, or 0, because everything is canceled. Why was he wrong?

$$B. \quad \frac{\cancel{2}}{\cancel{3}} \times \frac{\cancel{3}}{\cancel{2}} = 0$$

4. In working the problems below, Jack remembered the 1's instead of writing them. Find the answers:

(a) $6 \times \frac{5}{6} = \frac{\cancel{6} \times 5}{\cancel{6}} = ?$ (b) $\frac{1}{3} \times \frac{5}{6} = ?$ (c) $\frac{8}{5} \times \frac{\overset{3}{\cancel{15}}}{\cancel{8}} = ?$

After you have learned to multiply fractions, you may remember the 1's instead of putting them down. In working harder problems, however, you will avoid many mistakes if you write the 1's.

HARDER WORK IN MULTIPLYING FRACTIONS

Tell how each problem is done and give the result:

1. $\dfrac{1}{7} \times \dfrac{7}{8} = ?$

2. $\dfrac{4 \times 3}{4} = ?$

3. $\dfrac{1}{3} \times \dfrac{\overset{3}{9}}{10} = ?$

4. $\dfrac{5}{6} \times \dfrac{\overset{2}{12}}{5} = ?$

5. $\dfrac{4}{5} \times \dfrac{5}{4} = ?$

6. $\underset{2}{\dfrac{5}{6}} \times \underset{2}{\dfrac{3}{10}} = \mathbf{?}$

Exercises in Multiplying Fractions

Multiply, canceling when you can:

GROUP

C.   1. $\frac{1}{2} \times \frac{6}{7}$ 2. $\frac{1}{4} \times \frac{8}{5}$ 3. $\frac{1}{5} \times \frac{10}{3}$

E.   4. $28 \times \frac{3}{4}$ 5. $16 \times \frac{7}{8}$ 6. $\frac{1}{2} \times 18$

F.   7. $\frac{2}{3} \times \frac{9}{16}$ 8. $\frac{8}{9} \times \frac{3}{4}$ 9. $\frac{4}{5} \times \frac{15}{16}$

H.   10. $\frac{1}{4} \times \frac{4}{9}$ 11. $\frac{1}{6} \times \frac{6}{7}$ 12. $\frac{1}{5} \times \frac{5}{6}$

    13. $\frac{1}{8} \times \frac{8}{9}$ 14. $\frac{1}{7} \times \frac{7}{3}$ 15. $\frac{1}{4} \times \frac{4}{5}$

    16. $\frac{1}{3} \times \frac{3}{4}$ 17. $\frac{1}{2} \times \frac{2}{3}$ 18. $\frac{1}{9} \times \frac{9}{10}$

J.   19. $\frac{2}{5} \times \frac{5}{8}$ 20. $\frac{2}{9} \times \frac{3}{4}$ 21. $\frac{4}{5} \times \frac{5}{8}$

    22. $\frac{5}{9} \times \frac{3}{5}$ 23. $\frac{2}{3} \times \frac{3}{4}$ 24. $\frac{5}{6} \times \frac{3}{20}$

    25. $\frac{4}{9} \times \frac{3}{8}$ 26. $\frac{2}{5} \times \frac{5}{6}$ 27. $\frac{8}{9} \times \frac{3}{16}$

K.   28. $\frac{5}{2} \times \frac{12}{5}$ 29. $\frac{2}{3} \times \frac{15}{2}$ 30. $\frac{3}{4} \times \frac{8}{3}$

    31. $\frac{7}{8} \times \frac{16}{7}$ 32. $\frac{2}{3} \times \frac{9}{4}$ 33. $\frac{5}{8} \times \frac{16}{5}$

    34. $\frac{3}{4} \times \frac{16}{3}$ 35. $\frac{4}{5} \times \frac{15}{4}$ 36. $\frac{4}{3} \times \frac{15}{2}$

L.   37. $\frac{7}{8} \times \frac{8}{7}$ 38. $\frac{5}{9} \times \frac{9}{5}$ 39. $\frac{3}{4} \times \frac{4}{3}$

    40. $\frac{2}{9} \times \frac{9}{2}$ 41. $\frac{3}{8} \times \frac{8}{3}$ 42. $\frac{8}{9} \times \frac{9}{8}$

NOTE. Groups *C*, *E*, and *F* represent the same types of difficulty as those found in the corresponding groups on page 131.

CHANGING MIXED NUMBERS TO FRACTIONS

Betty's mother has $2\frac{5}{6}$ peach pies. How many girls will this serve if each girl gets $\frac{1}{6}$ of a pie?

Change $2\frac{5}{6}$ to sixths. Since 1 whole pie $= \frac{6}{6}$ pie, then 2 whole pies $= \frac{12}{6}$ pies. Hence $2\frac{5}{6} = \frac{12}{6} + \frac{5}{6}$, or $\frac{17}{6}$. Since there are 17 *sixths* in all, 17 girls can be served.

You see that to change $2\frac{5}{6}$ to $\frac{17}{6}$, you multiply 2 by 6 and add 5.

To change a mixed number to an improper fraction, multiply the whole number by the denominator, add the numerator, and place the result over the denominator.

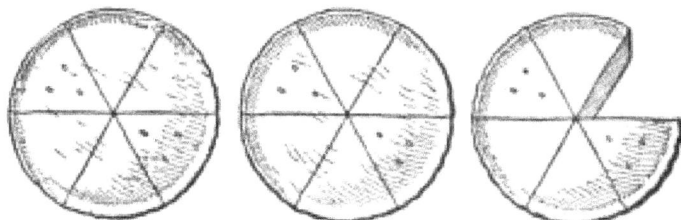

Exercises

Reduce the following to improper fractions:

1. $2\frac{2}{3}$	**6.** $4\frac{1}{2}$	**11.** $4\frac{3}{8}$	**16.** $1\frac{3}{16}$	**21.** $4\frac{1}{3}$
2. $9\frac{1}{3}$	**7.** $2\frac{7}{8}$	**12.** $5\frac{5}{8}$	**17.** $5\frac{1}{5}$	**22.** $6\frac{1}{4}$
3. $1\frac{5}{6}$	**8.** $7\frac{3}{4}$	**13.** $5\frac{3}{4}$	**18.** $8\frac{3}{4}$	**23.** $3\frac{5}{6}$
4. $2\frac{7}{10}$	**9.** $7\frac{1}{4}$	**14.** $1\frac{1}{16}$	**19.** $2\frac{3}{4}$	**24.** $7\frac{2}{3}$
5. $6\frac{1}{2}$	**10.** $2\frac{2}{5}$	**15.** $3\frac{2}{5}$	**20.** $9\frac{1}{2}$	**25.** $1\frac{3}{5}$

26. In Jane's sewing class the children are making scarfs, using $\frac{1}{2}$ yd. of silk for each. How many scarfs can be made from a piece of silk $3\frac{1}{2}$ yd. long? 8 yd. long?

27. How many boxes of candy, each containing $\frac{1}{8}$ lb., can be filled from $2\frac{1}{8}$ lb. of candy? from $1\frac{5}{8}$ lb.? $2\frac{7}{8}$ lb.?

★**28.** On a scale drawing of Henry's new house, $\frac{1}{2}$ in. represents 1 ft. If Henry's new room is $6\frac{1}{2}$ in. long and $4\frac{1}{2}$ in. wide on the drawing, how long and how wide is the room?

MULTIPLYING MIXED NUMBERS

1. Helen uses $\frac{2}{3}$ of a $3\frac{1}{2}$-pound bag of flour in making cake. How much flour does she use?

Change $3\frac{1}{2}$ to $\frac{7}{2}$. Then multiply $\frac{7}{2}$ by $\frac{2}{3}$. Always cancel when you can.

$$\frac{\cancel{2}}{3} \times \frac{7}{\cancel{2}} = \frac{7}{3} = 2\frac{1}{3}$$

You find that Helen uses $2\frac{1}{3}$ lb. of flour.

2. A farmer sows $3\frac{1}{2}$ qt. of clover seed on each acre of land. How many quarts does he need for $6\frac{2}{3}$ acres?

Change $3\frac{1}{2}$ to $\frac{7}{2}$ and $6\frac{2}{3}$ to $\frac{20}{3}$.

$$\frac{\overset{10}{\cancel{20}}}{3} \times \frac{7}{\cancel{2}} = \frac{70}{3} = 23\frac{1}{3}$$

To multiply a mixed number by a fraction or by another mixed number, first reduce each mixed number to an improper fraction and then multiply.

Problems

1. A recipe for cookies calls for $\frac{3}{4}$ lb. of sugar. Marie is making $2\frac{1}{2}$ times the amount of the recipe. How many pounds of sugar does she need?

2. A cake recipe calls for $1\frac{3}{4}$ cups of sugar. Louise is making $1\frac{1}{2}$ times the amount of the recipe. How many cups of sugar will she need?

3. How far can Mr. Jones travel in his car in $3\frac{1}{4}$ hr., if he averages $19\frac{1}{2}$ mi. an hour?

4. If Mr. Lane's car averages $17\frac{1}{2}$ mi. on 1 gal. of gasoline, how many miles can it go on $3\frac{1}{2}$ gal.?

5. There are $16\frac{1}{2}$ ft. in a rod. How many feet long is a fence that is $14\frac{2}{3}$ rd. long?

6. A farmer has $75\frac{1}{2}$ acres of wheat. How many bushels will he get if the average yield is $15\frac{3}{4}$ bu. per acre?

MULTIPLYING MIXED NUMBERS

Multiply. Check the work by going over it again:

GROUP

A. 1. $\frac{2}{5} \times 5\frac{1}{4}$　　　2. $\frac{2}{3} \times 2\frac{1}{8}$　　　3. $\frac{3}{5} \times 1\frac{5}{6}$

B. 4. $\frac{3}{4} \times 3\frac{1}{5}$　　　5. $\frac{3}{5} \times 7\frac{1}{2}$　　　6. $\frac{7}{8} \times 5\frac{1}{3}$

C. 7. $\frac{1}{8} \times 3\frac{1}{5}$　　　8. $\frac{4}{5} \times 7\frac{1}{4}$　　　9. $\frac{1}{3} \times 5\frac{1}{4}$

D. 10. $\frac{5}{6} \times 2\frac{1}{4}$　　11. $\frac{1}{4} \times 3\frac{1}{3}$　　12. $\frac{3}{8} \times 1\frac{1}{5}$

F. 13. $3\frac{1}{8} \times \frac{4}{5}$　　14. $1\frac{7}{8} \times \frac{2}{3}$　　15. $4\frac{1}{6} \times \frac{3}{5}$

G. 16. $4\frac{1}{6} \times \frac{4}{5}$　　17. $2\frac{2}{5} \times \frac{15}{16}$　　18. $1\frac{3}{5} \times \frac{5}{6}$

H. 19. $\frac{1}{5} \times 6\frac{1}{4}$　　20. $\frac{1}{8} \times 2\frac{2}{3}$　　21. $\frac{1}{2} \times 3\frac{3}{5}$

J. 22. $1\frac{1}{3} \times \frac{3}{16}$　　23. $1\frac{1}{3} \times \frac{3}{8}$　　24. $1\frac{2}{3} \times \frac{3}{10}$

K. 25. $7\frac{1}{2} \times \frac{4}{5}$　　26. $5\frac{1}{3} \times \frac{3}{4}$　　27. $4\frac{2}{7} \times \frac{7}{10}$

A. 28. $2\frac{1}{8} \times 1\frac{1}{3}$　　29. $1\frac{1}{2} \times 1\frac{1}{6}$　　30. $1\frac{1}{2} \times 1\frac{5}{6}$

B. 31. $2\frac{1}{4} \times 1\frac{3}{5}$　　32. $2\frac{1}{2} \times 2\frac{2}{3}$　　33. $4\frac{1}{2} \times 1\frac{3}{5}$

D. 34. $7\frac{1}{5} \times 2\frac{1}{8}$　　35. $2\frac{1}{4} \times 1\frac{1}{5}$　　36. $1\frac{1}{4} \times 3\frac{1}{3}$

F. 37. $1\frac{3}{5} \times 1\frac{9}{16}$　　38. $1\frac{1}{3} \times 1\frac{7}{8}$　　39. $1\frac{1}{3} \times 1\frac{1}{8}$

G. 40. $1\frac{1}{4} \times 1\frac{1}{5}$　　41. $3\frac{3}{4} \times 3\frac{1}{3}$　　42. $6\frac{1}{4} \times 3\frac{3}{5}$

K. 43. $8\frac{1}{3} \times 2\frac{2}{5}$　　44. $1\frac{2}{3} \times 1\frac{4}{5}$　　45. $7\frac{1}{2} \times 1\frac{3}{5}$

　　46. $4\frac{4}{5} \times 1\frac{2}{3}$　　47. $2\frac{1}{4} \times 2\frac{2}{3}$　　48. $4\frac{1}{2} \times 5\frac{1}{3}$

L. 49. $2\frac{1}{2} \times \frac{2}{5}$　　50. $1\frac{2}{3} \times \frac{3}{5}$　　51. $2\frac{1}{4} \times \frac{4}{9}$

NOTE. The above groups for mixed numbers correspond to those on pages 131 and 133 for fractions. Thus, Group *A* represents the same type of difficulty on all three pages.

DIAGNOSTIC TEST

If you miss exercises in any row, you need more practice. The Help Pages tell you where to find it.

Multiply the following and check the work:

				HELP PAGES
1.	$2 \times \frac{2}{5}$	$5 \times \frac{1}{6}$	$7 \times \frac{3}{4}$	$4 \times \frac{2}{3}$	116
2.	$9 \times \frac{1}{8}$	$8 \times \frac{3}{5}$	$4 \times \frac{5}{8}$	$7 \times \frac{5}{6}$	116
3.	$7 \times 2\frac{1}{2}$	$2 \times 3\frac{3}{5}$	$5 \times 2\frac{3}{4}$	$7 \times 1\frac{1}{6}$	117
4.	$8 \times 5\frac{3}{4}$	$4 \times 8\frac{1}{3}$	$9 \times 3\frac{3}{8}$	$6 \times 4\frac{1}{8}$	117
5.	$\frac{2}{5} \times 25$	$\frac{7}{8} \times 48$	$\frac{5}{6} \times 66$	$\frac{4}{5} \times 50$	118
6.	$\frac{3}{4} \times 20$	$\frac{2}{3} \times 51$	$\frac{3}{8} \times 32$	$\frac{3}{4} \times 76$	118
7.	$\frac{5}{8} \times 11$	$\frac{2}{5} \times 12$	$\frac{2}{3} \times 16$	$\frac{3}{4} \times 26$	119
8.	$\frac{3}{4} \times 17$	$\frac{5}{8} \times 20$	$\frac{4}{5} \times 19$	$\frac{7}{8} \times 30$	119
9.	$3\frac{1}{2} \times 18$	$2\frac{3}{4} \times 36$	$5\frac{1}{8} \times 44$	$6\frac{2}{5} \times 37$	121
10.	$5\frac{2}{3} \times 12$	$4\frac{5}{8} \times 56$	$7\frac{1}{3} \times 22$	$8\frac{5}{6} \times 33$	121
11.	$\frac{3}{4} \times \frac{5}{8}$	$\frac{1}{5} \times \frac{2}{3}$	$\frac{7}{8} \times \frac{3}{5}$	$\frac{5}{6} \times \frac{5}{8}$	129
12.	$\frac{5}{8} \times \frac{2}{3}$	$\frac{1}{3} \times \frac{9}{16}$	$16 \times \frac{5}{8}$	$\frac{9}{10} \times \frac{5}{6}$	131
13.	$\frac{1}{3} \times \frac{3}{5}$	$\frac{2}{3} \times \frac{3}{2}$	$\frac{4}{5} \times \frac{5}{8}$	$\frac{8}{3} \times \frac{9}{4}$	133
14.	$4\frac{1}{2} \times 3\frac{1}{3}$	$1\frac{1}{6} \times 1\frac{1}{2}$	$1\frac{7}{8} \times 1\frac{1}{5}$	$2\frac{2}{5} \times 1\frac{3}{8}$	136
15.	$3\frac{1}{3} \times 3\frac{4}{5}$	$1\frac{3}{5} \times 3\frac{3}{4}$	$5\frac{2}{5} \times 1\frac{1}{6}$	$1\frac{1}{8} \times 5\frac{1}{3}$	136

PROBLEM TEST B3

1. Ted's father is buying a house on the installment plan. He paid $1500 down when he bought it and agreed to pay $75 a month for 60 mo. How much will he pay in all for the house?

2. The 4 Lee boys put up a stand in front of their house and sold fruit and vegetables that grew in their father's garden. They got $2.48 for berries, $3.44 for fruit, and $2.52 for vegetables. If they shared the money equally, how much did each one get?

3. Mr. Carr used 24 gal. of gasoline when he made a trip of 432 mi. What was the average number of miles that he drove on each gallon?

4. Two boys earned money selling candy. Jim sold 9 boxes and earned $.48 on each box and Ned sold 250 bars and earned $.02 on each bar. How much more money did Ned earn than Jim?

5. Mrs. Jones bought $2\frac{1}{2}$ yd. of cloth for a dress for Ann and $3\frac{1}{4}$ yd. of the same kind of cloth for a dress for Nancy. How many yards did she buy in all?

6. A man sold $1\frac{1}{2}$ doz. roses at $2.00 a dozen and a plant for $1.25. How much did he get for them?

7. A bookstore had a sale and all books were sold for $\frac{1}{3}$ off the regular price. May bought a book that usually sold for $1.95. How much did she pay for it?

Standards	Excellent	Good	Fair	Poor
	7 right	5 or 6	4	0 to 3

This test is like Tests B1 and B2, pages 110 and 125. You should have all the problems right on this test.

IMPROVEMENT TEST NO. 7

Test 7 A — Addition (Time 4 min.)

1. $2\frac{1}{2}$
$7\frac{3}{4}$

2. $6\frac{1}{3}$
$3\frac{2}{3}$

3. $9\frac{5}{8}$
$6\frac{7}{8}$

4. $3\frac{1}{5}$
$5\frac{1}{2}$

5. $2\frac{1}{2}$
$4\frac{3}{8}$

6. $2\frac{2}{3}$
$9\frac{1}{6}$

7. $1\frac{7}{8}$
$4\frac{3}{4}$

8. $6\frac{1}{3}$
$7\frac{1}{2}$

9. 4
$9\frac{7}{12}$

10. $1\frac{3}{10}$
$8\frac{7}{10}$

11. $8\frac{1}{10}$
$5\frac{3}{5}$

12. $5\frac{1}{2}$
$6\frac{9}{16}$

Test 7 B — Subtraction (Time 4 min.)

1. $4\frac{7}{8}$
$2\frac{1}{8}$

2. $6\frac{3}{4}$
$2\frac{1}{2}$

3. $2\frac{3}{4}$
$2\frac{1}{3}$

4. 7
$5\frac{3}{5}$

5. $5\frac{1}{3}$
$1\frac{2}{3}$

6. $7\frac{1}{2}$
$3\frac{1}{3}$

7. $6\frac{2}{5}$
$1\frac{3}{10}$

8. $8\frac{1}{8}$
$6\frac{5}{8}$

9. $9\frac{7}{16}$
$4\frac{1}{2}$

10. $3\frac{7}{8}$
$2\frac{5}{16}$

11. $8\frac{3}{4}$
$3\frac{5}{12}$

12. $9\frac{7}{8}$
$7\frac{11}{16}$

Test 7 C — Multiplication (Time 4 min. after copying)

1. $14\frac{7}{8}$
8

2. 164
$3\frac{3}{4}$

3. 50
$12\frac{3}{8}$

4. $\frac{2}{3}$ of 27

5. $\frac{9}{10} \times \frac{5}{8}$

6. $15 \times \frac{3}{4}$

7. $\frac{3}{16}$ of 52

8. $\frac{9}{16} \times 6\frac{2}{5}$

9. $3\frac{1}{5} \times 3\frac{3}{4}$

NOTE. For a test in the multiplication or division of fractions, like Test 7 C, first copy all the examples on paper, allowing sufficient space for working them. The time allowance does not include the time required for copying.

MAKING CANDY

1. To try this recipe, Ellen is making only half the amount. How much of each ingredient should she use?

Butterscotch

2 cups brown sugar $\frac{1}{4}$ teaspoon salt
$\frac{1}{4}$ cup light corn sirup $\frac{1}{3}$ cup butter
1 cup water   4 drops oil of lemon

2. How much of each ingredient should Julia use to make $2\frac{1}{2}$ times the amount of this recipe?

Plain Chocolate Caramels

$2\frac{1}{2}$ cups sugar $2\frac{1}{2}$ cups milk
$\frac{3}{4}$ cup corn sirup $2\frac{1}{2}$ squares chocolate
$\frac{1}{2}$ cup butter   1 teaspoon vanilla
$\frac{1}{8}$ teaspoon cream of tartar

3. The recipe below calls for 4 qt. of popcorn. John has only 3 qt. If he uses the 3 qt. for popcorn balls, how much of each of the other ingredients should he use?

Chocolate Popcorn Balls

$1\frac{1}{2}$ cups sugar   4 qt. popcorn, well salted
$\frac{1}{3}$ cup corn sirup   3 tablespoons butter
$\frac{2}{3}$ cup water   3 squares chocolate
$\frac{1}{3}$ cup molasses   1 teaspoon vanilla

4. The following recipe will make 2 lb. of nut brittle. Write a new recipe to make 1 lb. ; to make 3 lb.

Nut Brittle

2 cups granulated sugar $\frac{1}{4}$ cup butter
1 cup brown sugar $\frac{1}{8}$ teaspoon soda
$\frac{1}{2}$ cup light corn sirup $\frac{1}{8}$ teaspoon salt
$\frac{1}{2}$ cup water $1\frac{1}{2}$ cups nut meats

WINTER SPORTS

1. The weights of the six children on a bobsled are 62½ lb., 85¾ lb., 91⅛ lb., 41¼ lb., 78⅝ lb., and 81½ lb. What is the total weight on the sled?

2. Frank coasts on a hill 45 ft. long. Tony, who lives in the country, coasts on a hill 1629 ft. long. Tony's hill is how many times as long as Frank's?

★3. There are 5280 ft. in a mile. The hill on which Amy goes coasting is 660 ft. long. Amy says that it is $\frac{660}{5280}$ of a mile long. Reduce this fraction to lowest terms.

4. It is 1¾ mi. around Shady Lake. If Ben skates around the lake 10 times a day, how far does he skate in a day? in 6 days?

5. Bill's ice boat has a mast 12½ ft. high. Martin's is only 11⅔ ft. high. How much taller is Bill's mast than Martin's?

6. Bill crosses the frozen bay in ½ hr. in his ice boat. He stays on the other side 2¼ hr. and takes ¾ hr. to get back. How long is he gone in all?

7. A fast skater goes 1320 ft. in 38 sec. How many feet per second does he go?

8. Our snowman was 8⅜ in. taller than Susan when we made him. Now he is only 4½ in. taller than Susan. How much shorter has he grown?

DIAGNOSTIC TEST

If you miss exercises in any row, you need more practice.
The Help Pages tell you where to find it.

Add and check the work: **HELP PAGES**

1.

$3\frac{3}{4}$	$1\frac{1}{8}$	$5\frac{5}{6}$	$9\frac{5}{16}$	$3\frac{1}{2}$	**70, 75**
$4\frac{1}{4}$	$8\frac{5}{8}$	$3\frac{5}{6}$	$4\frac{1}{16}$	$2\frac{1}{2}$	
$3\frac{3}{4}$	$2\frac{7}{8}$	$6\frac{5}{6}$	$1\frac{9}{16}$	$8\frac{1}{2}$	

2.

$4\frac{7}{8}$	$6\frac{1}{6}$	$1\frac{9}{10}$	$3\frac{3}{8}$	$4\frac{1}{2}$	**78, 93**
$4\frac{1}{2}$	$2\frac{2}{3}$	$8\frac{3}{5}$	$7\frac{5}{16}$	$2\frac{5}{6}$	**96**
$5\frac{3}{4}$	$4\frac{1}{2}$	$3\frac{1}{2}$	$2\frac{3}{4}$	$9\frac{1}{3}$	

3.

$1\frac{1}{2}$	$5\frac{5}{6}$	$9\frac{3}{4}$	$6\frac{5}{6}$	$8\frac{4}{5}$	**103, 104**
$1\frac{3}{4}$	$8\frac{1}{8}$	$2\frac{1}{3}$	$5\frac{1}{2}$	$1\frac{1}{2}$	
$4\frac{1}{5}$	$6\frac{2}{3}$	$7\frac{1}{6}$	$3\frac{1}{4}$	$4\frac{1}{3}$	

Subtract and check the work:

4.

$9\frac{3}{8}$	$6\frac{1}{2}$	$8\frac{3}{4}$	$7\frac{11}{16}$	$6\frac{7}{8}$	**84, 85**
$3\frac{1}{8}$	$6\frac{3}{16}$	$3\frac{1}{8}$	$4\frac{5}{16}$	$1\frac{1}{4}$	

5.

$5\frac{1}{2}$	$9\frac{3}{8}$	$7\frac{5}{16}$	$6\frac{1}{2}$	$8\frac{3}{4}$	**89**
$2\frac{3}{4}$	$5\frac{3}{4}$	$2\frac{7}{8}$	$3\frac{5}{8}$	$4\frac{15}{16}$	

6.

$4\frac{2}{3}$	$8\frac{1}{2}$	$6\frac{2}{3}$	$9\frac{1}{6}$	$7\frac{5}{6}$	**94**
$2\frac{5}{6}$	$6\frac{1}{3}$	$2\frac{1}{6}$	$7\frac{1}{3}$	$3\frac{1}{2}$	

7.

$9\frac{2}{3}$	$6\frac{1}{5}$	$8\frac{1}{2}$	$7\frac{1}{4}$	$4\frac{2}{3}$	**101**
$8\frac{3}{5}$	$4\frac{3}{4}$	$2\frac{1}{5}$	$5\frac{2}{3}$	$3\frac{5}{8}$	

MULTIPLICATION AND DIVISION

Multiply the following and check the work:

1. 345   578   169 $30.56 $91.24
   728   425   580   53   65

2. 653   214   789 $80.09 $90.03
   609   309   390   89   43

Divide the following and check the work:

3. $23)\overline{1173}$ $19)\overline{1699}$ $62)\overline{13206}$ $451)\overline{23928}$

4. $51)\overline{3386}$ $54)\overline{7567}$ $34)\overline{15761}$ $933)\overline{63444}$

5. $75)\overline{3525}$ $26)\overline{7904}$ $87)\overline{25839}$ $793)\overline{38886}$

6. $58)\overline{4234}$ $93)\overline{9765}$ $38)\overline{24189}$ $771)\overline{159597}$

MIXED PRACTICE

Find the answers to the following:

1. $7\frac{3}{4} - 2\frac{3}{8} = ?$ $\frac{5}{8}$ of $40 = ?$ $\frac{2}{3} \times \frac{1}{2} = ?$
2. $5\frac{1}{2} + 6\frac{7}{8} = ?$ $\frac{2}{3}$ of $14 = ?$ $\frac{3}{4} \times \frac{5}{9} = ?$
3. $2\frac{1}{2} \times 4\frac{2}{3} = ?$ $1\frac{2}{3} \times 6 = ?$ $\frac{1}{2}$ of $\frac{1}{4} = ?$
4. $8\frac{3}{4} - 5\frac{3}{4} = ?$ $4 \times 1\frac{3}{4} = ?$ $\frac{2}{3}$ of $\frac{3}{4} = ?$

5. $326 + 18 + 700 + 70 + 1405 + 610 = ?$
6. How much smaller is 5001 than 5401?
7. How many inches are there in $\frac{1}{4}$ yd.?
8. Change $\frac{3}{4}$ to a fraction having the same value as $\frac{3}{4}$ and also having a denominator of 8.

REVIEW OF FRACTIONS

Add.   Check the work by going over it again:

1. $8\frac{3}{4}$	**2.** $3\frac{1}{3}$	**3.** $9\frac{3}{4}$	**4.** $7\frac{3}{8}$	**5.** $3\frac{4}{5}$
$2\frac{1}{8}$	$4\frac{5}{6}$	$1\frac{2}{3}$	$9\frac{3}{4}$	$5\frac{1}{2}$
$6\frac{1}{8}$	$7\frac{1}{2}$	$5\frac{3}{4}$	$2\frac{3}{16}$	$6\frac{3}{5}$

Subtract.   Check the work by going over it again:

6. $3\frac{5}{8}$	**7.** $9\frac{1}{4}$	**8.** $4\frac{3}{5}$	**9.** $8\frac{2}{3}$	**10.** $6\frac{1}{2}$
$2\frac{1}{4}$	$6\frac{3}{4}$	$1\frac{1}{10}$	$4\frac{5}{6}$	$5\frac{9}{16}$

Multiply.   Check the work by going over it again:

11. $9 \times \frac{2}{3}$ **18.** $\frac{4}{7} \times 7$ **25.** $6\frac{1}{2} \times 3$ **32.** $12 \times 3\frac{1}{8}$

12. $6 \times \frac{3}{4}$ **19.** $\frac{1}{2} \times 5$ **26.** $3\frac{1}{2} \times 8$ **33.** $10 \times 1\frac{1}{2}$

13. $\frac{1}{2} \times \frac{4}{5}$ **20.** $\frac{5}{8} \times 6$ **27.** $2\frac{1}{6} \times 9$ **34.** $15 \times 2\frac{1}{4}$

14. $\frac{1}{4} \times \frac{1}{3}$ **21.** $\frac{3}{5} \times 2\frac{1}{2}$ **28.** $6\frac{1}{4} \times \frac{1}{5}$ **35.** $4\frac{3}{4} \times 7\frac{1}{2}$

15. $\frac{2}{9} \times \frac{9}{2}$ **22.** $\frac{7}{8} \times 5\frac{1}{3}$ **29.** $7\frac{1}{3} \times \frac{3}{4}$ **36.** $5\frac{7}{8} \times 64$

16. $\frac{3}{8} \times \frac{10}{9}$ **23.** $\frac{4}{5} \times 3\frac{3}{4}$ **30.** $1\frac{1}{2} \times \frac{1}{9}$ **37.** $4\frac{1}{2} \times 50$

17. $\frac{5}{6} \times \frac{3}{10}$ **24.** $\frac{8}{9} \times 5\frac{1}{4}$ **31.** $6\frac{3}{4} \times \frac{4}{9}$ **38.** $2\frac{3}{8} \times 75$

Multiply.   Check the work by going over it again:

39. 460	**40.** 207	**41.** 135	**42.** $61\frac{3}{4}$	**43.** $89\frac{7}{8}$
$14\frac{1}{4}$	$85\frac{2}{3}$	$17\frac{1}{8}$	24	69

Divide and check.   Express remainders as fractions in the quotients and reduce the fractions to lowest terms:

44. $1988 \div 56$ **48.** $5157 \div 216$ **52.** $8475 \div 175$

45. $3920 \div 42$ **49.** $9765 \div 420$ **53.** $9135 \div 630$

46. $4995 \div 75$ **50.** $6345 \div 675$ **54.** $2520 \div 576$

47. $1611 \div 27$ **51.** $9728 \div 768$ **55.** $6944 \div 896$

ANSWERS TO
STRAYER-UPTON PRACTICAL ARITHMETICS
SECOND BOOK

Page 1. — **1.** $1.75; $7.00.   **2.** $6.64.   **3.** $.36.

Page 3. — **1.** Cash on hand, $.89.   **2.** Cash on hand, $3.34.
3. Cash on hand, $3.59.

Page 4. — **2.** Yes.   **3.** Cash on hand, Sept. 30, $2.15.   **4.** $5.36.

Page 5. — **1.** 26.   **2.** 20.   **3.** 22.   **4.** 21.   **5.** 26.   **6.** 27.
7. 26.   **8.** 25.   **9.** 23.   **10.** 29.   **11.** 21.   **12.** 27.
13. 23.   **14.** 21.   **15.** 21.   **16.** 23.   **17.** 26.   **18.** 22.
19. 23.   **20.** 28.   **21.** 27.   **22.** 23.   **23.** 28.   **24.** 22.
25. 289.   **26.** 250.   **27.** 282.   **28.** 308.   **29.** 322.   **30.** 321.
31. 240.   **32.** 225.   **33.** 304.   **34.** 236.   **35.** 269.   **36.** 204.

Page 6. — **1.** 33.   **2.** 37.   **3.** 46.   **4.** 33.   **5.** 33.   **6.** 37.
7. 39.   **8.** 38.   **9.** 372.   **10.** 344.   **11.** 304.   **12.** 221.
13. 279.   **14.** 364.   **15.** 382.   **16.** 364.   **17.** 398.   **18.** 355.
19. 318.   **20.** 374.   **21.** 2178.   **22.** 2734.   **23.** 2442.
24. 2984.   **25.** 3202.   **26.** 2314.

Page 7. — **1.** 2658.   **2.** 2522.   **3.** 3898.   **4.** 3239.   **5.** 3945.
6. 4078.   **7.** 3789.   **8.** 4167.   **9.** 3271.   **10.** 3391.
11. 3763.   **12.** 3103.   **13.** 3775.   **14.** 5168.   **15.** 4855.
16. 4283.   **17.** 3484.   **18.** 3012.   **19.** 4299.   **20.** 4295.
21. 4371.   **22.** 4132.   **23.** 4120.   **24.** 4966.

Page 8. — **1.** $392.94.   **2.** $309.19.   **3.** $335.56.   **4.** $305.44.
5. $420.10.   **6.** $305.70.   **7.** $289.30.   **8.** $367.69.   **9.** $573.81.
10. $659.86.   **11.** $656.52.   **12.** $548.99.   **13.** $513.22.

Page 9. — **3.** $2.08.   **4.** $5.45.   **5.** 56 yr.   **6.** 753 mi.

Page 10. — **1.** 2382.   **2.** 5637.   **3.** 3481.   **4.** 805.   **5.** 6929.
6. 7770.   **7.** 1973.   **8.** 6584.   **9.** 4680.   **10.** 3245.   **11.** 1670.
12. 1762.   **13.** 5259.   **14.** 4780.   **15.** 4976.   **16.** 7481.   **17.** 7941.
18. 1392.   **19.** 632.   **20.** 2531.   **21.** 3551.   **22.** 3189.   **23.** 5454.
24. 3026.   **25.** 8329.   **26.** 5669.   **27.** 823.   **28.** 1540.

Page 11. — **1.** $29.77. **2.** $60.95. **3.** $26.17. **4.** $18.57.
5. $34.38. **6.** $37.56. **7.** $46.86. **8.** $36.97. **9.** $58.01.
10. $63.95. **11.** $59.46. **12.** $29.68. **13.** $31.79. **14.** $24.92.
15. $42.40. **16.** $78.49. **17.** $123.59. **18.** $252.38.
19. $718.75. **20.** $137.86. **21.** $410.28. **22.** $485.68.
23. $134.66. **24.** $407.04. **25.** $548.71. **26.** $385.99.
27. $253.60. **28.** $812.98. **29.** $457.60. **30.** $656.49.
31. $42.98. **32.** $377.98.

Page 12. — **1.** 56 acres. **2.** 82 bu. **3.** 140 qt. **4.** 77 qt.
5. 102 crates. **6.** 7 lb.

Page 13. — **1.** 69, 70, 75, 1 dollar; yes. **2.** 7, 10, 15, 25¢.
3. No; 1 dime, 1 quarter, 1 half dollar. **4.** 2 cents, 1 nickel, 1 dime.
5. 3 cents, 1 quarter, 1 half dollar. **6.** 1 cent, 1 nickel, 1 dime, 1 quarter.
7. 4 cents, 1 nickel, 1 half dollar. **8.** 4 cents, 1 nickel. **9.** 1 cent,
2 dimes, 1 half dollar. **10.** 3 cents, 1 quarter. **11.** 2 cents, 1 nickel,
1 dime, 1 half dollar. **12.** 2 cents, 1 nickel, 1 quarter. **13.** 1 cent,
1 nickel, 1 dime, 1 quarter, 1 half dollar. **14.** 1 nickel, 1 dime,
1 quarter. **15.** 4 cents, 1 nickel, 1 quarter, 1 half dollar.
16. 2 cents, 1 quarter, 1 half dollar, 3 dollars. **17.** 3 cents,
1 nickel, 1 dime, 1 quarter, 1 half dollar, 2 dollars. **18.** 3 cents,
1 dime, 1 quarter, 1 half dollar, 1 dollar. **19.** 2 cents, 2 dimes,
1 half dollar, 2 dollars. **20.** 1 cent, 1 dime, 1 quarter, 1 dollar.

Page 14. — **1.** $.43. **2.** 19¢. **3.** $.42. **4.** $.15. **5.** $2.33.

Page 15. — **1.** 7 fish. **2.** 64¢. **3.** 13 eggs. **4.** $.70.
5. 275 stamps. **6.** $2.86. **7.** 45¢. **8.** 12¢. **9.** $1.44.

Page 17. — *See page* xlii.

Page 22. — **2.** $44.45. **3.** $56.16. **4.** $79.80. **5.** $26.66.
6. $9.00. **7.** $6.96. **8.** $8.10. **9.** $25.92.

Page 23. — **1.** 24,768. **2.** 23,650. **3.** 9342. **4.** 25,724.
5. 44,499. **6.** 21,025. **7.** 29,469. **8.** 12,008. **9.** 52,585.
10. 38,963. **11.** 75,276. **12.** 59,346. **13.** 45,828. **14.** 21,112.
15. 12,596. **16.** 64,650. **17.** 18,644. **18.** 20,584. **19.** 35,121.
20. 16,184. **21.** 37,305. **22.** 23,142. **23.** 19,432. **24.** 16,065
25. 23,983. **26.** $2437.89. **27.** $3848.26. **28.** $1819.29
29. $4087.56. **30.** $1619.52. **31.** $3188.25. **32.** $1693.44.
33. $3198.35. **34.** $456.48. **35.** $1748.95. **36.** $1281.60.
37. $5853.16. **38.** $2812.69. **39.** $3827.04. **40.** $1422.22.
41. $6161.32.

Page 24. — **1.** 5292. **2.** 3268. **3.** 2496. **4.** 1352. **5.** 1653.
6. 3145. **7.** 612,365. **8.** 210,382. **9.** 292,192. **10.** 56,340.
11. 433,976. **12.** 16,942. **13.** 3472. **14.** 18,601. **15.** 51,709.
16. 53,334. **17.** 158,627. **18.** 156,978. **19.** 280,932.
20. 133,856. **21.** 551,304.

Page 25. — **1.** 44,100 papers. **2.** $42,945. **3.** 24,840 flowers. **4.** 505,420. **5.** 174,420. **6.** 233,130. **7.** 447,810. **8.** 130,780. **9.** 710,600. **10.** 489,027. **11.** 60,494. **12.** 229,871. **13.** 236,232. **14.** 145,314. **15.** 358,248. **16.** 145,299. **17.** 50,960. **18.** 201,777.

Page 26. — **1.** $240. **2.** 608 yd. **3.** $27.75. **4.** 3612 chickens. **5.** 744 hr. **6.** 6307 ft. **7.** 1485 yd. **8.** $364. **9.** $780. **10.** $2456. **11.** $12.96. **12.** $11.48. **13.** $14.19.

Page 27. — **1.** $9.12. **2.** $5.20. **3.** 117 lb. **4.** $24.13. **5.** $65.61. **6.** 7350 mints; 10,500 mints; 21,000 mints; 26,250 mints. **7.** $.06.

Page 30. — **1.** 24; 10; 321; 403; 210. **2.** 43; 31; 110; 221; 302. **3.** 28; 12; 68; 105; 106. **4.** 15; 12; 63; 72; 48. **5.** 12; 24; 120; 103; 106. **6.** 15; 13; 95; 82; 95. **7.** 18; 16; 88; 108; 102.

Page 31. — **2.** $2.65; $2.50. **3.** $2.03. **4.** $1.90.

1. $.49. **2.** A little over 32 mi. **3.** $4.05. **4.** 32 rows, 2 girls left.

Page 32. — **1.** 54; 142 R2; 671; 1060; 1070. **2.** 63; 39 R4; 270 R5; 340; 760 R3. **3.** 72; 40 R7; 207; 209 R2; 593. **4.** 68; 59 R3; 850; 506 R2; 601. **5.** 105; 289; 619 R2; 316; 749. **6.** 84; 164 R2; 1008; 1006; 408. **7.** 60; 69 R3; 405; 435 R4; 1000 R1. **8.** 75; 54 R6; 237; 417; 875. **9.** 28 R3; 109; 1030; 809; 624 R2.

Page 33. — *See page* xlii.

Page 34. — **1.** 3896; 3023; 3450; 3502; 3005. **2.** 6884; 2016; 2699; 2940. **3.** 7848; 32,870; 66,015; 170,496. **4.** 264,176; 444,996; 373,226; 146,740. **5.** 26; 150; 102; 1530. **6.** 17 R2; 201 R3; 133 R5; 321 R7.

Page 35. — **1.** 2999. **2.** 3573. **3.** 3727. **4.** $1344.88. **5.** $274.92. **6.** 213. **7.** 587. **8.** 1174. **9.** 161,028. **10.** 2. **11.** 31 in. **12.** 10. **13.** 1000. **16.** 82. **17.** 115. **18.** 36. **19.** 3115. **20.** 165. **21.** 102. **22.** 45. **23.** 91 R5. **24.** 41. **25.** 22. **26.** 134,420. **27.** 692. **28.** 165. **29.** 101.

Page 36. — **1.** $.35. **2.** 16 stamps; 2¢ left. **3.** $.40. **4.** $4.67. **5.** 8 pieces. **6.** $9.75. **7.** $1.06. **8.** 78 tickets. **9.** $4.75; $9.50. **10.** $2.69.

Page 37. — **1.** 375 mi. **2.** $.37. **3.** $1.50. **4.** 930 mi. **5.** $3.43. **6.** $6.80. **7.** 55 in. **8.** 13 oranges; 3¢ left.

Page 39. — **1.** 224 mi. **2.** 44 mi. **3.** 148 da.

1. 244. **2.** 223. **3.** 72. **4.** 42. **5.** 231. **6.** 122. **7.** 98 R11. **8.** 51 R13. **9.** 93. **10.** 71. **11.** 123 R23.

Page 39 (*continued*). — **12.** 91.   **13.** 35 R10.   **14.** 231 R28.
15. 45.   **16.** 136 R7.   **17.** 52 R36.   **18.** 378.   **19.** 293 R18.
20. 58.   **21.** 19.   **22.** 291.   **23.** 438.   **24.** 297.   **25.** 395 R26.
26. 288.   **27.** 916.   **28.** 472.   **29.** 253.   **30.** 736.   **31.** 453.
32. 367.   **33.** 529.

Page 40. — **1.** 21 R10.   **2.** 44 R26.   **3.** 349 R20.   **4.** 78 R30.
5. 78 R54.   **6.** 18 R33.   **7.** 47 R4.   **8.** 34.   **9.** 81 R3.   **10.** 85.
11. 434 R12.   **12.** 509 R33.   **13.** 726.   **14.** 678.   **15.** 359.

Page 41. — **1.** 245.   **2.** 241.   **3.** 37.   **4.** 62 R6.   **5.** 31 R21.
6. 36.   **7.** 31 R15.   **8.** 113.   **9.** 142.   **10.** 19.   **11.** 68.
12. 97 R20.   **13.** 73 R21.   **14.** 178 R39.   **15.** 62.   **16.** 267.
17. 46 R18.   **18.** 73 R12.   **19.** 81 R3.   **20.** 92.   **21.** 21.
22. 298.   **23.** 225 R19.   **24.** 64 R11.   **25.** 64.   **26.** 178 R25
27. 186.   **28.** 86 R15.   **29.** 32 R9.   **30.** 68.   **31.** 143 R23.
32. 145 R15.   **33.** 49 R2.   **34.** 74 R26.   **35.** 71 R15.
36. 151.   **37.** 374 R13.   **38.** 77 R26.   **39.** 73 R10.
40. 64.   **41.** 277 R10.   **42.** 69 R25.   **43.** 125 R21.
44. 76.   **45.** 472.   **46.** 436.   **47.** 573 R28.   **48.** 434 R12
49. 604.   **50.** 413.   **51.** 183.   **52.** 514.   **53.** 278 R12.
54. 386.   **55.** 697.   **56.** 518.   **57.** 821 R10.   **58.** 621
59. 635 R31.   **60.** 741.   **61.** 318 R7.   **62.** 737 R8.
63. 402 R11.   **64.** 334 R20.   **65.** 211 R18.   **66.** 642 R12.

Page 42. — **1.** 309.   **2.** 90.   **3.** 103.   **4.** 208.   **5.** 106.
6. 305.   **7.** 207 R15.   **8.** 307.   **9.** 109.   **10.** 103.   **11.** 150.
12. 10 R31.   **13.** 380.   **14.** 503.   **15.** 390.   **16.** 504.
17. 840.   **18.** 410.

Page 43. — **2.** $1.06.   **3.** $.19 ; $4.86.   **4.** $1.51.   **5.** $.19.
6. $.05.   **7.** $.55.

Page 44. — **1.** 193 R15.   **2.** 363.   **3.** 43.   **4.** 171.   **5.** 19.
6. 160.   **7.** 32.   **8.** 47.   **9.** 211.   **10.** 186.   **11.** 249 R23.
12. 45.   **13.** 122.   **14.** 185.   **15.** 408.   **16.** 377 R6.
17. 176 R19.   **18.** 52.   **19.** 323.   **20.** 556.   **21.** 76.   **22.** 62.
23. 403.   **24.** 335.   **25.** 79.   **26.** 31 R46.   **27.** 192.
28. 347 R19.   **29.** 648.   **30.** 115 R23.   **31.** 128 R33.
32. 292 R14.   **33.** 256 R20.   **34.** 31 R21.   **35.** 343.
36. 234 R18.   **37.** 135.   **38.** 75.   **39.** 436.   **40.** 206 R11.
41. 140.   **42.** 114.   **43.** 221.   **44.** 430.   **45.** 134 R33.   **46.** 73.
47. 322 R9.   **48.** 134.   **49.** 79.   **50.** 64.   **51.** $5.33 R56¢.
52. $6.11.   **53.** $2.16.   **54.** $7.23.   **55.** $6.31.   **56.** $6.42 R9¢.
57. $9.20.   **58.** $5.26 R27¢.   **59.** $3.80.   **60.** $8.63 R16¢.
61. $5.26.   **62.** $8.54 R26¢.   **63.** $2.24.   **64.** $9.32.
65. $2.44 R26¢.   **66.** $3.22.   **67.** $4.08.   **68.** $5.77 R30¢.
69. $9.31.   **70.** $8.18.   **71.** $8.60.   **72.** $6.08.   **73.** $5.20.
74. $9.52.   **75.** $6.54.

ANSWERS

Page 45. — **1.** $1.01. **2.** $.23. **3.** $.24. **4.** $2.18. **5.** $.50.

Page 46. — **1.** 13. **2.** 17. **3.** 24. **4.** 19. **5.** 23 R83.
6. 24 R3. **7.** 27. **8.** 24. **9.** 17. **10.** 13. **11.** 16.
12. 23 R23. **13.** 212 R65. **14.** 367. **15.** 79. **16.** 214 R17.
17. 41 R301. **18.** 85. **19.** 76. **20.** 53. **21.** 26. **22.** 51.
23. 62. **24.** 74. **25.** 51. **26.** 69. **27.** 73 R40. **28.** 53.
29. 41 R20. **30.** 72. **31.** 74. **32.** 351. **33.** 194. **34.** 214.
35. 441. **36.** 531.

Page 47. — **1.** 506. **2.** 52. **3.** 51 R18. **4.** 306. **5.** 50 R40.
6. 104. **7.** 53 R22. **8.** 207 R75. **9.** 81 R25. **10.** 209.
11. 250 R83. **12.** 63 R46. **13.** 303 R16. **14.** 330 R88.
15. 120 R9. **16.** 201. **17.** 118 R8. **18.** $7.07. **19.** $6.02.
20. $6.60 R$3.20. **21.** $5.06 R32¢. **22.** $6.10. **23.** $8.40.
24. $5.09 R$1.11. **25.** $3.60. **26.** $3.04. **27.** $4.80. **28.** $2.08.
29. $4.30. **30.** $5.40. **31.** $6.10. **32.** $8.03. **33.** $9.70 R34¢.
34. $4.06.

Page 48. — **1.** 22 R78. **2.** 26. **3.** 20. **4.** 14 R125.
5. 24 R118. **6.** 31. **7.** 21. **8.** 26. **9.** 24 R15. **10.** 16.
11. 17. **12.** 61. **13.** 208. **14.** 204. **15.** 39 R53. **16.** 71 R42.
17. 52. **18.** 25 R25. **19.** 97 R800. **20.** 55. **21.** 73 R120.
22. 84. **23.** 37. **24.** 333 R120. **25.** 209. **26.** 64.
27. 417 R70. **28.** 210. **29.** 108. **30.** 73 R125. **31.** 240.
32. 34. **33.** 247 R22.

Page 49. — **1.** 918. **2.** 547. **3.** 844 R61. **4.** 357. **5.** 441.
6. 916 R15. **7.** 573 R19. **8.** 458. **9.** 989. **10.** 444. **11.** 531.
12. 308 R100. **13.** 624. **14.** 275. **15.** 477. **16.** 415 R117.
17. 254. **18.** 309. **19.** 637. **20.** 557 R20. **21.** 472. **22.** 207.
23. 324. **24.** 321 R52. **25.** 418. **26.** $5.41. **27.** $5.40.
28. $7.45. **29.** $7.05 R18¢. **30.** $7.06. **31.** $6.74 R$3.50.
32. $7.38. **33.** $6.69 R63¢. **34.** $4.20. **35.** $7.62. **36.** $9.05.
37. $3.66. **38.** $9.46 R88¢. **39.** $5.40. **40.** $7.52 R2¢.
41. $6.86. **42.** $3.60. **43.** $3.21 R$2.08. **44.** $2.24.
45. $3.06. **46.** $7.46 R44¢. **47.** $9.60. **48.** $8.51 R10¢.
49. $6.69. **50.** $5.06.

Page 50. — **1.** 322; 532; 672 R8. **2.** 234 R12; 766; 314 R24.
3. 63; 445; 466. **4.** 68 R18; 263; 549 R30. **5.** 230; 407 R13; 470.
6. 207; 609; 550 R9. **7.** 61; 74; 64 R126. **8.** 57; 327 R50; 85.
9. 41 R110; 81; 267 R5. **10.** 58; 66; 221 R115. **11.** 63 R25;
217 R211; 86 R80. **12.** 73; 93; 223. **13.** 409; 230; 107 R230.

Page 51. — *See page* xlii.

Page 52. — **1.** $5.50. **2.** 47 children. **3.** 1096 mi. **4.** 24 times.
5. 20 automobiles; $360 left. **6.** $12.50. **7.** $20.16. **8.** $.89.
9. $1.52. **10.** $4.30.

Page 53. — **1.** About 50¢; about 75¢; about $1.00.   **2.** 2 records; yes.   **3.** About $2.00; smaller.   **4.** $60; estimate is larger. **5.** Betty's.   **6.** 5 uniforms.   **7.** No.

Page 54. — **1.** Less; 28¢ less.   **2.** No; estimate, $4.00; exact change, $4.04.   **3.** Estimate, 1500 children; exact answer, 1530 children. **4.** Estimate, $20.00; exact answer, $20.47.   **5.** Estimate, 20 hr.; exact answer, 19 hr.

Page 55. — **2.** 295 mi.   **3.** 79 lb.   **4.** $1.63.   **5.** 112 mi.   **6.** $28.

Page 57. — **1.** $1.07.   **2.** 102 jars.   **3.** $20.80.   **4.** 8 wk. **5.** $.05.   **6.** $61.48.   **7.** $.09.

Page 58. — **1.** $45.64.   **2.** 66,822.   **3.** 312.   **4.** 3823. **5.** 457 R28.   **6.** $26.00.   **7.** 940.   **8.** 48 times.   **9.** 39. **10.** 210.   **11.** 76.   **12.** 1600.   **13.** $5.24.   **14.** $7.91. **15.** 1208.   **16.** Yes.

Page 59. — **1.** $14.   **2.** 18 cookies.   **3.** $3.15.   **4.** $7.75. **5.** $5.37.   **6.** 12 badges; 2 in. left.   **7.** $3.86.   **8.** $1.69.

Page 61. — **1.** 85 pages.   **2.** 25.   **3.** 19.   **4.** 45.   **5.** 64. **6.** 71.   **7.** 99.   **8.** 303.   **9.** 456.   **10.** 1800.   **11.** 1492. **12.** 1905.   **13.** 1929.   **14.** V.   **15.** 1793.

Page 63. — **1.** 4 oz.; 12 oz.; 2 oz.; 10 oz.; 16 oz.   **2.** 45¢. **3.** 9 in.; 27 in.   **4.** 36¢.   **5.** 6; 12.   **6.** 8; 24.   **7.** 4; 20. **8.** $.20; $.60.   **9.** 7; 14; 21.   **10.** 7; 14; 35.   **11.** 9; 45; 63. **12.** $.40; $.80; $.90.

Page 64. — **2.** $7.20.   **3.** $18.60.   **4.** $2.00.   **5.** $2.50. **6.** $3.75.   **7.** $1.80.   **8.** $.90.   **9.** $1.50.

Page 65. — **1.** $\frac{1}{3}$.   **2.** $\frac{2}{3}$.   **3.** $\frac{1}{6}$.   **4.** $\frac{5}{6}$.   **5.** $\frac{2}{5}$.   **7.** $\frac{7}{8}$. **8.** $\frac{2}{3}$.   **9.** $\frac{1}{2}$.   **10.** $\frac{7}{1}$.   **11.** $\frac{20}{5}$.   **12.** $\frac{10}{2}$.   **13.** $\frac{18}{5}$.   **14.** $\frac{27}{9}$. **15.** $\frac{18}{1}$.   **16.** $\frac{5}{1}$.   **17.** $\frac{8}{1}$.   **18.** $\frac{2}{1}$.

Page 66. — **2.** $4\frac{2}{3}$ yd.   **3.** $13\frac{1}{2}$.   **4.** $8\frac{1}{4}$.   **5.** $14\frac{1}{3}$.   **6.** $15\frac{3}{4}$. **7.** $11\frac{7}{8}$.   **8.** $13\frac{5}{8}$.   **9.** $64\frac{3}{5}$.   **10.** $54\frac{3}{8}$.   **11.** $39\frac{3}{4}$.   **12.** $74\frac{2}{3}$.

Page 68. — **1.** $4\frac{1}{2}$.   **2.** 1.   **3.** $1\frac{3}{4}$.   **4.** $4\frac{2}{3}$.   **5.** $7\frac{1}{2}$.   **6.** $2\frac{1}{8}$. **7.** 15.   **8.** $5\frac{3}{4}$.   **9.** $4\frac{3}{4}$.   **10.** $2\frac{5}{8}$.   **11.** $3\frac{1}{5}$.   **12.** 2.   **13.** $10\frac{1}{4}$. **14.** 10.   **15.** $3\frac{7}{10}$.   **16.** $5\frac{1}{8}$.   **17.** $5\frac{1}{8}$.   **18.** $4\frac{1}{6}$.   **19.** $3\frac{1}{8}$. **20.** $10\frac{1}{2}$.   **21.** $5\frac{1}{5}$.   **22.** 5.   **23.** $4\frac{5}{8}$.   **24.** 3.   **25.** $3\frac{1}{2}$ lb. **26.** $2\frac{1}{2}$ hr.   **27.** $9\frac{1}{4}$.

Page 69. — **4.** $\frac{3}{8}$; $\frac{7}{8}$; $\frac{2}{3}$.   **5.** $\frac{5}{8}$.   **6.** 1.   **7.** $\frac{4}{5}$.   **8.** $\frac{3}{8}$.   **9.** $\frac{9}{16}$. **10.** $\frac{9}{10}$.   **11.** $1\frac{1}{4}$.   **12.** $1\frac{1}{8}$.   **13.** 1.   **14.** $1\frac{3}{8}$.   **15.** $1\frac{1}{3}$. **16.** 1.   **17.** 1.

Page 70. — **3.** $9\frac{1}{4}$ mi. **4.** $5\frac{1}{4}$. **5.** $3\frac{3}{4}$. **6.** 2. **7.** 4.
8. 13. **9.** 6. **10.** 11. **11.** $7\frac{1}{4}$. **12.** $6\frac{3}{8}$. **13.** $13\frac{1}{2}$.
14. 20. **15.** $15\frac{5}{8}$. **16.** 21. **17.** $9\frac{7}{8}$. **18.** $7\frac{1}{4}$. **19.** $8\frac{3}{4}$.
20. $19\frac{3}{4}$. **21.** 14. **22.** $8\frac{1}{2}$. **23.** $19\frac{3}{8}$.

Page 71. — **3.** $1\frac{3}{4}$. **4.** $10\frac{1}{4}$. **5.** $17\frac{3}{4}$. **6.** $3\frac{3}{4}$. **7.** $6\frac{1}{4}$.
8. 17. **9.** $21\frac{1}{4}$. **10.** $11\frac{3}{4}$. **11.** 15. **12.** $15\frac{3}{4}$.

Page 73. — **1.** $\frac{1}{2}$. **2.** $\frac{1}{4}$. **3.** $\frac{1}{4}$. **4.** $\frac{1}{2}$. **5.** $\frac{1}{8}$. **6.** $\frac{3}{8}$.
7. $\frac{5}{8}$. **8.** $\frac{3}{4}$. **9.** $\frac{7}{8}$. **10.** 1. **11.** $\frac{2}{3}$ ft. **12.** No; correct
answer $\frac{1}{2}$. **13.** $\frac{4}{16}$; $\frac{12}{16}$.

Page 74. — **2.** $1\frac{1}{2}$ yd. **4.** $3\frac{1}{2}$ yd.
1. $\frac{3}{4}$. **2.** $\frac{3}{4}$. **3.** $\frac{1}{2}$. **4.** $4\frac{1}{2}$. **5.** $11\frac{3}{4}$. **6.** $\frac{1}{2}$. **7.** $1\frac{1}{4}$.
8. $1\frac{1}{8}$. **9.** $7\frac{1}{4}$. **10.** $15\frac{3}{4}$. **11.** $\frac{1}{2}$. **12.** $1\frac{3}{4}$. **13.** $\frac{1}{2}$.
14. $12\frac{5}{8}$. **15.** $8\frac{1}{2}$. **16.** $\frac{1}{2}$. **17.** $\frac{3}{4}$. **18.** $\frac{3}{4}$. **19.** $13\frac{1}{2}$.
20. $7\frac{5}{8}$.

Page 75. — **2.** $5\frac{1}{4}$ lb. **3.** $8\frac{3}{4}$ lb.
1. 7. **2.** 17. **3.** $10\frac{1}{2}$. **4.** 12. **5.** $13\frac{1}{4}$. **6.** $9\frac{7}{8}$. **7.** 12.
8. 10. **9.** $16\frac{1}{4}$. **10.** $7\frac{3}{4}$. **11.** 21. **12.** $22\frac{3}{8}$. **13.** $20\frac{1}{8}$.
14. $19\frac{1}{2}$. **15.** 19. **16.** $20\frac{1}{4}$. **17.** $22\frac{7}{8}$. **18.** $23\frac{1}{4}$. **19.** $29\frac{1}{2}$.
20. $27\frac{3}{8}$.

Page 76. — **2.** 8; yes. **3.** Numerator is multiplied by 2 and
denominator by 4. **4.** 2. **5.** 4. **6.** 6. **7.** 16. **8.** 8.
9. 2. **10.** 4. **11.** 10. **12.** 16. **13.** 8. **14.** 12. **15.** 6.
16. 14. **17.** 4. **18.** 4. **19.** 16. **20.** 2. **21.** 8. **22.** 20.
23. 4.

Page 77. — **1.** $5\frac{7}{8}$ yd. **2.** $\frac{7}{8}$. **3.** $\frac{5}{8}$. **4.** $\frac{7}{8}$. **5.** $\frac{3}{8}$. **6.** $\frac{5}{8}$.
7. $1\frac{3}{8}$. **8.** $1\frac{1}{8}$. **9.** $1\frac{1}{8}$. **10.** $1\frac{1}{8}$. **11.** $\frac{7}{8}$. **12.** $1\frac{3}{8}$. **13.** $1\frac{5}{8}$.

Page 78. — **2.** $13\frac{7}{8}$ acres. **3.** $13\frac{3}{8}$ acres.
1. $21\frac{7}{8}$. **2.** $6\frac{7}{8}$. **3.** $22\frac{7}{8}$. **4.** $17\frac{3}{8}$. **5.** 23. **6.** $11\frac{3}{8}$.
7. $17\frac{5}{8}$. **8.** 15. **9.** $23\frac{3}{8}$. **10.** $12\frac{1}{2}$. **11.** $3\frac{5}{16}$. **12.** $10\frac{11}{16}$.
13. $8\frac{3}{16}$. **14.** $10\frac{5}{16}$. **15.** $7\frac{9}{16}$. **16.** $6\frac{7}{16}$. **17.** $4\frac{5}{16}$. **18.** $8\frac{3}{16}$.
19. $10\frac{9}{16}$. **20.** $13\frac{1}{16}$.

Page 79. — **1.** $\frac{2}{3}$; $\frac{5}{8}$; 1; $1\frac{1}{16}$; $1\frac{3}{8}$. **2.** $12\frac{3}{4}$; $14\frac{7}{8}$; 11; $8\frac{5}{8}$; 17.
3. $7\frac{1}{4}$; $10\frac{3}{4}$; 14; $13\frac{3}{4}$; $13\frac{1}{4}$. **4.** $1\frac{1}{8}$; $\frac{5}{8}$; $\frac{7}{8}$; $1\frac{1}{8}$; $1\frac{3}{8}$. **5.** $\frac{5}{8}$; $1\frac{1}{4}$;
$13\frac{1}{2}$; $6\frac{7}{8}$; $13\frac{1}{4}$. **6.** $\frac{2}{8}$; $\frac{3}{8}$; $11\frac{1}{4}$; $11\frac{1}{8}$; $9\frac{1}{2}$. **7.** $15\frac{13}{16}$; $15\frac{13}{16}$; $12\frac{1}{16}$;
$10\frac{5}{16}$; $18\frac{5}{16}$. **8.** $11\frac{5}{8}$; $18\frac{3}{8}$; 13; $14\frac{3}{4}$; $8\frac{7}{8}$.

Page 80. — **1.** 1972 lb. **2.** 108 lb. **3.** About 12 dolphins.
4. About 2 times. **5.** About 35 times; about $25\frac{1}{2}$ times.

Page 81. — **1.** 164,250. **2.** 76. **3.** 513. **4.** $10.00. **5.** 1.
6. $3\frac{1}{4}$. **7.** 6. **8.** 3. **9.** $1\frac{5}{8}$. **10.** 19. **11.** $1\frac{1}{16}$. **12.** 18.
13. XLII; LVII; XCVIII; CXLVIII; DCCCLXII; MCMXXXIV.
14. $11\frac{7}{8}$. **15.** $\frac{2}{3}$. **16.** $\frac{9}{12}$. **17.** $11\frac{11}{16}$. **18.** 588. **19.** No.
21. $4\frac{1}{4}$; 7; $2\frac{3}{8}$; 2; $2\frac{1}{2}$; $3\frac{1}{8}$; 1. **23.** 159. **25.** 118.

Page 82. — 1. $4.67. **2.** $15.42. **3.** $.15. **4.** 58 rows; yes; 3 children. **5.** $24. **6.** 276 pupils. **7.** $4.55. **8.** 70 min.

Page 83. — *See pages* xlii *and* xliii.

Page 84. — 1. $\frac{1}{2}$ lb. **2.** $\frac{1}{2}$ mi. **3.** $6\frac{1}{4}$ lb. **4.** $\frac{1}{4}$. **5.** $\frac{1}{4}$. **6.** 0. **7.** $\frac{3}{8}$. **8.** $\frac{1}{4}$. **9.** $\frac{3}{4}$. **10.** $1\frac{1}{16}$. **11.** $\frac{3}{4}$. **12.** $\frac{5}{8}$. **13.** $\frac{3}{4}$. **14.** $\frac{3}{4}$. **15.** $\frac{1}{2}$. **16.** $\frac{1}{8}$; $\frac{3}{4}$; $\frac{1}{4}$; $\frac{1}{2}$; $\frac{5}{8}$; $\frac{15}{16}$; $\frac{11}{16}$.

Page 85. — 2. $3\frac{1}{8}$ lb.; no. **3.** $1\frac{5}{8}$ lb.

1. $6\frac{1}{4}$ sec. **2.** $1\frac{1}{4}$ hr. **3.** $1\frac{1}{4}$. **4.** $4\frac{3}{8}$. **5.** $1\frac{5}{8}$. **6.** $2\frac{3}{8}$. **7.** $3\frac{7}{16}$. **8.** $2\frac{1}{8}$. **9.** $5\frac{1}{4}$. **10.** $4\frac{1}{8}$. **11.** $2\frac{5}{16}$. **12.** $1\frac{1}{16}$. **13.** $2\frac{1}{8}$. **14.** $4\frac{3}{8}$. **15.** $4\frac{1}{8}$. **16.** $6\frac{1}{8}$. **17.** $3\frac{3}{16}$.

Page 86. — 3. 4. **4.** 2. **5.** 5. **6.** 3. **7.** 5. **8.** 5. **9.** $\frac{1}{10}$; $\frac{1}{20}$. **10.** 10. **11.** 20. **12.** 11. **13.** 4. **14.** 8. **15.** 2. **16.** 8. **17.** 4. **18.** 16. **19.** 3. **20.** 5. **21.** 7. **22.** 11. **23.** 9. **24.** 19. **25.** $5\frac{2}{8} = 4\frac{10}{8}$. **26.** $8\frac{4}{8} = 7\frac{12}{8}$. **27.** $6\frac{2}{4} = 5\frac{6}{4}$. **28.** $4\frac{2}{8} = 3\frac{10}{8}$. **29.** $7\frac{6}{8} = 6\frac{14}{8}$. **30.** $3\frac{2}{16} = 2\frac{18}{16}$.

Page 88. — 3. $\frac{3}{4}$ lb. **4.** $1\frac{1}{2}$ lb.

1. $1\frac{1}{2}$ sec. **2.** $\frac{3}{4}$ lb. **3.** $4\frac{1}{2}$. **4.** $2\frac{1}{4}$. **5.** $1\frac{7}{8}$. **6.** $5\frac{1}{2}$. **7.** $2\frac{1}{4}$. **8.** $2\frac{3}{4}$. **9.** $2\frac{1}{8}$. **10.** $2\frac{1}{2}$. **11.** $1\frac{1}{2}$. **12.** $2\frac{3}{4}$.

Page 89. — 2. $78\frac{3}{4}$ lb.

1. $2\frac{3}{4}$. **2.** $4\frac{5}{8}$. **3.** $3\frac{3}{8}$. **4.** $8\frac{1}{8}$. **5.** $1\frac{5}{8}$. **6.** $2\frac{7}{8}$. **7.** $1\frac{3}{8}$. **8.** $6\frac{7}{8}$. **9.** $5\frac{3}{4}$. **10.** $\frac{5}{8}$.

Page 90. — 1. $4\frac{7}{8}$ lb. **2.** $76\frac{3}{4}$ lb. **3.** $3\frac{3}{4}$ lb. **4.** $4\frac{1}{4}$ lb.

1. $6\frac{1}{2}$; $1\frac{1}{4}$; $6\frac{1}{2}$; $\frac{3}{8}$; $1\frac{7}{8}$; $7\frac{3}{4}$. **2.** $2\frac{1}{2}$; $3\frac{15}{16}$; $\frac{11}{16}$; $5\frac{1}{2}$; $2\frac{5}{8}$; $11\frac{13}{16}$. **3.** $5\frac{3}{8}$; $2\frac{13}{16}$; $4\frac{1}{2}$; $7\frac{5}{8}$; $3\frac{3}{8}$; $5\frac{13}{16}$. **4.** $4\frac{5}{8}$; $\frac{3}{4}$; $3\frac{7}{8}$; $5\frac{13}{16}$; $3\frac{3}{8}$; $9\frac{3}{8}$. **5.** $5\frac{1}{2}$; $2\frac{9}{16}$; $3\frac{15}{16}$; $2\frac{1}{8}$; $1\frac{5}{8}$; $8\frac{9}{16}$.

Page 91. — 1. $\frac{1}{2}$; $\frac{1}{2}$; $\frac{1}{2}$; $\frac{5}{16}$; $\frac{1}{2}$. **2.** $4\frac{5}{16}$; $4\frac{1}{8}$; $4\frac{5}{16}$; $7\frac{1}{8}$; $4\frac{3}{16}$. **3.** $2\frac{5}{8}$; $5\frac{1}{16}$; $5\frac{7}{16}$; $3\frac{1}{8}$; $2\frac{5}{16}$. **4.** $4\frac{3}{8}$; $2\frac{1}{8}$; $3\frac{3}{4}$; $\frac{1}{4}$; $4\frac{3}{4}$. **5.** $\frac{3}{4}$; $2\frac{1}{2}$; $1\frac{1}{2}$; $2\frac{5}{8}$; $5\frac{1}{4}$. **6.** $\frac{7}{8}$; $5\frac{13}{16}$; $1\frac{7}{8}$; $1\frac{13}{16}$; $2\frac{5}{16}$. **7.** $1\frac{5}{8}$; $5\frac{13}{16}$; $7\frac{7}{8}$; $2\frac{9}{16}$; $1\frac{13}{16}$.

Page 92. — 9. $\frac{1}{4}$; $\frac{6}{12}$ doz.; $\frac{4}{12}$ doz.; $\frac{8}{12}$ doz.; $\frac{2}{12}$ doz.; $\frac{10}{12}$ doz.; $\frac{9}{12}$ doz. **10.** $\frac{1}{3}$ ft.; $\frac{5}{6}$ ft.; $\frac{1}{2}$ ft. **11.** $\frac{2}{6} = \frac{1}{3}$; $\frac{10}{12} = \frac{5}{6}$; $\frac{3}{6} = \frac{1}{2}$; $\frac{3}{12} = \frac{1}{4}$; $\frac{4}{6} = \frac{2}{3}$; $\frac{6}{12} = \frac{1}{2}$. **12.** $\frac{8}{12} = \frac{2}{3}$; $\frac{9}{12} = \frac{3}{4}$; $\frac{4}{12} = \frac{1}{3}$.

Page 93. — 1. $6\frac{2}{3}$ hr. **2.** $8\frac{1}{3}$ hr. **3.** $9\frac{1}{2}$. **4.** $5\frac{2}{3}$. **5.** $10\frac{5}{8}$. **6.** $18\frac{1}{6}$. **7.** $15\frac{1}{3}$. **8.** $12\frac{2}{3}$. **9.** $13\frac{5}{8}$. **10.** $8\frac{1}{6}$. **11.** $13\frac{1}{2}$. **12.** $16\frac{5}{8}$. **13.** 16. **14.** $17\frac{1}{6}$. **15.** $16\frac{2}{3}$. **16.** $22\frac{1}{2}$. **17.** 18. **18.** $18\frac{2}{3}$. **19.** 15. **20.** 11. **21.** $20\frac{1}{6}$. **22.** $22\frac{1}{2}$.

Page 94. — 2. $14\frac{5}{6}$ ft. **3.** The running high jump; $1\frac{1}{8}$ ft.

1. $5\frac{2}{3}$. **2.** $2\frac{1}{3}$. **3.** $7\frac{2}{3}$. **4.** $4\frac{1}{8}$. **5.** $3\frac{1}{2}$. **6.** $5\frac{2}{3}$. **7.** $4\frac{1}{8}$. **8.** $1\frac{5}{6}$. **9.** $2\frac{5}{6}$. **10.** $3\frac{5}{8}$. **11.** $\frac{1}{3}$. **12.** $1\frac{1}{2}$. **13.** $6\frac{1}{6}$. **14.** $1\frac{5}{6}$. **15.** $1\frac{2}{3}$. **16.** $1\frac{1}{6}$. **17.** $2\frac{1}{6}$. **18.** $4\frac{1}{3}$. **19.** $\frac{1}{6}$. **20.** $\frac{5}{8}$.

Page 95. — **9.** No; correct answer $148\frac{2}{5}$ mi. **10.** $\frac{1}{20}$ of a dollar.
16. $\frac{8}{12} = \frac{2}{3}$; $\frac{4}{6} = \frac{2}{3}$; $\frac{20}{30} = \frac{2}{3}$; $\frac{8}{20} = \frac{2}{5}$. **17.** $\frac{16}{100} = \frac{4}{25}$; $\frac{6}{8} = \frac{3}{4}$; $\frac{10}{20} = \frac{1}{2}$; $\frac{12}{16} = \frac{3}{4}$.

Page 96. — **2.** $31\frac{3}{5}$ sec. **3.** $31\frac{3}{10}$ sec. **4.** $32\frac{2}{5}$ sec.
5. Midget team.
1. $13\frac{3}{10}$. **2.** $10\frac{4}{5}$. **3.** $13\frac{9}{10}$. **4.** $9\frac{1}{10}$. **5.** $6\frac{3}{5}$. **6.** $11\frac{7}{10}$.
7. $17\frac{3}{10}$. **8.** $15\frac{1}{10}$. **9.** $11\frac{9}{10}$. **10.** $11\frac{3}{10}$. **11.** $17\frac{3}{10}$. **12.** 25.
13. $16\frac{2}{5}$. **14.** $13\frac{2}{5}$. **15.** $18\frac{2}{5}$.

Page 97. — **2.** $102\frac{9}{10}$ mi. **3.** $\frac{1}{2}$ sec. **4.** $4\frac{3}{10}$ mi. **5.** $2\frac{7}{10}$.
6. $1\frac{7}{10}$. **7.** $2\frac{4}{5}$. **8.** $4\frac{9}{10}$. **9.** $5\frac{3}{10}$. **10.** $5\frac{7}{10}$. **11.** $4\frac{4}{5}$.
12. $2\frac{3}{10}$. **13.** $2\frac{1}{10}$. **14.** $5\frac{8}{10}$. **15.** $1\frac{9}{10}$. **16.** $2\frac{1}{10}$. **17.** $1\frac{1}{10}$
18. $4\frac{3}{10}$. **19.** $5\frac{7}{10}$. **20.** $1\frac{7}{10}$ sec.

Page 99. — **1.** Larger; 4426 sq. mi. larger. **2.** The states on the Atlantic; 48,835 sq. mi. greater. **3.** Almost $\frac{1}{8}$.

Page 100. — **2.** $\frac{5}{6}$. **3.** $\frac{11}{15}$. **4.** $\frac{23}{30}$. **5.** $\frac{13}{20}$. **6.** $\frac{19}{20}$. **7.** $\frac{11}{18}$.
8. $\frac{11}{12}$. **9.** $1\frac{1}{12}$. **10.** $1\frac{1}{8}$. **11.** $\frac{11}{30}$. **12.** $1\frac{1}{15}$. **13.** $\frac{17}{24}$.
14. $1\frac{1}{10}$. **15.** $\frac{19}{30}$. **16.** $\frac{7}{12}$. **17.** $\frac{19}{24}$. **18.** $1\frac{7}{24}$. **19.** $1\frac{2}{15}$.

Page 101. — **1.** $7\frac{3}{4}$ lb. **2.** $1\frac{19}{24}$. **3.** $6\frac{9}{20}$. **4.** $1\frac{23}{30}$. **5.** $2\frac{1}{30}$.
6. $5\frac{9}{10}$. **7.** $2\frac{11}{30}$. **8.** $2\frac{3}{10}$. **9.** $4\frac{7}{40}$. **10.** $2\frac{7}{24}$. **11.** $4\frac{7}{15}$.
12. $5\frac{11}{30}$. **13.** $2\frac{13}{15}$. **14.** $1\frac{4}{15}$. **15.** $5\frac{1}{20}$. **16.** $7\frac{5}{12}$.

1. $15\frac{1}{8}$. **2.** $17\frac{7}{8}$. **3.** $16\frac{4}{5}$. **4.** $15\frac{7}{8}$. **5.** $16\frac{3}{16}$. **6.** 19.
7. $20\frac{2}{3}$. **8.** $10\frac{3}{16}$. **9.** $15\frac{4}{5}$. **10.** $27\frac{1}{3}$. **11.** $2\frac{7}{8}$. **12.** $5\frac{2}{3}$.
13. $3\frac{5}{12}$. **14.** $1\frac{9}{10}$. **15.** $5\frac{7}{8}$. **16.** $4\frac{1}{2}$. **17.** $1\frac{7}{10}$. **18.** $6\frac{5}{16}$.
19. $5\frac{1}{2}$. **20.** $3\frac{2}{15}$.

Page 102. — **1.** $1\frac{1}{12}$. **2.** $\frac{7}{24}$. **3.** $\frac{14}{15}$. **4.** $\frac{5}{18}$. **5.** $\frac{29}{40}$. **6.** $11\frac{13}{24}$.
7. $11\frac{37}{40}$. **8.** $9\frac{13}{24}$. **9.** $11\frac{5}{12}$. **10.** $10\frac{1}{15}$.

Page 103. — **1.** $8\frac{11}{30}$. **2.** $13\frac{7}{12}$. **3.** $17\frac{17}{24}$. **4.** $12\frac{13}{18}$. **5.** $14\frac{11}{12}$.
6. $15\frac{8}{15}$. **7.** $6\frac{7}{40}$. **8.** $12\frac{11}{24}$. **9.** $19\frac{5}{24}$. **10.** $9\frac{7}{12}$. **11.** 17.
12. $13\frac{5}{12}$. **13.** $25\frac{3}{4}$. **14.** 19. **15.** $12\frac{13}{24}$.

Page 104. — **1.** $11\frac{11}{16}$. **2.** $20\frac{1}{12}$. **3.** $20\frac{5}{12}$. **4.** $19\frac{11}{20}$. **5.** 13.
6. $23\frac{29}{30}$. **7.** $18\frac{5}{18}$. **8.** $11\frac{17}{18}$. **9.** $21\frac{13}{24}$. **10.** $18\frac{7}{8}$. **11.** $24\frac{5}{8}$.
12. $20\frac{1}{4}$. **13.** $17\frac{19}{24}$. **14.** $21\frac{5}{36}$. **15.** $21\frac{1}{48}$. **16.** Tenths of a pound scale; $\frac{3}{20}$ lb. **17.** $\frac{5}{8}$ in. **18.** $30\frac{41}{60}$ min.

Page 105. — *See page* xliii.

Page 106. — **2.** All six sums = 2. **3.** All six sums = 1. **4.** Six sums are not equal. No. 4 is not a magic square. **5.** All six sums = 2. **6.** $A = \frac{3}{4}$, $B = \frac{5}{8}$, $C = \frac{1}{2}$, $D = \frac{1}{2}$, $E = \frac{7}{8}$.

Page 107. — **1.** $A = \frac{3}{4}$, $B = \frac{5}{8}$, $C = \frac{1}{4}$, $D = \frac{1}{4}$, $E = \frac{1}{8}$. **2.** $A = \frac{7}{16}$, $B = \frac{3}{8}$, $C = \frac{1}{8}$, $D = \frac{9}{16}$, $E = \frac{1}{4}$. **3.** $A = \frac{1}{4}$, $B = \frac{1}{8}$, $C = \frac{1}{2}$, $D = \frac{3}{8}$, $E = \frac{1}{4}$. **4.** $A = \frac{1}{5}$, $B = \frac{9}{10}$, $C = \frac{1}{10}$, $D = \frac{4}{5}$, $E = \frac{3}{10}$.

Page 107 (*continued*).—**5.** $A = \frac{1}{2}$, $B = \frac{5}{12}$, $C = \frac{1}{4}$, $D = \frac{7}{12}$, $E = \frac{1}{3}$.
6. $A = \frac{1}{2}$, $B = \frac{3}{8}$, $C = \frac{3}{4}$, $D = \frac{3}{8}$, $E = \frac{1}{2}$.   **7.** $A = \frac{3}{16}$, $B = \frac{3}{16}$,
$C = \frac{5}{16}$, $D = \frac{1}{8}$, $E = \frac{1}{4}$.   **8.** $A = \frac{7}{16}$, $B = \frac{7}{16}$, $C = \frac{5}{8}$, $D = \frac{5}{16}$, $E = \frac{7}{16}$.

Page 108.—**1.** 17.   **2.** 350.   **3.** 18.   **4.** 378.   **5.** 41.
6. 160.   **7.** 7980.   **8.** $1\frac{7}{8}$.   **9.** $6\frac{1}{4}$.   **10.** $\frac{3}{4}$; $\frac{11}{16}$; $\frac{4}{5}$; $\frac{3}{8}$; $\frac{5}{8}$; $\frac{7}{16}$.
11. 1938.   **12.** $1.28.   **13.** 63 in.   **14.** CXVI; CXV.
15. $\frac{4}{8}$; $\frac{6}{8}$; $\frac{7}{8}$; $\frac{2}{8}$.   **16.** $\frac{7}{8}$.   **17.** 48.   **18.** 1288.   **19.** 146.
20. 12.   **21.** 63.   **22.** $18\frac{1}{2}$.   **23.** 11.   **24.** $23\frac{2}{3}$.   **25.** $19\frac{7}{8}$.   **26.** 0.

Page 109.—**1.** $12\frac{1}{2}$; $8\frac{1}{6}$; $14\frac{2}{3}$; $10\frac{1}{3}$; $16\frac{1}{2}$.   **2.** $9\frac{9}{10}$; $5\frac{1}{2}$; $15\frac{1}{3}$;
$9\frac{1}{10}$; $11\frac{9}{10}$.   **3.** $1\frac{1}{6}$; $1\frac{4}{15}$; $7\frac{7}{24}$; $5\frac{7}{12}$; $12\frac{7}{30}$.   **4.** $7\frac{17}{24}$; $15\frac{11}{12}$; $14\frac{25}{48}$;
$9\frac{1}{12}$; $11\frac{23}{30}$.   **5.** $7\frac{1}{2}$; $3\frac{2}{3}$; $3\frac{1}{6}$; $3\frac{2}{3}$; $3\frac{5}{8}$.   **6.** $\frac{3}{10}$; $4\frac{1}{5}$; $1\frac{1}{2}$; $3\frac{3}{10}$; $2\frac{1}{2}$.
7. $2\frac{1}{6}$; $4\frac{29}{40}$; $5\frac{7}{10}$; $1\frac{23}{24}$; $3\frac{7}{15}$.

Page 110.—**1.** $14\frac{3}{4}$ mi.   **2.** $840.   **3.** $.10.   **4.** $93.
5. $6.45.   **6.** $.16.   **7.** $9.75.

Page 111.—Divisible by 9: No. 2, 4, 6, 7, 9, 10, 11, 12, 14, 15;
not divisible by 9: No. 1, 3, 5, 8, 13.   **16.** No; yes; no; yes.

Page 112.—**1.** Yes; yes; no.

Page 113.—**5.** $\frac{3}{4}$.   **6.** $\frac{4}{5}$.   **7.** $\frac{2}{3}$.   **8.** $\frac{9}{10}$.   **9.** $\frac{8}{11}$.   **10.** $\frac{1}{2}$.
11. $\frac{3}{4}$.   **12.** $\frac{1}{2}$.   **13.** $\frac{4}{5}$.   **14.** $\frac{2}{5}$.   **15.** $\frac{1}{3}$.   **16.** $\frac{9}{16}$.   **17.** $\frac{1}{3}$.
18. $\frac{4}{5}$.   **19.** $\frac{5}{16}$.   **20.** $\frac{3}{16}$.   **21.** $\frac{1}{4}$.   **22.** $\frac{3}{8}$.

Page 114.—**1.** Yes; yes. No; yes; yes; yes; no; yes.   **2.** $\frac{3}{5}$.
3. $\frac{1}{2}$.   **4.** $\frac{1}{3}$.   **5.** $\frac{6}{13}$.   **6.** $\frac{7}{12}$.   **7.** $\frac{17}{25}$.   **8.** $\frac{8}{15}$.   **9.** $\frac{14}{25}$.
10. $\frac{7}{8}$.   **11.** $\frac{37}{101}$.   **12.** $\frac{22}{25}$.   **13.** $\frac{7}{19}$.   **14.** $\frac{4}{7}$.   **15.** $\frac{1}{3}$.   **16.** $\frac{5}{7}$.
17. $58\frac{3}{4}$.   **18.** $133\frac{1}{4}$.   **19.** $110\frac{1}{3}$.   **20.** $42\frac{1}{3}$.   **21.** $22\frac{13}{40}$.   **22.** $5\frac{5}{16}$.
23. $14\frac{8}{27}$.   **24.** $14\frac{5}{8}$.   **25.** $17\frac{11}{16}$.

Page 115.—**1.** 4727.   **2.** 5026.   **3.** 3021.   **4.** 4085.   **5.** 4349.
6. 5423.   **7.** 4901.   **8.** 4141.   **9.** 4545.   **10.** 5043.
11. $676.81.   **12.** $241.03.   **13.** $559.87.   **14.** $448.34.
15. $317.89.   **16.** $352.49.   **17.** $399.78.   **18.** $598.65.
19. $246.92.   **20.** $155.46.   **21.** $404.69.   **22.** $687.36.

Page 116.—**1.** $\frac{3}{4}$.   **2.** $\frac{2}{3}$.   **3.** $\frac{4}{5}$.   **4.** $3\frac{1}{3}$.   **5.** $1\frac{1}{2}$.   **6.** $1\frac{1}{5}$.
7. $2\frac{1}{2}$.   **8.** $\frac{2}{3}$.   **9.** 6.   **10.** $4\frac{1}{2}$.   **11.** 2.   **12.** $2\frac{2}{5}$.   **13.** $1\frac{1}{2}$.
14. $4\frac{3}{8}$.   **15.** 4.   **16.** 4.   **17.** 3.   **18.** $1\frac{1}{4}$.   **19.** 6.   **20.** $\frac{1}{2}$.
21. $\frac{1}{2}$.   **22.** $2\frac{1}{4}$.   **23.** $2\frac{2}{3}$.   **24.** $\frac{2}{5}$.   **25.** $2\frac{2}{3}$.   **26.** $1\frac{3}{4}$.   **27.** 1.
28. $\frac{5}{6}$.   **29.** 1.   **30.** $1\frac{4}{5}$.   **31.** $\frac{3}{4}$.   **32.** $2\frac{2}{3}$.   **33.** $3\frac{2}{3}$.   **34.** $3\frac{1}{3}$.
35. $1\frac{2}{3}$.   **36.** $5\frac{1}{3}$.   **37.** $5\frac{1}{4}$ yd.

Page 117.—**2.** 385 mi.   **3.** $1347\frac{1}{2}$ mi.

1. 21.   **2.** $45\frac{1}{3}$.   **3.** 15.   **4.** $10\frac{7}{8}$.   **5.** $45\frac{1}{2}$.   **6.** 60.
7. $46\frac{1}{4}$.   **8.** 63.   **9.** $43\frac{1}{3}$.   **10.** $38\frac{1}{2}$.   **11.** $15\frac{3}{4}$.   **12.** 44.
13. $86\frac{1}{4}$.   **14.** $100\frac{4}{5}$.   **15.** 35.   **16.** 94.   **17.** $108\frac{1}{2}$.   **18.** $67\frac{1}{3}$.
19. $51\frac{2}{3}$.   **20.** $91\frac{1}{4}$.   **21.** $122\frac{2}{5}$.   **22.** $73\frac{1}{2}$.   **23.** 166.   **24.** 177.

25. 833.   **26.** $382\frac{2}{3}$.   **27.** $427\frac{1}{2}$.   **28.** 306.   **29.** $422\frac{5}{8}$.   **30.** 340.
31. 1128.   **32.** 243.   **33.** 315.   **34.** $235\frac{1}{8}$.   **35.** 297.   **36.** 394.

Page 118. — **2.** 4; 12.   **3.** 6; 18.   **4.** 12; 24; 6; 30.   **5.** 45¢.
6. 30¢.   **7.** 9.   **8.** 14.   **9.** 28.   **10.** 60.   **11.** 18.   **12.** 15.
13. 6.   **14.** 36.   **15.** 21.   **16.** 12.   **17.** 10.   **18.** 6.   **19** 35.
20. 50.   **21.** 22.   **22.** 90.   **23.** 100.   **24.** 200.   **25.** 75.
26. 280.

Page 119. — **1.** $5\frac{1}{3}$.   **2.** $4\frac{1}{2}$.   **3.** $6\frac{2}{3}$.   **4.** $3\frac{3}{8}$.   **5.** $3\frac{1}{3}$.   **6.** $3\frac{1}{3}$.
7. $9\frac{1}{5}$.   **8.** $22\frac{1}{2}$.   **9.** $11\frac{1}{3}$.   **10.** $13\frac{1}{2}$.   **11.** $6\frac{2}{3}$.   **12.** $28\frac{1}{8}$.
13. $56\frac{1}{4}$.   **14.** $43\frac{3}{4}$.   **15.** $15\frac{5}{8}$.   **16.** $11\frac{1}{4}$.   **17.** $18\frac{3}{4}$.   **18.** $108\frac{1}{2}$.
19. $131\frac{1}{5}$.   **20.** $93\frac{3}{4}$.

Page 120. — **1.** $18.75; $15.63; $12.50; $9.38; $6.25; $3.13.
2. $1.13.   **3.** $11.63.   **4.** $.52; $.54.

1. $5\frac{1}{4}$ yd.   **2.** $23\frac{3}{4}$ hr.   **3.** 10.   **4.** $8\frac{3}{4}$.   **5.** $13\frac{1}{3}$.   **6.** 35.
7. $18\frac{3}{4}$.   **8.** 40.   **9.** 60.   **10.** 16.   **11.** $63\frac{3}{4}$.   **12.** 24.
13. $9\frac{3}{8}$.   **14.** $46\frac{7}{8}$.   **15.** $27\frac{7}{8}$.   **16.** 25.   **17.** $26\frac{1}{4}$.   **18.** 35.
19. $31\frac{1}{2}$.   **20.** $78\frac{2}{5}$.   **21.** 45.   **22.** 36.   **23.** 40.   **24.** $39\frac{3}{8}$.
25. 81.   **26.** 15.   **27.** 105.   **28.** $131\frac{1}{4}$.   **29.** 100.   **30.** $82\frac{1}{2}$.
31. 150.   **32.** 220.   **33.** 160.   **34.** 30.

Page 121. — **1.** 252.   **2.** $76\frac{2}{3}$.   **3.** 285.   **4.** $140\frac{2}{5}$.   **5.** 215.
6. 150.   **7.** $43\frac{1}{8}$.   **8.** 156.   **9.** 270.   **10.** $108\frac{1}{3}$.   **11.** $202\frac{1}{2}$.
12. $234\frac{3}{8}$.   **13.** $203\frac{2}{3}$.   **14.** $86\frac{2}{3}$.   **15.** 120.   **16.** 272.   **17.** 87.
18. $116\frac{2}{3}$.   **19.** 260.   **20.** 368.   **21.** $118\frac{1}{8}$.   **22.** 370.   **23.** $37\frac{1}{2}$.
24. $89\frac{1}{4}$.   **25.** $194\frac{2}{5}$.   **26.** 210.   **27.** 253.   **28.** $132\frac{13}{16}$.   **29.** 238.
30. 159.   **31.** $11.88.   **32.** $24.17.   **33.** $14.34.   **34.** $17.63.
35. $2.34.   **36.** $17.50.   **37.** $8.29.   **38.** $13.23.   **39.** $28.75.
40. $32.50.   **41.** $16.63.   **42.** $7.00.   **43.** $7.30.   **44.** $24.00.
45. $39.00.

Page 122. — **1.** $1.48.   **2.** $10.25.   **3.** $3.72.   **4.** $3.81.
5. 53¢.   **6.** $2.16.   **7.** $2.48.   **8.** 50¢.   **9.** $9.30.

Page 123. — **4.** 1.   **5.** 1.   **6.** 30.   **7.** 4.   **8.** 1.   **9.** 1.
10. 1.   **11.** 1.   **12.** 1.   **13.** 1.   **14.** 5.   **15.** 3.   **16.** 2.
17. 10.   **18.** 1.   **19.** $\frac{1}{4}$.   **20.** 1; 1; 1.   **21.** All three right.
22. $\dfrac{7 \times 1}{7} + 7 = 8; \quad \dfrac{7}{7} + \dfrac{7}{1} = 8; \quad \dfrac{1 \times 1}{1} + \dfrac{1}{1} + \dfrac{1}{1} + \dfrac{1}{1} = 4.$

Page 124. — **1.** $.30.   **2.** 15¢.   **3.** 32¢.   **4.** $8.80.   **5.** $58.03.
6. $13.86.

Page 125. — **1.** $1.14.   **2.** $2.75.   **3.** $5\frac{3}{4}$ lb.   **4.** $6.37.
5. 32 mi.   **6.** $50.   **7.** $3.00.

Page 127. — *See page* xliii.

Page 129. — **1.** $\frac{3}{8}$ pt. **2.** $\frac{1}{4}$ bu. **3.** $\frac{1}{2}$ cup. **4.** $\frac{1}{8}$ hr. **5.** $\frac{5}{16}$ lb.
6. $\frac{1}{8}$ yd. **7.** $\frac{1}{8}$. **8.** $\frac{1}{4}$. **9.** $\frac{1}{6}$. **10.** $\frac{3}{8}$. **11.** $\frac{1}{8}$. **12.** $\frac{3}{16}$.
13. $\frac{3}{10}$. **14.** $\frac{1}{12}$. **15.** $\frac{1}{5}$. **16.** $\frac{4}{15}$. **17.** $\frac{7}{16}$. **18.** $\frac{1}{6}$. **19.** $\frac{1}{4}$.
20. $\frac{2}{15}$. **21.** $\frac{1}{10}$. **22.** $\frac{1}{24}$. **23.** $\frac{3}{16}$. **24.** $\frac{1}{8}$. **25.** $\frac{3}{16}$. **26.** $\frac{1}{15}$.
27. $\frac{1}{8}$. **28.** $\frac{3}{10}$. **29.** $\frac{9}{20}$. **30.** $\frac{8}{15}$. **31.** $\frac{5}{16}$. **32.** $\frac{2}{15}$. **33.** $\frac{1}{3}$.
34. $\frac{1}{2}$. **35.** $\frac{5}{12}$. **36.** $\frac{1}{16}$. **37.** $\frac{1}{5}$. **38.** $\frac{3}{16}$. **39.** $\frac{3}{8}$. **40.** $\frac{1}{6}$.
41. $\frac{3}{10}$. **42.** $\frac{2}{25}$. **43.** $\frac{1}{2}$. **44.** $\frac{3}{5}$. **45.** $\frac{7}{12}$. **46.** $\frac{2}{5}$.

Page 131. — **1.** $\frac{3}{10}$. **2.** $\frac{5}{8}$. **3.** $\frac{7}{12}$. **4.** $\frac{3}{10}$. **5.** $\frac{5}{12}$. **6.** $\frac{5}{8}$.
7. $\frac{4}{7}$. **8.** $\frac{9}{16}$. **9.** $\frac{4}{15}$. **10.** $2\frac{2}{3}$. **11.** $2\frac{2}{8}$. **12.** $4\frac{2}{3}$. **13.** $\frac{3}{10}$.
14. $\frac{2}{11}$. **15.** $\frac{2}{5}$. **16.** $\frac{2}{9}$. **17.** $\frac{2}{7}$. **18.** $\frac{4}{9}$. **19.** $\frac{3}{8}$. **20.** $\frac{5}{12}$.
21. $\frac{3}{8}$. **22.** $\frac{9}{14}$. **23.** $\frac{3}{20}$. **24.** $\frac{9}{10}$. **25.** $\frac{2}{15}$. **26.** $\frac{3}{32}$. **27.** $7\frac{1}{2}$.
28. $\frac{5}{8}$. **29.** $3\frac{3}{4}$. **30.** $2\frac{1}{12}$. **31.** $3\frac{3}{4}$. **32.** $7\frac{1}{2}$. **33.** $\frac{3}{20}$.
34. $13\frac{1}{3}$. **35.** $4\frac{1}{2}$. **36.** $4\frac{1}{2}$. **37.** 21. **38.** 6. **39.** 18.
40. 12. **41.** 15. **42.** 14. **43.** $\frac{2}{5}$. **44.** $\frac{5}{8}$. **45.** $\frac{3}{4}$.
46. $\frac{3}{5}$. **47.** $1\frac{1}{2}$. **48.** $1\frac{1}{2}$. **49.** $\frac{3}{4}$. **50.** $2\frac{1}{2}$. **51.** $3\frac{1}{3}$.
52. $1\frac{1}{4}$. **53.** $\frac{2}{3}$. **54.** $\frac{9}{20}$.

Page 133. — **1.** $\frac{1}{8}$. **2.** 3. **3.** $\frac{3}{10}$. **4.** 2. **5.** 1. **6.** $\frac{1}{4}$.
1. $\frac{3}{4}$. **2.** $\frac{2}{5}$. **3.** $\frac{2}{3}$. **4.** 21. **5.** 14. **6.** 9. **7.** $\frac{3}{8}$.
8. $\frac{2}{3}$. **9.** $\frac{3}{4}$. **10.** $\frac{1}{5}$. **11.** $\frac{1}{7}$. **12.** $\frac{1}{6}$. **13.** $\frac{1}{9}$. **14.** $\frac{1}{3}$.
15. $\frac{1}{5}$. **16.** $\frac{1}{4}$. **17.** $\frac{1}{3}$. **18.** $\frac{1}{10}$. **19.** $\frac{1}{4}$. **20.** $\frac{1}{8}$. **21.** $\frac{1}{2}$.
22. $\frac{1}{3}$. **23.** $\frac{1}{6}$. **24.** $\frac{1}{8}$. **25.** $\frac{1}{6}$. **26.** $\frac{1}{6}$. **27.** $\frac{1}{6}$. **28.** 6.
29. 5. **30.** 2. **31.** 2. **32.** $1\frac{1}{2}$. **33.** 2. **34.** 4. **35.** 3.
36. 10. **37.** 1. **38.** 1. **39.** 1. **40.** 1. **41.** 1. **42.** 1.

Page 134. — **1.** $\frac{8}{3}$. **2.** $\frac{23}{3}$. **3.** $\frac{11}{6}$. **4.** $\frac{27}{10}$. **5.** $\frac{13}{2}$. **6.** $\frac{9}{2}$.
7. $\frac{23}{8}$. **8.** $\frac{31}{4}$. **9.** $\frac{29}{5}$. **10.** $\frac{12}{5}$. **11.** $\frac{35}{8}$. **12.** $\frac{45}{8}$. **13.** $\frac{23}{4}$.
14. $\frac{17}{16}$. **15.** $\frac{17}{5}$. **16.** $\frac{19}{16}$. **17.** $\frac{28}{5}$. **18.** $\frac{35}{4}$. **19.** $\frac{11}{4}$.
20. $\frac{18}{5}$. **21.** $\frac{13}{3}$. **22.** $\frac{25}{4}$. **23.** $\frac{23}{6}$. **24.** $\frac{23}{3}$. **25.** $\frac{8}{3}$.
26. 7 scarfs; 16 scarfs. **27.** 17 boxes; 13 boxes; 23 boxes.
28. 13 ft. long, 9 ft. wide.

Page 135. — **1.** $1\frac{7}{8}$ lb. **2.** $2\frac{4}{5}$ cups. **3.** $63\frac{3}{8}$ mi. **4.** $61\frac{1}{4}$ mi.
5. 242 ft. **6.** $1189\frac{1}{8}$ bu.

Page 136. — **1.** $2\frac{1}{10}$. **2.** $1\frac{5}{12}$. **3.** $1\frac{1}{10}$. **4.** $2\frac{2}{3}$. **5.** $4\frac{1}{2}$.
6. $4\frac{2}{3}$. **7.** $\frac{2}{5}$. **8.** $5\frac{1}{5}$. **9.** $1\frac{3}{4}$. **10.** $1\frac{7}{8}$. **11.** $\frac{5}{6}$. **12.** $\frac{9}{20}$.
13. $2\frac{1}{2}$. **14.** $1\frac{1}{4}$. **15.** $2\frac{1}{2}$. **16.** $3\frac{1}{3}$. **17.** $2\frac{1}{4}$. **18.** $1\frac{1}{3}$.
19. $1\frac{1}{4}$. **20.** $\frac{1}{3}$. **21.** $1\frac{1}{5}$. **22.** $\frac{1}{4}$. **23.** $\frac{1}{2}$. **24.** $\frac{1}{3}$. **25.** 6.
26. 4. **27.** 3. **28.** $2\frac{5}{8}$. **29.** $1\frac{3}{4}$. **30.** $2\frac{3}{4}$. **31.** $3\frac{3}{5}$. **32.** $6\frac{2}{3}$.
33. $7\frac{1}{5}$. **34.** $15\frac{3}{10}$. **35.** $2\frac{7}{10}$. **36.** $4\frac{1}{8}$. **37.** $2\frac{1}{2}$. **38.** $2\frac{1}{2}$.
39. $1\frac{1}{2}$. **40.** $1\frac{1}{2}$. **41.** $12\frac{1}{2}$. **42.** $22\frac{1}{2}$. **43.** 20. **44.** 3.
45. 12. **46.** 8. **47.** 6. **48.** 24. **49.** 1. **50.** 1. **51.** 1.

Page 137. — **1.** $\frac{4}{5}$; $\frac{5}{6}$; $5\frac{1}{4}$; $2\frac{2}{3}$. **2.** $1\frac{1}{8}$; $4\frac{4}{5}$; $2\frac{1}{2}$; $5\frac{5}{8}$. **3.** $17\frac{1}{2}$; $7\frac{1}{5}$;
$13\frac{3}{4}$; $8\frac{1}{6}$. **4.** 46; $33\frac{1}{3}$; $30\frac{2}{3}$; $24\frac{3}{4}$. **5.** 10; 42; 55; 40.
6. 15; 34; 12; 57. **7.** $6\frac{7}{8}$; $4\frac{4}{5}$; $10\frac{2}{3}$; $19\frac{1}{2}$. **8.** $12\frac{3}{4}$; $12\frac{1}{2}$; $15\frac{1}{5}$; $26\frac{1}{4}$.
9. 63; 99; $225\frac{1}{2}$; $236\frac{4}{5}$. **10.** 68; 259; $161\frac{1}{3}$; $291\frac{1}{2}$.

11. $\frac{15}{32}$; $\frac{2}{15}$; $\frac{21}{40}$; $\frac{25}{48}$.   **12.** $\frac{5}{12}$; $\frac{3}{16}$; 10; $\frac{3}{4}$.   **13.** $\frac{1}{5}$; 1; $\frac{1}{2}$; 6.
14. 15; $1\frac{3}{4}$; $2\frac{1}{4}$; $3\frac{3}{10}$.   **15.** $12\frac{2}{3}$; 6; $6\frac{3}{10}$; 6.

Page 138. — **1.** $6000.   **2.** $2.11.   **3.** 18 mi.   **4.** $.68.
5. $5\frac{3}{4}$ yd.   **6.** $4.25.   **7.** $1.30.

Page 139. — *See page* xliii.

Page 140. — **1.** 1 cup sugar, $\frac{1}{8}$ cup sirup, $\frac{1}{2}$ cup water, $\frac{1}{8}$ ts. salt, $\frac{1}{8}$ cup butter, 2 drops oil of lemon.   **2.** $6\frac{1}{4}$ cups sugar, $1\frac{7}{8}$ cups sirup, $1\frac{1}{4}$ cups butter, $6\frac{1}{4}$ cups milk, $6\frac{1}{4}$ squares chocolate, $2\frac{1}{2}$ ts. vanilla, $\frac{5}{16}$ ts. cream of tartar.   **3.** $1\frac{1}{8}$ cups sugar, $\frac{1}{4}$ cup sirup, $\frac{1}{2}$ cup water, $\frac{1}{4}$ cup molasses, 3 qt. popcorn, $2\frac{1}{4}$ tb. butter, $2\frac{1}{4}$ squares chocolate, $\frac{3}{4}$ ts. vanilla.   **4.** For 1 lb. of brittle: 1 cup granulated sugar, $\frac{1}{2}$ cup brown sugar, $\frac{1}{4}$ cup sirup, $\frac{1}{4}$ cup water, $\frac{1}{8}$ cup butter, $\frac{1}{16}$ ts. soda, $\frac{1}{16}$ ts. salt, $\frac{3}{4}$ cup nut meats; for 3 lb. of brittle: 3 cups granulated sugar, $1\frac{1}{2}$ cups brown sugar, $\frac{3}{4}$ cup sirup, $\frac{3}{4}$ cup water, $\frac{3}{8}$ cup butter, $\frac{3}{16}$ ts. soda, $\frac{3}{16}$ ts. salt, $2\frac{1}{4}$ cups nut meats.

Page 141. — **1.** $440\frac{3}{4}$ lb.   **2.** $36\frac{1}{5}$ times.   **3.** $\frac{1}{8}$ mi.   **4.** $17\frac{1}{2}$ mi.; 105 mi.   **5.** $\frac{5}{8}$ ft.   **6.** $3\frac{1}{2}$ hr.   **7.** $34\frac{14}{16}$ ft.   **8.** $3\frac{7}{8}$ in.

Page 142. — **1.** $11\frac{3}{4}$; $12\frac{5}{8}$; $16\frac{1}{2}$; $14\frac{15}{18}$; $14\frac{1}{2}$.   **2.** $15\frac{1}{8}$; $13\frac{1}{3}$; 14; $13\frac{7}{16}$; $16\frac{2}{3}$.   **3.** $7\frac{9}{20}$; $20\frac{5}{8}$; $19\frac{1}{4}$; $15\frac{7}{12}$; $14\frac{19}{30}$.   **4.** $6\frac{1}{4}$; $\frac{5}{16}$; $5\frac{5}{8}$; $3\frac{3}{8}$; $5\frac{5}{8}$.   **5.** $2\frac{3}{4}$; $3\frac{5}{8}$; $4\frac{7}{16}$; $2\frac{7}{8}$; $3\frac{13}{16}$.   **6.** $1\frac{5}{6}$; $2\frac{1}{6}$; $4\frac{1}{2}$; $1\frac{5}{6}$; $4\frac{1}{3}$.   **7.** $1\frac{1}{15}$; $1\frac{9}{20}$; $6\frac{3}{16}$; $1\frac{7}{12}$; $1\frac{1}{24}$.

Page 143. — **1.** 251,160; 245,650; 98,020; $1619.68; $5930.60.   **2.** 397,677; 66,126; 307,710; $7128.01; $3871.29.   **3.** 51; 89 R8; 213; 53 R25.   **4.** 66 R20; 140 R7; 463 R19; 68.   **5.** 47; 304; 297; 49 R29.   **6.** 73; 105; 636 R21; 207.

1. $5\frac{3}{8}$; 25; $\frac{1}{3}$.   **2.** $12\frac{3}{8}$; $9\frac{1}{3}$; $\frac{5}{12}$.   **3.** $11\frac{2}{3}$; 10; $\frac{1}{8}$.   **4.** 3; 7; $\frac{1}{2}$.
5. 3129.   **6.** 400.   **7.** 9 in.   **8.** $\frac{6}{8}$.

Page 144. — **1.** 17.   **2.** $15\frac{2}{3}$.   **3.** $17\frac{1}{8}$.   **4.** $19\frac{5}{16}$.   **5.** $15\frac{9}{10}$.
6. $1\frac{3}{8}$.   **7.** $2\frac{1}{2}$.   **8.** $3\frac{1}{2}$.   **9.** $3\frac{5}{8}$.   **10.** $\frac{15}{18}$.   **11.** 6.   **12.** $4\frac{1}{4}$.
13. $\frac{2}{5}$.   **14.** $\frac{1}{12}$.   **15.** 1.   **16.** $\frac{5}{12}$.   **17.** $\frac{1}{4}$.   **18.** 4.   **19.** $2\frac{1}{2}$.
20. $3\frac{3}{4}$.   **21.** $1\frac{1}{2}$.   **22.** $4\frac{2}{3}$.   **23.** 3.   **24.** $4\frac{2}{3}$.   **25.** $19\frac{1}{2}$.
26. 28.   **27.** $19\frac{1}{2}$.   **28.** $1\frac{1}{4}$.   **29.** $5\frac{1}{2}$.   **30.** $\frac{1}{6}$.   **31.** 3.
32. $37\frac{1}{2}$.   **33.** 15.   **34.** $33\frac{3}{4}$.   **35.** $35\frac{5}{8}$.   **36.** 376.   **37.** 225.
38. $178\frac{1}{8}$.   **39.** 6555.   **40.** 17,733.   **41.** $2311\frac{7}{8}$.   **42.** 1482.
43. $6201\frac{3}{8}$.   **44.** $35\frac{1}{2}$.   **45.** $93\frac{1}{3}$.   **46.** $66\frac{2}{3}$.   **47.** $59\frac{2}{3}$.   **48.** $23\frac{7}{8}$.
49. $23\frac{1}{4}$.   **50.** $9\frac{2}{5}$.   **51.** $12\frac{2}{3}$.   **52.** $48\frac{3}{7}$.   **53.** $14\frac{1}{2}$.   **54.** $4\frac{3}{8}$.
55. $7\frac{3}{4}$.

www.ingramcontent.com/pod-product-compliance
Lightning Source LLC
Chambersburg PA
CBHW081230090426
42738CB00016B/3244